# Praise for *The Power of a*

CU00703806

"To say Jennifer Forster has 'nailed it' is an understatement. Finally, a beautiful book that honours the feminine energy holistically and gives all women permission to allow their gentle yet incredibly strong nature to shine.

With her open heart, beautiful stories and generous vulnerability, Jennifer guides her reader to realise that no matter what's happened, no matter what story or drama we're living, we each have the tools within to climb up, out, over and through these challenges with a sense of dignity, peace, calm and love.

This book will encourage you to create deeper, more profound relationships in every area of your life. You'll see how easy it is to create a more loving trust in yourself. And most of all, this book will give you the courage to make all decisions from this moment on with a resounding belief in the spirit of what it truly means to be a powerful, peaceful woman.

I cannot recommend it highly enough."

**Kim Morrison**
International speaker, founder of Twenty-8 and author
of the bestselling book *Like Chocolate for Women*
and the award-winning *The Art of Self Love*

"Wow! What a powerful chronicle of a life that has led to so many profound and timely lessons! As I turned each page and explored the glory of each lesson, I found myself diving deep into the corners that have been calling for light.

Through these pages, I know that readers will find themselves 'rescued' from the suffering that has been their conditioning; and through the peaceful way, a brighter light will beam for all to warm their hearts!

Thank you for the effort of putting this gem together. Through the practical resource you've created, I can see, feel and KNOW that lives will be changed and minds will be freed."

**Carren Smith**
International speaker, author of the bestseller
*Soul Survivor* and founder of Spirit Hive

"This is a powerful book and it will impact many lives. It's a beautiful collection of stories, insights, inspiration, lessons, humour, wisdom and real-world strategies that will empower people to explore their power, potential, possibilities and purpose.

I personally love the writing style, the lack of *fluff,* and the real-ness and raw-ness. Jen has managed to navigate and simplify subject matter which can, at times, be slippery and confusing in a way which is practical, understandable and useable.

I believe this book will be a turning point for many people."

**Craig Harper**
Author, speaker and media presenter

"Jen has been an influential woman in my life for around ten years. Her raw, heartfelt and genuine passion for life has guided me to see my full potential.

I recently truly understood and 'heard' what Jen had been saying all along. Now, I'm no longer searching for a destination or a person I need to become. I'm already 'me' and I'm already 'there'...

Loosen your grip on life and watch it unfold just as it's meant to. Thank you, Jen, from the bottom of my heart."

**Sarah Hansen**
Client and friend

The Power of a Peaceful Woman

The following page is left blank.

**For Alexander and Isobel:** Thank you for letting me practise being a mum with you both (even though most of the time we all knew I had no idea what I was doing, you still let me pretend I did).

**For Elizabeth (Liz) Gilbert:** Thank you for being my human muse and the 'grand meister' of permission granting.

**And for you, the beautiful woman who's holding this book:** Thank you for awakening your heart to the power of a peaceful woman.

# *The* POWER *of a* Peaceful Woman

49 WAYS TO DROP THE ARMOUR AND DEFUSE THE DRAMA

# JENNIFER FORSTER

The Power of a Peaceful Woman: 49 ways to drop the armour and defuse the drama

© Jennifer Forster 2019

www.jenniferforster.com

This book is sold with the understanding that the author is not offering specific personal advice to the reader. For professional advice, seek the services of a suitable, qualified practitioner. The author disclaims any responsibility for liability, loss or risk, personal or otherwise, that happens as a consequence of the use and application of any of the contents of this book.

All rights reserved. This book may not be reproduced in whole or part, stored, posted on the internet, or transmitted in any form or by any means, electronic, mechanical, photocopying, recording, or other, without permission from the author of this book.

Editing, design and publishing support by
www.AuthorSupportServices.com

ISBN: 978-0-6483917-4-6

A catalogue record for this book is available from the National Library of Australia

NATIONAL LIBRARY OF AUSTRALIA

# Foreword

*by Linda Pesavento*

'There are some people
who will only hear the
truth the way you tell it.'

When I was an anxious, reluctant first-time author and speaker, these words of strength and empowerment from a friend gave me the courage to write my first book. In the 15 years that have passed since then, I've continued to write and speak. And I've now shared that same quote with thousands of women from all over the world, including my fabulous friend Jen Forster.

The book you have in your hands is rich with life, humility, courage and hard-won wisdom.

It's a testimony to the courage of a woman who's not afraid to make tough choices, learn hard lessons and persist in order to create a life that's uniquely beautiful and free.

I'm convinced that honouring and sharing our unique stories is an act of bravery and generosity that has the power to bring hope and healing to others. I know that Jen's story will enlarge your heart and enrich your life.

**Linda Pesavento**
Author, speaker and founder of The She Is Project

# Preface

What you're holding in your hands is a treasure, as was the notebook I held in my hands years before.

And just like that notebook was made especially for me, I've made this book especially for you.

Turn the pages slowly and gently, with love and tenderness. It's our life, beautiful woman, that you're holding in your hands.

## It's 19 May, 2016

**Tomorrow, I'll be 50.**

And here I am, alone, sleeping on a mattress on the floor.

I'm in the spare room of the house I own. Across the hallway in the master bedroom, my ex-husband and his fiancée are sleeping peacefully.

In my bed.

Later, I'll share the details of this moment, but for right now, it doesn't matter. What's important for you to know is that as I look up at the ceiling, I can't wipe the smile off my face.

I realise with every cell of my body that I've *genuinely* never been happier, more peaceful, and more certain of myself and who I am than in this very moment.

I'm giggling like a child as I realise the absurdity that other people might find in this moment.

Truth be told, if present-day me had travelled back in time and told 39-year-old me that this was how I'd spend the eve of such a major milestone birthday, I'd probably have punched her in the face. Followed closely by shouting, "WTF?! How did we screw THAT up?"

Back on my mattress, my smile widens to an open-mouthed grin at that thought.

I'm so ridiculously delighted and filled with joy at the way my life has turned out... And it's a true testament to how much I've learnt, unlearnt and relearnt about myself in that time.

For more than a decade, I'd made my life into a living classroom.

It was one in which I was, at times, a slow learner, but I was always relentless and persistent nonetheless. You see, I knew the kind of life I wanted for myself. I just didn't know how to create it. And over that time, I've learnt SO much about what it takes to really transform a life.

Then, as you do when you're hovering on the edge of sleep, I start to drift back over the lessons I've learnt, trying to figure out the moment it had all started.

## I remember when it all began

It's 2005, and I'm sitting at my desk in the childcare centre where I work as a childcare coordinator.

I'm gasping for air. It feels like someone is standing on my chest wearing size-13 steel cap boots. It's like a giant hand has reached into my chest and squeezed my heart in a vice-like grip. My heartbeat is racing as I desperately try to breathe.

I want to cry but the tears just won't come. Why can't I cry? Tears would be so much easier than this! Had it really just been a few weeks earlier that I was 'living the dream' (at least from the outside)?

I was married with two beautiful children – a boy and a girl – and living in a wonderful home on the Sunshine Coast. We were the perfect family: a mum, dad and two kids with successful careers and a lovingly renovated home.

**From the outside looking in, it truly looked like we had it all.**

However, beneath the surface, things weren't so perfect. Cracks in our relationship that had started as microfissures in the early days of our marriage had just kept deepening. Destructive behaviours, past experiences, old habits and our 'stories' would repeatedly reveal themselves.

And as time went on, as so often happens, we both changed.

Now, just before I would turn 40, I'd made the decision to end my marriage. And there at my desk, I was experiencing what I'd later discover was my first ever panic attack.

At the time, I just wondered how I could arrive at 39 years of age and suddenly feel so sure and yet so lost.

How could I feel so certain and yet so off course?

## Everyone needs a 'Mr Miyagi' in their life

**Remember the 1984 box office success *The Karate Kid*?**

If you've never seen it, the movie tells the story of a boy called Daniel who is bullied by members of a karate club. Mr Miyagi is the janitor in Daniel's building who – after much coercion – agrees to help train Daniel in karate. As he does, and as the movie goes on to reveal, what's far more impactful for Daniel is Mr Miyagi's shared wisdom, practices, culture and friendship.

Well, as it turned out, my very own Mr Miyagi (or perhaps I should call her 'Mrs Miyagi') would appear.

**Her name was Fran and she was, at that point in my life, the wisest person I'd ever met.**

She was kind, funny, peaceful, generous, compassionate and empathetic. She carried a heart and soul that held so much wisdom about life that I'd often ask her how she knew what she knew. Much of it, she'd tell me, she'd learnt from her grandmother.

The wisdom Fran shared with me began as conversations during morning tea and lunch breaks.

On many days, I'd arrive at work feeling anxious, angry, sad or afraid. And Fran would *always* share just the right words with me to help access my inner reason and return to a sense of peace.

Some days, I'd only be able to momentarily absorb Fran's words and fleetingly see the situation from a different perspective. Remarkably, on other days I could feel my new-found wisdom physically shift something within me.

## One day, I arrived at work to find a notebook on my desk

**The notebook cover was colourful and it read 'Recipe for Life'.**

Tied to the front of the book with maroon ribbon was a wooden spoon. Inside the book, Fran had written, "Good morning, Sunshine. Today is the first day of the rest of your life."

The rest of the notebook was empty.

At morning tea, I caught up with Fran and asked her about the mysterious notebook. She told me that the book would be on my desk every day with a new piece of wisdom in it for me to practise.

**The only rule was that the book had to remain on my desk: I wasn't to take it home.**

As the days rolled on, my 'Recipe for Life' notebook gradually filled up with new quotes, pearls of wisdom, reminders, colourful drawings and short anecdotes from Fran.

Each daily entry was always *perfectly* aligned to whatever I was experiencing in my world. Regardless of whether I was navigating being a solo mum, a divorced woman or my first new relationship, it was always relevant.

## The days turned into weeks, and the weeks turned into months

**I read my entry each morning and we'd chat about it over morning tea and lunch.**

We talked about where Fran learnt it, how she applied it to her life and what triggers reminded her of it. And then it was my turn to do the same.

What I came to learn is that wisdom alone is useless. We can intellectually understand something, but only when we apply action to the wisdom can it permeate and change our lives.

Applying Fran's wisdom to my life and then creating a reminder to practise it was the foundation – and the beginning – of my profound transformation.

But, like with anything in life, mastery comes with constant practice.

(Of course, your very own Mr Miyagi helps too.)

**At the end of the year, my 'Recipe for Life' notebook was full.**

On my desk that day was a note telling me I was ready. I was ready to take this precious chronicle of wisdom home. This was the start of my relentless quest to transform my life. The wisdom in that notebook had opened a part of my mind that was previously closed.

My awareness had been nudged and had awoken. I now knew stuff I couldn't 'unknow'.

And I realised that, with practice, I could create the peaceful, happy and fun-filled life I'd always dreamed of. I could fill it with wholehearted connections and relationships, and live from a space of complete peace and calm. I could recognise when fear and ego were taking me off course and how love would always guide me home.

Or I could choose not to. And as it would turn out, often did.

## The great circle of life

**I eventually left my job at the childcare centre.**

A little while later, Fran moved interstate – and without the assistance of social media, which we're all so familiar with today, we lost contact. It's crazy to realise this, given the profound impact she had on my life.

I tried searching for her, but could never track her down.

It reminds me of a line from a poem by an anonymous author.

> *"People come into your life for a reason, a season, or a lifetime...*
> *When you figure out which it is, you know exactly what to do."*

**Then, over a decade later, I was scrolling Facebook, and my attention was caught by the cleverness of a dancing realtor.**

The guy was busting out some seriously funky dance moves, and I recognised him instantly. It was Fran's son. So I immediately messaged him and asked if he could put me in contact with his mum. He did, and we arranged to meet.

I was so excited to reunite with my old friend and mentor. The day finally arrived and just as I was about to leave to meet her, I remembered my notebook.

A couple of years earlier, I'd worked in Saudi Arabia (more about this later). During that time, I'd packed all my possessions up in my garage. Crap! How would I ever find it? And by now, I was running late!

I ran into the garage, closed my eyes and took a deep breath. I asked to be shown the box it was in; sure enough, there it was in the very first box I opened!

**I made it to lunch only slightly late and burst into tears when I saw Fran!**

She looked exactly the same. My heart overflowed with love for this beautiful woman who'd so profoundly impacted my life. And completely consumed with catching up, I forgot about the notebook.

We began with me. I shared everything that had happened to me in the decade since I'd seen her. I told her what my kids were doing and about my new-found, peaceful relationship with their dad and his beautiful fiancée (now stepmum to our kids).

I told her about my transition out of an 11-year relationship that had taught me so much about love, heartbreak and, most of all, myself.

And, of course, I told her about the incredible career opportunities that had come my way.

My life was amazing, and Fran had been such a role model for me at a critical and pivotal point in my journey of self-exploration and transformation. So I chatted on and on madly with complete exuberance as I held her hands.

Then I sat back, smiled and sighed happily as I asked her about her life. What had she been up to over the past decade?

Her first words were, "Jen, where do I begin?"

She told me about her marriage ending and then shared the most crushing news that she'd buried her youngest son 18 months earlier. I had no words in those next moments, just more tears.

We both cried together.

## Then I remembered the notebook

**I looked at her and squeezed her hands again.**

Smiling through my tears, I said, "I have something for you, something that I know will bring you comfort. And I know this because that's what it did for me when you wrote it!"

I pulled out the notebook and she just stared at it with shocked disbelief.

She couldn't believe I still had it, so I let her know it had lived on my bedside table right up until I'd packed up my home to work in Saudi. I also told her that finding it was the reason I'd been late for lunch that day.

**Together we pored over the pages.**

We both remembered the wisdom, love, guidance and practices that Fran herself had lovingly written on those pages.

I wanted her to have the notebook but she declined. Seeing it had been impact enough to remind her of what she already knew.

She did ask me to send her photos of random pages from it from time to time as a gentle reminder though.

## That notebook had just been the beginning

**The life lessons I'd learnt over time had encompassed so much more than Fran's original wisdom.**

Lying on that mattress in my spare room, I realised the life lessons that had brought me to this moment had indeed started with that notebook.

However, it was my relentless curiosity to hone my awareness, embrace acceptance, let go of what I couldn't control and actualise it all into my life that had transformed me. That was what had changed me from the woman who'd had that very first panic attack to the powerfully peaceful woman on that mattress.

In the decade after Fran had moved away, I met many more teachers, guides, friends and mentors. I read countless books, attended numerous workshops and seminars, studied self-development and eventually worked in the field of fitness and coaching.

But that notebook had been pivotal in my quest for the peaceful, happy, fun-filled life I wanted. And when I reconnected with Fran, I came to understand that wisdom alone is powerless without daily practice.

**So as I approached my major birthday milestone, something in me knew I needed to create a notebook of my own.**

I wanted to create something that I too could pass on to another woman who might also be at a pivotal point in her life.

The next day, I started brainstorming all the life lessons I'd learnt, unlearnt and relearnt. I started documenting how I'd learnt them and the daily practices I'd implemented to bring them into my life.

Because the truth is that wisdom is all around us. It's in the people we know, the books we read, the movies we watch and the stories we hear. It's readily available and accessible to everyone.

**But transformation doesn't come from wisdom.**

Transformation only occurs when wisdom is practised. In other words, transformation is wisdom that's been learnt and then experientially applied.

Here's the thing about transformation: it's not a single, one-off thing – it's a continuous action and one that's available to us in every moment of every day.

By continuous, I mean that it's constant and ongoing. It's a work in progress: an everyday thing, not a 'one-day' thing. My transformation is occurring every second that I'm alive and yours will too. And it will start (if it hasn't already) from within the pages of this book.

## So, beautiful woman, now you know

**Now you know why I made this book especially for you.**

But there's so much more within these pages that I can't wait for you to discover. The wisdom and practices in this book offer you an opportunity to transform something – maybe many things – in your life. They'll help you to create the life you want.

They'll also awaken you to a life where you can drop your armour and defuse *any* drama. That, in turn, means you can start each thought, moment, sentence or day peacefully and powerfully.

My life was never the same again after receiving my notebook from Fran. That's how I know yours won't be either by the time you finish this book.

# Contents

## STAGE 2: ACCEPTANCE

## STAGE 3: AREA OF CONTROL

# STAGE 4: ACTUALISATION

# Introduction

"She is your light and she is your shadow.
She is your voice and she is your wisdom.
She is your peace and she is your power.
And She knows the way."

# Welcome to the first day of the rest of your life

"Hello, beautiful woman. Welcome to the first day of the rest of your life..."

This phrase was shared with me well over a decade ago, and reading it back then became a turning point in my life. So it seems appropriate to share it with you now as I welcome you to the pages of this book in what I hope will become a pivotal moment in *your* life too.

Because today – and any day – IS the first day of the rest of your life.

Although I have to admit that all those years ago I found it hard to imagine just how I'd survive one day, much less the rest of my life.

**Back then, I was lost, confused and asking myself how on earth my life had turned out this way.**

How had all the hopes and dreams I'd had in my twenties and thirties turned into a life I now barely recognised as my own? I wasn't *living* my life. I was just clinging to it by my fingernails, uncertain whether to hang on or let go.

There I was, on the eve of my fortieth birthday, a single, divorced mum of two young kids. I was working a job I didn't particularly love to pay the mortgage and all of the other bills that were piling up. And although I was grateful for everything and everyone in my life, the daily dramas and responsibilities seemed burdensome.

I'd often find myself screaming, "Stop the ride, I want to get off!" in my head.

**But every day, I'd wake up to find I was still 'on the ride'.**

I can remember the first thoughts I had when I woke up most days. They were the same thoughts that kept me from sleeping peacefully each night – my daily dramas, driven by my fear that:

- I'd be alone for the rest of my life.

- I wouldn't be able to pay the bills.

- I wouldn't be able to give my kids all the opportunities I wanted them to have.

- They'd hate me for breaking up our family.

- I was a bad mother.

- I'd never find my purpose.

- I had to make all of the decisions alone from now on.

And underneath all of these fears was my biggest fear – that I'd screw it all up and fail.

**Not knowing any other way, I'd put on my armour each morning and brace for the day's dramas.**

Most days, it felt like I was viewing the world through a sheet of plate glass. Everyone else on the other side looked happy, peaceful and in love with life. And I desperately wanted to be that way too. But no matter how hard or how wildly I banged on the glass with my armour-clad fist, I couldn't break through.

That is until I discovered all the practices I'm going to share with you in this book.

Surrendering to my fears has taken me into some pretty dark and mostly ignored corners of my being. I've travelled back in time to my childhood, revisited all kinds of memories, and sought counsel from the wisdom of countless books, seminars, articles, podcasts, mentors and friends.

**Through the practices I share, you'll discover how to drop your own armour and defuse your dramas.**

These practices have changed the way I work, the way I parent, the way I live and the way I love. And they can do that for you too. They'll teach you how to open your heart when fear closes it and to trust in your inner peace as your greatest source of power.

Imagine having the power to transform every relationship in your life from a constant argument, battle or drama to one filled with peace, love and complete happiness. That includes relationships:

- with your partner (past or present)
- with your kids
- with your family
- with your friends
- with your colleagues
- with yourself (most importantly)!

**You'll no longer wonder 'Who am I?'**

Instead, you'll understand that if you live from the peaceful foundations of your heart, you can't be anything but YOU. None of us can.

This is your purpose: to let go of how things are 'supposed to be' and live a life that fully reflects who you're here to be.

I believe that every single woman is being called to rise. Do you feel that too?

But we can't do it from our angst and dramas. Instead, we need to connect to our open hearts and share our truths that exist there. To connect to *that* message that's within each of us – the one that's uniquely ours to bring to the world. And to do so peacefully and powerfully.

## It won't happen overnight...

**It's OK if you've wandered off course. We all do sometimes.**

If you're at a place in your life where you're burnt out, lost, confused or overwhelmed, I'm here to tell you, "I get it! I get you! I was and am you!"

That feeling you have is the same feeling I carried around with me for years. I always knew I was here to make a difference. But instead of listening (and I mean truly listening) to my heart, I allowed my mind to navigate all my decisions and reactions.

I made those decisions and reacted from fear, instead of from love.

**Just like with Pantene shampoo, changing this didn't happen for me overnight.**

I had to become relentless in my quest to transform my life and bust through the plate glass wall that held me prisoner. I had to study what was happening, putting it under a microscope, dissecting it, and learning, unlearning and relearning everything I ever knew about myself.

In other words, I had to deconstruct my life.

I unpacked my memories, beliefs and stories. And after tears, laughter, acceptance (of myself and others), surprises, doubt, tantrums, procrastination and fear (lots and lots of fear), I reconstructed the woman I am today.

So now I can experience joy, peace and happiness on a daily basis.

## ... but it will happen

**What I've created in this book is an array of tools, practices and exercises that I use myself daily.**

They help me to navigate my life and ensure that no matter what comes at me, I always choose to respond with an open heart. Whilst I know my mind will always be with me, I also know that under no circumstances does it EVER get to drive.

So how do you know whether your heart or mind is in the driver's seat? To answer that, I'll share a quick tip with you. It's a simple one to help you figure this out.

**Take a step back and ask yourself, "How do I feel right now?"**

If you're experiencing fear, anger, sadness, judgement, jealousy, resentment, disturbance or any kind of upset, you're in your mind. Your mind is driving the 'YOU' car. That means whatever you do next will be a fear-based decision or reaction that will move you in a direction you don't want to go.

However, if you're experiencing a sense of joy, happiness, deep inner peace, love, compassion, empathy or calm knowing, trust that your heart is at the wheel. Even if you're only feeling this fleetingly, whatever decision or reaction you choose in that moment will move you in the direction you do want to go.

Your heart uses inner peace, love and happiness as her true north. And SHE knows the way as long as you let her drive.

## This book is written for women by a woman

**I've written this book for women.**

That's not because it's not suitable for men (it absolutely is, and I encourage all men to read it). Rather, it's because I'm a woman, so I believe other women will relate more to the personal stories I share.

I also believe that we're at a pivotal point in history, and women have an incredible opportunity before them to 'be the change' that humanity needs.

**Somehow, women have taken on the idea that navigating this world requires them to fight or to be strong, fierce and in control.**

If this is something you've learnt, I invite you to keep both an open mind *and* an open heart throughout this book, and consider that as women:

- We can be both strong AND delicate.
- We can be both fierce AND gentle.
- We can be both selfish AND selfless.
- We can be both powerful AND peaceful.

None of these traits make us right or wrong, good or bad. And none of them are specifically masculine or feminine either. They're all part of being human.

**This is not a book about gender, equality or fairness.**

Instead, it's an invitation to you, as a woman, to lay down your weapons and step out of your armour. It's an invitation to rise above all the drama to 'get it right', 'to fight for your life' or to be 'perfect' – or to be 'enough'.

For the next few hundred pages, I invite your heart to listen.

Because what I know for sure is that SHE knows the way.

## A map for your journey

I've designed this book to be read from cover to cover, one section at a time.

Or you could simply open the book randomly at any lesson. Each one is a complete lesson that ends with a practice for you to try, which will then help you to embed a new awareness into your daily life.

However, to make the journey easier and to guide you step by step, I've divided the book into four distinct stages: Awareness, Acceptance, Area of Control and Actualisation.

These are what I call the 'Four Stages of Experiential Transformation'.

**Experiential transformation is transformation in action.**

What I mean is that for these practices to create any change in your life, you'll need to apply them to your *own* life experiences. It's not enough to simply read about them.

Each of these four stages and the practices contained within them are the cornerstones of the foundations from which any woman can rise – peacefully and powerfully.

Here's a little more about these four stages.

### Awareness

**The book begins by helping you to discover your awareness spotlight.**

Imagine your whole life is contained in a giant room with no windows. You can't see a thing – it's all completely dark.

Awareness is like a golden spotlight in the corner of that room. When you turn it on and gradually increase its power, it will first light up one aspect of the room, then another and then another. Eventually, you'll be able to clearly see everything that's contained within it.

In this stage, we'll dive into what awareness is and how to turn on your spotlight and *keep* it turned on. In its light, you'll begin to notice things you didn't even know were there.

## Acceptance

**The next stage invites acceptance to the table.**

Lack of acceptance can show up as avoiding or resisting people or situations. It may also show up as being stuck in a repeating pattern or fixed way of being.

You'll learn about how accepting 'what is' actually helps you to let go of all your struggles and dramas. It's not about being complacent or giving in. Rather, it's about rising above your judgements about how things 'should be' and moving towards being peaceful with how things 'are'.

## Area of Control

**So often, we all waste precious energy trying to control things we have absolutely no control over.**

It's all too easy to get bogged down in trying to keep everything perfectly aligned in our lives. This stage helps you to focus in on the places you're doing this in a futile attempt to control external factors that simply aren't controllable.

It helps you to focus instead on the things that *are* within your area of control and let go of anything that isn't. You'll understand that the life you want is absolutely possible but that creating it is an inside job that has nothing to do with what's going on around you.

## Actualisation

**In this final stage, you'll focus on and pay attention to the practices that allow you to be in the flow of your life.**

By this point, you're aware of who you are and what's important in your life. You've learnt to accept 'what is' without judgement or resistance. And you're clear on what is and isn't within your area of control.

This stage now shares practices that will act as a maintenance kit. Using them every day will help you to *keep* the experiential transformation process occurring and continue evolving your peaceful power.

# Are you ready to begin?

**I can't tell you how profoundly changed your life will be by the end of this book.**

Nor can I tell you how excited I am for you to discover the power that comes from a calm mind and a peaceful, happy, open heart.

And the most wonderful part of the whole process is that it will all happen from within your beautiful self. Your heart and soul will shine so brightly that the whole world will feel the radiance of the powerfully, peaceful you.

Before we begin, I want to say thank you.

- Thank you for choosing to reconnect with YOU.

- Thank you for choosing to open your heart.

- Thank you for 'being the change'.

- And, most of all, thank you for trusting me to guide you.

So are you ready?

OK, let's begin.

*Jen* x

# Stage 1:
# Awareness

"There is nothing more
important to true growth than
realizing that you are not
the voice of the mind – you
are the one who hears it."

– Michael A Singer

## Transformation begins with awareness

**What do you think about when you hear the word 'transformation'?**

The Oxford dictionary defines transformation as 'a marked change in form, nature or appearance'; it's something that many of us covet. We especially want it in the context of happiness; peaceful, loving relationships; successful, prosperous careers; and purpose-filled, abundant lives.

So it's no surprise that, in the world of personal development, transformation is – at least in theory – alluring for anyone seeking any kind of change.

**But as nothing more than a theory, transformation is powerless.**

To be a tool for change with any kind of impact, transformation *must* become an experiential process, not an intellectual one.

What I mean by this is that simply reading self-help books (even this one) won't create any kind of change in your life. Nor will just attending workshops or seminars, or trying to understand transformation as a concept.

**Rather, transformation requires *applying* knowledge.**

And whilst many people continue to search outside of themselves, the answers they seek externally are often already within them.

Those answers are completely accessible with just one thing... awareness.

## What IS awareness?

**When it comes to creating any kind of change, your awareness is a superpower.**

It's like a powerful spotlight that lights up your internal wisdom.

Remember the classic film *The Wizard of Oz*? In the beginning, Dorothy's world was a monotone of black and white until she landed in Munchkin Land and met Glinda the Good Witch. Suddenly, she could see everything around her in vibrant technicolour, and she couldn't help noticing what had always been there.

**Similarly, once you turn on your awareness, you can see everything.**

And if you're looking with an open and honest mind, you may not like all that you see.

However, your awareness isn't a tool to beat yourself up with. It's not there to create opportunities to make yourself – or anyone else – right (or wrong).

Instead, it's a tool to reveal the complete picture.

When I first began honing my awareness, I discovered things I hadn't known and saw things I'd never before seen. And that's when my own transformation began.

**I also discovered a few things about transformation itself.**

The first thing I realised is that transformation requires action. The second is that it's constant. It's a work in progress. It's not somewhere you arrive where you're all of a sudden – ta-da! – 'transformed'.

Instead, as your awareness spotlight becomes stronger and shines more brightly, you'll notice that your life will simply continuously transform.

## Join me in a journey to – and through – awareness

**Firing up your awareness is about widening the beam on your inner spotlight and then shining it brightly on everything in your life.**

So as you work through this stage, I invite you to keep your heart and mind open.

Try to avoid judging yourself and, instead, allow yourself to view whatever you become aware of with a sense of wonder and gratitude.

**The fact that you picked up this book tells me that you're just like me.**

You know that there's something 'there', but you can't see what it is. You know it though because deep down you can feel it. And I acknowledge you for being brave enough (and possibly *sassy* enough) to want to turn your own awareness spotlight on.

When you harness your awareness superpower, you'll be amazed at the new level of happiness, peacefulness and love you'll experience. You'll see it in all your relationships, your business and career, and – well – your entire life.

And then you'll be ready to move on to Stage 2: Acceptance.

# Lesson 1

## AWARENESS IS THE KEY TO TRANSFORMATION

 AKA Turn your spotlight inwards

### Awareness has the power to transform your entire life

I've mentioned already that transformation requires you to *apply* knowledge.

That knowledge may well already be within you – and it's completely accessible the moment you become aware of it.

Sometimes your awareness of that knowledge is subtle and gentle. Other times it's forthright and profound. Regardless, you can't access transformation without first accessing your inner awareness.

**'Inner awareness' is a concept that I'll repeat constantly throughout this book.**

It's also exactly where I'm going to begin. So often, when we want to change something, we start by looking for 'what's wrong' externally and then try to fix that.

But awareness is NOT about looking outside of yourself for knowledge. Rather, it's like a beautiful spotlight that you turn inwards to illuminate the transformation process.

So let's take a look at your 'awareness spotlight' and how you can activate its power.

## How do you activate your awareness?

**What do you already know you know?**

You know you know how to walk, how to talk, how to breathe and how to blink your eyes. You know that you know all those things, right? So you're fully aware of what you know.

**There are also things you know you don't know.**

Personally, I know that I don't know how to speak Japanese. I also know I don't know how to fly a plane. I know I don't know how to perform open heart surgery. So I'm also aware of what I don't know.

But here's where it gets really interesting.

**There's also all the stuff you don't know you don't know.**

For example, I didn't know I was allergic to sea scallops until I ate them and threw up for 24 hours. In fact, it wasn't until I ate them a second time (and threw up for *another* 24 hours) that my awareness kicked in.

**So this is now something I know that I know.**

And now, with this new awareness, I can respond differently when sea scallops are on the menu!

## What if the signs aren't quite so obvious?

My awareness of sea scallops was reasonably easy to develop because of the physical effects that triggered it. However, sometimes your 'side effects' won't be so obvious, so you may continue to repeat behaviours that keep you from an outcome you want. In short, you may inadvertently block the very change you seek. For example:

- **You may find that certain people annoy you, so you avoid them.** The side-effect may be that you miss out on a relationship or friendship, despite your belief that you 'have no close friends'.

- **You may use humour to defuse awkward situations.** The side-effect may be that you avoid being vulnerable and opening yourself up to deeper conversations, despite your belief that 'you've never found your soul mate'.

- **Perhaps you find being spontaneous unsettling.** Instead, you'd prefer order and certainty. The side-effect may be that you miss out on unexpected opportunities, despite your belief that 'you're never lucky'.

With my sea scallop allergy, the best option *was* to simply not eat sea scallops. However, when you begin to really hone your awareness, you'll come to see that what it actually gives you is the power to choose.

So how do you uncover what you don't know you don't know?

(And why do you even *need* to know what you don't know you don't know?)

# Nothing changes if you don't know it needs to change

Another way to say the above is that 'nothing changes if nothing changes', and nothing will change unless you're aware that you want it to change.

**Awareness begins with noticing.**

It's about noticing repeated things you do and simply pausing to ask yourself, "Why do I do that?" And then it's about being open and honest with what you notice.

For example, in 2016, I had returned to Australia after a life-changing experience in Saudi Arabia. I'd spent my time there pioneering a health and fitness program at a vocational college for women.

**As was my 'thing', I began to plan out everything I wanted to achieve in 2017.**

I'd done this every year for more than a decade. But over the years the list had become bigger and bigger. Here's what was on there for 2017:

- Complete my MBA (in 12 months, which equated to studying full-time).

- Successfully launch a company from a business plan for two private entrepreneurs (which also required working in excess of full-time hours to project manage, launch and make it financially viable within six months of the doors opening).

- Trek to Everest Base Camp (which required hours of hiking training each week).

- Run a 100km ultramarathon (which required hours of trail running training each week).

True to form, I ticked each thing off my list one by one.

At the end of November that same year, I returned from my MBA graduation ceremony in Adelaide... but within a few days, I began to feel depressed.

**I couldn't understand it. Why wasn't I on cloud nine?**

I'd just completed one of the most successful years of my life, yet I felt underwhelmed, unfulfilled and unable to escape a nagging, uncomfortable feeling. Was there something I didn't know that I didn't know? If so, was it unconsciously running my life?

So I turned on my awareness spotlight and shone it inwards. I asked myself, "Why do you love to set goals and achieve them?"

**And I realised it had begun when I was five years old.**

My family and I were attending the end-of-school-year presentation for my first year of school. I was sitting with them and suddenly heard my name called out.

I walked up on the stage, feeling very small and confused, and was handed the most beautiful book I'd ever seen. When I got back to my seat, I opened it, and saw inside that it said 'Citizenship Award presented to Jennifer Shade'.

I recall thinking at first that there *must* have been a mistake. But what I truly remember was how good it felt and how happy everyone around me was.

So, in my five-year-old-mind that day, I decided that winning meant everybody loved me. I also decided that not winning would perhaps mean I wouldn't be loved.

Looking back now as a wiser and older adult, I know that before receiving the citizenship award, the five-year-old I'd been had had no concept of winning meaning anything. Then suddenly, with that beautiful book in her lap, she did.

She knew that winning brought an abundance of love. And what became the true catalyst for her need to achieve was her fear of not receiving that love.

**Enter the overachiever.**

As an adult, I knew that I liked to win, achieve and succeed. What I *didn't* know was why – at least until I turned my awareness spotlight inwards and started to investigate.

Once I developed this new awareness, the nagging feeling that used to drive me to seek out goal after goal to achieve disappeared. I could see what was hidden – what I didn't know I didn't know. And with this new awareness, I now had access to a clear, peaceful and open mind to choose my goals with purposeful intention, instead of to receive love.

## Becoming aware means you get to CHOOSE

The important part of this life lesson is that you always have a choice about what you do with your awareness.

For example, shining your awareness spotlight onto a habit or behaviour that you 'always do' doesn't mean you must stop doing it.

**What awareness gives you is the power to consciously choose your actions.**

For example, if humour is your thing, not being humorous would be like cutting away a part of you. But if humour is also your shield against any kind of vulnerability, awareness gives you the power to control when you utilise humour and when you don't.

In my case, as a 'goal-setting overachiever', being driven and determined has served me well in my life. However, when I turned my awareness spotlight on, I could begin to consciously choose which goals I set for myself and why I set them. I stopped jumping from goal to goal to unconsciously fulfil a five-year-old's made-up story of being loved for winning and started choosing my goals for the purpose of their outcomes.

**When you don't know what you don't know, you can't see what's truly driving your behaviours.**

You have no idea of what you may be really looking to gain, resist or avoid in life.

And perhaps most importantly, you don't know whether the thing you're doing has control over you or you have control over it.

Setting goals became an unconscious behaviour of mine. It was just something I did – something I was good at. And when I pondered what it would feel like to *not* set goals, it freaked me out.

In the same way, shining your awareness spotlight may feel clunky and awkward at first. But then with practice, just like with learning anything else new, it will soon become effortless.

If you want to see the view you have to physically open your eyes.

## The Practice – Developing awareness

Nothing changes until you're aware of what you want to change.

To start becoming aware of what you want to change in your life, take out your journal (or pull up a file on your computer).

Ask yourself the following questions and write down your responses.

Step 1: Have you noticed a recurring pattern or way of being in your life? It might be something you love, something that 'always happens to you', or something you're known for or have taken on as an identity.

Here are some possible examples:

- Perhaps you've always been the class clown or used humour to combat difficult situations?

- Maybe you need complete order and structure in your day-to-day life?

- Perhaps you always pick the wrong partner?

- Maybe you avoid confrontation or difficult conversations?

Step 2: Now write down 3–5 recent examples of when you recall this pattern occurring.

Step 3: See if you can recall the first time in your life it occurred, and write down whatever you can remember about it.

Step 4: Consider and journal about what it would feel like to choose the complete opposite in both your recent examples and your memory. Would you be comfortable with this? If not, begin to notice why not.

Step 5: Ask yourself whether this situation or pattern has control over your actions or whether you're consciously choosing it.

Step 6: Then, over the coming week, simply notice (without getting upset with yourself) when this pattern or behaviour occurs.

If you catch it, ask yourself, "Can I choose a different response?"

# Lesson 2

## BE CURIOUS

 AKA Notice the nudge

## Staying curious keeps your awareness spotlight on

I've chosen to make 'being curious' the next practice because, without curiosity, your awareness tends to start dimming.

And whilst this book is filled with every practice you could ever need to switch on your awareness spotlight, staying curious is what *keeps* it on full beam.

That's why I tell you to 'notice the nudge'.

Then, when you feel it, get curious about what's causing it.

## Have you ever noticed an awareness 'nudge' in your body?

This nudge might feel physical, mental or emotional.

It might show up in your back, your gut, your mind, the back of your head or your heart. It doesn't matter *where* you feel it. It only matters that you notice it when you do.

Your nudge may be soft and gentle, or it may be a full-on shove. It may feel mildly uncomfortable or like the sharp pain of a nerve being touched. It might feel like a minor disturbance or a major upset. In any case, it will almost always feel unpleasant, uncomfortable, irritating and annoying.

Whatever the sensation, it's imperative to acknowledge it.

That's because however you feel it, that nudge *is* your awareness. It's also your biggest opportunity to wrap your hands around a transformative moment.

**You may notice this nudge as you work your way through this book.**

But it's also OK if you don't notice the nudge in every lesson. It's natural for some parts of the book to resonate greatly, while others not as much. Our minds can only deal with so much at once, especially at this level of inner work.

There may even be parts of you that aren't ready to go inwards on certain aspects of your life. That's also perfectly OK!

**Sometimes, that nudge of awareness can have you running for the hills.**

It can be the catalyst for a shopping spree, a glass of wine, a cigarette, a sedative, housework, exercise, setting a new goal or even cleaning the oven.

Anything, in other words, to avoid leaning into your curiosity.

Because sometimes it feels like shit and you just don't want to go there. So instead, you choose to do something that will block, mask or push it away.

I get it! I really do. But unless you get curious about the nudge, you lose the chance to uncover what it's trying to show you about yourself.

## Here's what happened when I leaned into curiosity

**My nudge of awareness uncovered the way I reacted whenever I was challenged by someone.**

This reaction happened whenever I got into any kind of argument or confrontation, and most often with my kids or partner. If the person I was arguing with didn't see things my way, I'd inevitably walk out on the conversation – often midway through them speaking. I'd go to my room and lock the door, drive off, or just pull an Elvis and 'leave the building'.

My awareness nudge came one day when my daughter said to me, mid-argument, JUST as I turned my back on her, "Why do you always do that? Why do you always walk away?"

Of course, that just pissed me off even more, so I ignored her and kept walking.

**But I felt the nudge, and it was sharp and painful.**

It told me that she was, of course, right. This *is* what I always did.

Now, I could have done one of two things here. I could have ignored the nudge (and my daughter) and continued to repeat my pattern of walking away from arguments OR I could *be curious* and take a look.

On that day, I chose to lean into curiosity. And, for the first time in my life (although everyone else had already known it), I suddenly knew something about myself that I'd never previously been aware of.

With that new awareness, I had a new conscious choice available to me when I was in that situation. If I walked away, I was now aware of what I was doing. And that, of course, brought with it the choice not to.

## With choice comes the possibility of change

**You don't have to take on everything in this book at once.**

I've developed all of the practices in this book over the past 10-15 years.

I've utilised them relentlessly to unpack my entire life, scrutinise memories and put my behaviours under the microscope. I've tested theories on myself, examined my beliefs, deconstructed what didn't serve me and reconstructed new ways of being that did.

I've used these practices as a map to help me continually return to a place of peace, joy, love, trust and support. (At least, I have when I've turned on my awareness spotlight.)

**But every single practice requires one vital ingredient: a *willingness* to be curious.**

There are many definitions of curiosity, but *'an eager desire to know or learn something'* summarises it well.

In fact, if I were to put my own spin on the definition, it would be *'an eager desire to learn, unlearn and relearn something'*.

**Because being curious is an infinite process.**

Being curious is also an ideal antidote to the tendency many women (including me in the past) have to be judgemental and beat themselves up for making a mistake or getting it 'wrong'. Neither of these tendencies is conducive to creating a healthy awareness or any kind of transformation.

**Initially, your curiosity may tend to focus outwards to the world around you.**

This is also completely normal as you begin to hone your awareness. Just remember, though, that the outer world is a mirror (more about this in Lesson 4). It's a reflection of you. So whatever you see outside yourself is also occurring within you.

And if you turn your awareness spotlight inwards and get curious about what you see, I promise that's where you'll make your most profound discoveries.

## The Practice – Leaning into curiosity

**The following is a list of questions for inner exploration and reflection.**

Use them as journaling prompts whenever you feel your own nudges of awareness.

- What is this here to show me?
- What am I unable or unwilling to see?
- Who would I be if I was not this?
- How can I let this go?
- What unhealed wound (upset) is this here to show me?
- What would Love do?

# Lesson 3

## WOULD YOU ASK FOR ONE MORE WEEK?

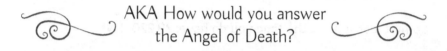 AKA How would you answer the Angel of Death?

### Are you aware of time?

**We know that time is infinite (well, according to the 'science-y' dudes it is).**

But time is NOT infinite for *us*. We – by which I mean you and me – only have a certain amount of time on this planet. But I know you already know this.

What you might not know is that if we each lived until we were 80, that would be 29,220 days.

So does it *really* matter if a few of these days slip through our fingers?

It's not really life or death, is it?

## Knowing how many days you have can be life-changing

**Time is the most valuable, irreplaceable thing you have.**

If you waste it, you don't get more. If it's stolen from you, it can't be returned. If you spend it somewhere and change your mind, you don't get a refund. And you can't take out an insurance policy for it either.

From the day you're born, the clock is ticking...

**So first let's look at the time you do have: 29,220 days.**

That's how many days you receive if you live until you're 80, right? That also accounts for the extra day you get in each leap year... which isn't too bad when you think about it.

For the purpose of easy maths, let's call it 30,000 days.

BUT maybe you're 40ish years old now. If so, you need to immediately *halve* that number. Wait, what?! Yep. You need to cut that down to 15,000 days.

**Shit just got real, didn't it?**

Personally, I'm now 50ish. And while I suck at maths, it only took me a second to realise that my 'Day Bank' is now roughly down to only 11,000 days...

AND IT'S COUNTING DOWN!

How many days do you have in YOUR Day Bank?

# Being aware of this changed my relationship with time

**Understanding the reality of my Day Bank balance shrinking each night when I closed my eyes was daunting.**

But I still didn't fully comprehend the reality of where I was spending all my time.

Realising *that* literally changed the course of my life. It's even why I'm writing this book. Because it not only highlights the importance of being aware of my Day Bank but it also magnifies the importance of taking responsibility for it.

**What triggered my realisation was imagining the Angel of Death.**

A little while ago, I was listening to an interview between Oprah Winfrey and Michael A Singer, author of *The Untethered Soul*. I highly recommend that every human studies Michael's book in its entirety, but one particular part became my literal reason for writing my own book.

In this interview, Michael shared a story about the Angel of Death. He asked me, as a listener, to imagine that I was in the middle of my day when suddenly, out of the blue, the Angel of Death appeared before me.

**Then he asked me to imagine the Angel saying, "Jen, giddy up! It's time to go!"**

Of course, I'd be startled by the Angel's arrival, so back when I first listened to this story, I'd have probably responded with, "Wait! What?"

And then I'd have thought, "Really?"

"Just like that? It's time to go?"

"Don't I get a warning?"

"Can't you give me a warning?"

"I'm sure you're supposed to give me a warning!"

"Can I just have one more week?"

"Then I'll be ready for sure, I promise!"

**Of course, I could imagine the Angel of Death standing there, looking at me, bemused.**

Clearly they'd have seen this kind of reaction millions of times before. And then, with a wry smile, they'd turn to me and say, "But, Jen, I gave you 52 weeks this past year alone. Why do you need one more week?"

BOOM! And there it was!

When I listened to this part of the interview, I actually felt something massive physically shift inside me.

I rewound the interview and listened to it again.

And again.

And *again*.

With each replay, the shift became deeper and more profound as I imagined that scene playing out in my mind.

Suddenly, without any warning, I discovered I now knew something I couldn't unknow. I'd learnt something I couldn't unlearn. I'd seen something I couldn't unsee.

**My awareness of time – and where I was spending it – smacked me hard.**

I thought about where I'd be going and what I'd be doing on that particular day; I imagined the Angel of Death appearing before me in any second during that day.

As I did, I wondered, "Is this *really* what I want to be doing in my life when I exit the Earth? Would I actually need one more week to ensure I'd ticked off all my dreams?"

And what I knew for sure in that moment was that the way I was about to spend my time would totally have me asking for another week!

**So I decided then and there to make sure I'd never need to ask for one more week ever again.**

I decided to make sure that whatever I was doing and however I was spending my time, I'd be able to say, "Yep, I'm ready!" if the Angel of Death appeared.

To ensure that happened, I became more conscious of my choices around my time. Whenever I needed to decide how I was about to spend my time, I'd pause and imagine the Angel of Death appearing.

You see, if it really *was* my time to exit Earth, this made my decisions effortless to make.

It truly simplified everything.

## Would you ask for one more week?

**This practice has helped me to make some big decisions, including the decision to write this book.**

It's helped me with small decisions too. In fact, it's an especially helpful tool if you're someone who has trouble saying no or someone who often finds yourself doing things you don't actually want to do.

Remember, time is *the* most precious resource you have, so it's important to be highly aware of how you spend it.

**There are NO refunds if you change your mind.**

So think about it. If the Angel of Death appeared before you right now, would you ask for another week? If so, ask yourself:

- Is where you're spending your time a place that you'd be happy for your life to have its end point?
- Is the work you're doing your dream job?
- Do you have unreconciled relationships that you'll 'deal with later'?
- Are there places you haven't yet been that you want to visit 'one day'.
- Do you have an unrealised dream that may die with you if the Angel of Death appears?

If any of this resonates, realise that you have the choice *right now* to ensure the life you're living is the exact one you want to live. So much so that you'd never, ever need to ask for 'one more week'.

Sometimes, with the busy-ness of life, it's easy to get caught up in living your life on autopilot. You can become almost robotic in your day-to-day tasks, duties and responsibilities.

**To break this autopilot mode, it's important to press pause.**

It's important to reflect and connect to your dreams, desires and spirit of adventure.

In fact, I highly recommend putting a reminder in your calendar to do this every 90 days. We're all such creatures of habit that we can easily fall back into our autopilot tendencies.

Perhaps you may discover you don't want to change a thing. But in case you do, pausing and reflecting will help to ensure that whatever you were planning to do, if the Angel of Death appeared, you *wouldn't* need to ask for one more week.

## The Practice – Writing a letter to yourself from your 'Spirit of Adventure'

This practice will help you to interrupt the autopilot I mentioned above.

Step 1: First, take out your journal or open a document on your computer to write a letter to yourself from your Spirit of Adventure.

Step 2: Start it like this:

"Dear [insert your name]
This is your Spirit of Adventure, and I'm writing to remind you of all the things you've always longed to do, said you would do and aren't yet doing..."

Step 3: Write, write and then write some more. Allow your adventurous spirit to openly and freely shine a light on all the things you love to do and have longed to do, but maybe have forgotten about.

Step 4: Sign it:

*"Giddy up, girl!*

*Love, Your Spirit of Adventure."*

# Lesson 4

## THE WORLD IS A MIRROR

 AKA What is the world reflecting back at you?

### What you see in others is a reflection of you

**Everything you see outside of yourself mirrors what's inside you.**

And whilst this is true for the stuff you see that you love in others, the real opportunity comes when you recognise that everything you don't love is you too.

For example, if you're a parent, you may have noticed that your kids seem to take on your moods. When you're calm and happy, they seem to be too. But if you're stressed and wigged out, they seem to become that way as well.

**Of course, this doesn't *just* relate to your kids.**

Some of us seem to only be surrounded by good and kind people, whilst others seem to attract complete arseholes. Constantly.

Have you ever noticed any of this?

40

# What you do with that reflection is up to you

During my decade working in the field of coaching, I effortlessly saw greatness in every person I worked with... even when they didn't see it for themselves.

However, until I fully understood that the world was a mirror, I was blindly unaware of my own greatness.

**Whatever you experience in another person is simply a reflection of you.**

But here's where it becomes tricky. As I said above, this isn't just true for the admirable qualities. It's true for all the qualities you dislike as well. Often, though, it's easier to turn away from someone who displays qualities you dislike. You might even tell others what you dislike about that person too.

All the while, you fail to recognise that those qualities exist in you.

**If they didn't, you wouldn't even notice them.**

The truth is that everything – the stuff you love in others and the stuff you don't love – is *all* you. So this lesson is an opportunity to bring awareness and, ultimately, peace to every part of you.

Sometimes the reflection you see is a reminder. Other times it's there to teach you something.

But in almost all cases, it's an opportunity to hone your awareness of your automatic view of the world. And from that place, you can potentially learn, heal, expand and grow.

Perhaps the most important part of this practice is that it also gives you the opportunity to become aware of where you're judging the world around you, other people or yourself.

# You can't notice something in someone else that doesn't already exist in you

**I once coached someone who had a visual impairment disability.**

I saw this person's potential and, by giving them the right encouragement and support, I helped them to achieve some extraordinary things. They ran a 5km race, climbed a mountain, kayaked, played team sports and took part in an obstacle race, to name just a few of their physical accomplishments.

Additionally, they radically improved their health, which quite literally changed them from the inside out. They also operated their own business in the music industry as a booking agent for bands, singers and musicians.

The thing I loved the most about this person was that being visually impaired didn't stop them from doing the things they loved. Not only that, but they also managed to support themselves in the process.

So we became great friends and hung out together often.

**However, there was one aspect of this person's life that irritated the *hell* out of me.**

Not only did they derive an income from their small business but they also received a disability payment from the government. In doing so, over their lifetime, they'd managed to travel the world, create a financial portfolio and live comfortably.

Despite the fact that they were entitled to do both and weren't in any way breaking any laws, I decided that they were rorting the system.

I believed that they should have worked harder to build their business up to the point that they no longer needed the disability payment.

After all, I'd seen how capable they were. Why would they *want* to receive a handout?

We'd often end up in extremely heated debates about this. And although we'd agree to disagree, it would work me into a frenzy. I was so sure I was right about it (Lesson 16 holds the gold about this topic!)

**I knew I'd need to dig into my toolkit of practices to find a way past this.**

Of course, these days I can totally see how judgemental this bugbear of mine was. But at the time, I could only *feel* how pissed off I was.

That's the thing: there's always something to learn when someone else annoys, irritates or pisses us off. The good news is that the opposite of 'pissed off' is 'peaceful', and that's what these lessons are designed to give you access to becoming.

## Start by asking what's upsetting you

When something or someone rubs you the wrong way or irritates the shit out of you, the first thing to ask is this:

**"What about this situation is upsetting me?"**

In my story, I was upset because I felt that my friend was getting an easy ride.

To me, they were rorting the system; if they could create a profitable business, why should they have access to disability support?

**And, of course, *I* would *never* 'be like that'.**

Whenever you hear yourself using the words, "I would never do that/ say that/think that!" or, "They always do that/say that/think that!" it means you're strongly resisting something. That, in turn, means you're probably judging not only the other person but yourself in some way too.

Which is actually great – as long as you first recognise that you're doing it and then acknowledge, learn from and make peace with it. (And the making peace part is for you, not the other person!)

**Remember: being pissed off is a cue for you to notice that there's something your awareness wants you to see.**

I knew I was the only person who had a strong issue with my friend's choices. And even if I *had* convinced other people to agree with me, the fact that I was so upset was a cue from my awareness. It was my nudge to be curious.

It was an immediate warning bell that my strong reaction wasn't about my friend. The reaction was about me.

Only when you can be completely honest with yourself about what's at the heart of your annoyance can you ask the next powerful question:

**"Where in my life am I doing this or something similar?"**

Or said another way, "What is it about me that's being reflected through this situation?"

Ouch! This is a tough question to ask yourself.

And, at first, the answer may not come easily to you. Because why would you be pissed off in the first place if you did the same thing?

When I first asked myself this question, I refused to entertain the idea that I'd ever done the same thing my client did. I'd worked *damn* hard for everything I had!

And you'll probably find your answer just as difficult to acknowledge. Because again, something will only annoy, irritate or piss you off if it reflects something in you.

**Let me give you an example you might be able to relate to.**

Have you ever noticed someone and immediately thought, "Gee, they look bit dodgy"? You have no evidence to support the feeling, but they just look like they're up to something. Is it the hoodie they're wearing? How they're walking? Or do they just generally seem 'dodgy' to you?

I'm sure we've all spotted someone dodgy before.

Now ask yourself this question: "Where in my life am *I* dodgy?"

I bet your first reaction to this is, "I am NOT dodgy!"

But now, think about all the 'good chocolate' you hide in the back of the fridge. The secret stash of treats on the shelf in the cupboard that's too high for the kids to see. The garbage bag you put in your neighbour's wheelie bin late one night because yours is full.

And to be clear, this is not about whether that 'dodgy' person was actually up to something or not. It's about your automatic judgement that they are.

**So when I took an honest look at myself in relation to rorting the system, imagine my surprise at what I discovered.**

At one point, when I owned my own business, I'd also received a parental support benefit from the government for being a solo mum. I'd told myself I was entitled to it. And the truth is that I was.

Now, when I first realised this, I argued internally that it was just not the same as my friend's situation. But as I sat with the discovery, I could acknowledge that it was. It was exactly the same.

45

Perhaps you justify *your* 'dodginess' the same way I justified my parental payment.

Accepting that answer then allowed me to ask the next question.

**"What about this situation do I want to hide from myself and/or the world?"**

Here's what I uncovered when I asked that question:

- embarrassment that I'd needed that money
- shame that I couldn't support my kids without it
- guilt for being in a situation where I'd needed to accept it.

**And suddenly, there it was.**

I had something I wanted to keep hidden from the world, so I used judging others as a tool to hide it and prove to myself that I wasn't 'like them'.

When I chose to stop unknowingly judging both myself and my friend, I noticed some other things too:

- I blamed myself that we didn't have the money for fancy holidays and I'd had to say, "No, that's not in our budget," as often as I did.
- I blamed myself that we often lived pay cheque to pay cheque.
- I blamed myself that the small savings I had kept going to 'emergencies'.
- In short, I blamed myself that we needed to accept the parental payment from the government.

Being able to see this for the first time brought me to my knees and I wept.

Rather than pushing it away, I allowed myself to see it and feel it for several days.

I didn't try to suppress it or judge myself for it.

I felt it. I invited it in. I made peace with it.

And finally, I gave gratitude to myself and to my friend: them, for being the mirror that reflected this unhealed wound to me, and me, for being brave enough to do the work to see it and heal it.

Sometimes the things you become aware of when you start paying attention to whatever the world reflects back at you are just small, like hiding the good chocolate.

However, with practice, you might discover some big things too.

And once you recognise and let go of them, they'll move you one step closer to a more peaceful you.

## The Practice – Investigating the reflection

Next time you find something really irritating you, try the following practice.

Step 1: Take out your journal and answer the three questions from above:

1. What about this situation is upsetting me?

2. Where in my life am I doing something similar? Or, said another way, what is it about me that is being reflected through this situation? (If the answer doesn't come immediately, keep looking.)

3. What about this situation do I want to hide from myself and/or the world?

**Step 2:** As you write your answers, you may well find – like I did – that it brings up a lot of strong emotion.

It's OK if so – just let yourself feel it.

**Step 3:** Forgive yourself for judging yourself and judging the reflection.

**Step 4:** Finally, allow yourself to feel deeply grateful, both to whoever irritated you and to yourself for being responsible enough to heal it.

**If you find the concept of forgiving yourself difficult, try the Ho'oponopono prayer.**

This ancient Hawaiian practice of reconciliation and forgiveness is beautiful either as a meditation or a spoken practice while looking into your own eyes in a mirror.

To do it, simply repeat the following prayer over and over:

*"I'm sorry.*
*Please forgive me.*
*Thank you.*
*I love you."*

# Lesson 5

## NO MATTER THE QUESTION, LOVE IS THE ANSWER

 AKA All you need is love

### If this sounds a little too woo-woo, bear with me!

**So far, the lessons you've read have been practical.**

They haven't been based on 'peace, love and mung beans' ideals. Rather, they've been based on your mindset, thoughts and actions. And when you change *these,* you have the power to completely transform your life.

So I can understand your reaction if the title of this life lesson seems a little 'John and Yoko'! If so, allow me to explain what it's really about. (Although for the record, I love John and Yoko, and I speak fluent woo-woo!)

**Sometimes practical tools just won't create a shift!**

For those times, this lesson will offer you a different (and sometimes necessary) angle to come from in order to shift back into your peaceful power.

## That voice in your head isn't *actually* you

The question this life lesson addresses is the battle that arises between your head and your heart. It's about listening for the quiet voice in your heart, which is often drowned out by the extremely loud voice in your head.

**You see, we all have a little voice inside our head that never shuts up.**

It chatters away all day, nonstop.

Do you know the voice I'm referring to?

Yep, that one! I know it sounds like your own voice, but it's not really you.

Remember Michael A Singer's bestseller *The Untethered Soul* from Lesson 3? In it, Michael says, *"The voice in your head isn't you: you're just the one that hears it."*

Day after day, you might notice your little voice not only incessantly asking questions but answering them too. It narrates your life all day long!

**And that voice you keep hearing is ACTUALLY the voice of your ego.**

Your little voice, aka your ego, is trying to protect you from a story – sometimes many stories – that you made up long ago about something that did or didn't happen. (And for more about how and why we make up stories, see Lesson 30.)

So what does your ego have to do with the idea of 'love being the answer'?

Well, as adults, our default operating systems are almost always our egos. Our little voices tend to run the show without our awareness. But back when we were born, our default operating systems were love.

Now, we'll talk more about what exactly your 'ego' and 'love' are in Lesson 15. For now, though, think of your ego as the part of you that just cares about Number One, ie. YOU! Love, on the other hand, is the part of you that wants the best for everyone.

**So when I say, "No matter the question, love is the answer," it's a reminder to always check in with your ego.**

When you do, ask yourself questions like:

- "Am I operating from ego or from love?"
- "Am I about to do/say/think something because my little voice is in control?"
- "Am I choosing an outcome that's for everyone's highest good or to avoid something I fear?"

If your ego is in control, you might find that what's driving your thoughts and actions is actually fear, anger, jealousy, or shifting blame or responsibility away from yourself. In other words, you may be attempting to (consciously or not) manipulate the outcome to neutralise your fear.

However, if you're responding from love, you'll find that you're operating from your heart. This means you can let go of any fears, be true to your values (what's most important to you in life) and accept an outcome that's for the highest good of all concerned.

No matter what.

## Making decisions from love

**If I asked any parent whether they loved their kids, of course they'd say, "Yes."**

But sometimes, as any parent knows, the decisions we make because we love our kids don't *feel* like love to them.

Which is exactly what my daughter experienced from me.

You see, near the end of her first year in high school, my daughter did something that resulted in her feeling deeply betrayed and humiliated. And, of course, in high school, this can seem like the end of the world.

So her solution was to ask to move to Melbourne to live with her dad and go to school there the following year.

**During this time, her dad and I lived in separate states.**

However, we were united in wanting our kids to know they always had a choice about which parent they lived with.

I knew that they both loved spending every school holiday with their dad and grandparents. So when her request came, it wasn't completely out of the blue – except at this stage, I was totally unaware of the circumstances that had prompted it.

Initially, I asked the usual questions that most parents might ask. I asked how long she'd been thinking about it and whether she'd thought about the challenges of starting at a new school. I also asked whether she'd miss her friends here.

She said she'd thought about it all, but she still wanted to move to Melbourne.

**So after some long discussions with her and her dad, we all agreed that she'd go.**

Of course, my heart was torn, as any solo mum's heart would be.

But I loved my daughter enough to want the very best for her. I knew the school in Melbourne had a wonderful drama program, which would support her in doing what she loved. Plus, she had her dad, stepmum and grandparents there, as well as opportunities that she wanted to pursue.

If it had just been about what was best for me, she'd never have gone. But I firmly reminded myself that 'love is always the answer'.

**Then, a couple of days later, the real reason behind her decision to move came to light.**

Now, with this new information, was love *still* the answer?

Just like any mum, my first reaction was to feel my heart breaking as I heard about her experience. But I also knew I needed to talk to her about running away from her problems versus facing them.

She, of course, insisted that I had no idea of the gossip and humiliation she was dealing with. She swore she never wanted to return to her school again and moving to Melbourne was the only solution.

**I sat with this new information for most of the next day.**

As a mum, I could feel her pain, and I just wanted to protect her from it. And I knew that her moving to Melbourne was the easiest option for all of us.

But I *also* knew in my heart that it wouldn't be love making that decision. It would be fear: my fear that she'd hate me forever if I didn't let her go. Love knew how to support my daughter; fear just wanted to pretend it had never happened.

So, that afternoon, when she came home from school, I broke the news to her. I told her that she wouldn't be moving to Melbourne after all.

**Of course, she flipped her lid!**

She told me she hated me, that I was ruining her life and that she just wouldn't go to school next year.

And she *did* hate me for a while.

But, in time, she eventually realised that this situation had been a huge turning point for her. It had helped her to discover that facing her adversity was her fast track to defusing it. She also realised that if she'd taken the easy way out by moving the issue would simply have moved with her and perhaps never been resolved.

**Still, making that decision for her to stay was one of the hardest times in my life.**

I knew, however, that I'd made it *because* I loved her. Had I let her go, it would have only been because I was scared that she'd hate me if I didn't.

And I knew that wherever there was fear, my ego was almost always in control, which meant love wasn't present.

## Sometimes, ego can look like love (at least on the surface)

What I know for sure is this: if your ego is present, love is not. So if you're making a decision because you fear the outcome, then love is absolutely not the operating system at work.

**Sometimes, ego can be really obvious.**

For example, here are a few clear phrases you may recognise that make no room for love to be the answer:

- "Because I said so!"
- "If you love me, you'll say yes/no."
- "If you do that, I'll never speak to you again."
- "I don't want you to be mad at me."
- "I *forbid* you to speak to that person."
- "It's my way or the highway."

**Other times, however, ego can masquerade as love.**

That's what was going on in my story above. On the surface, wanting to let my daughter go to Melbourne was about sparing her more pain and humiliation because I loved her. It wasn't until I dug down that I realised how much that desire was coming from fear.

LOVE is ALWAYS the answer. Period.

But, beware of your ego masquerading in a bright red heart costume!

## The Practice – How to respond from love

Whilst the concept that 'love is the answer' is simple, we've established that it can sometimes be shadowed by your ego and fear.

Use the following questions to help you identify when and where this might be occurring for you.

- Is what I'm about to say or do motivated by avoiding or creating a particular outcome?

- Will what I'm about to say be for the highest good of everyone concerned or just me (or them)?

- What would love do right now?

- What would love choose right now?

- What would love say right now?

Journal your responses to help you create clarity, a new perspective and perhaps a deeper awareness of the situation.

# Lesson 6

## TRUST YOUR GUT AND FOLLOW YOUR HEART

 AKA Your inner GPS knows the way home

### Human instinct is not a brain function, it's a *deep-down* feeling

If I asked you whether you knew what a gut instinct was or if your heart had ever spoken to you, I'm confident you'd say, "Yes."

However, if I also asked you whether you'd ever ignored your gut instinct or your heart's desire, I feel extremely confident you'd also say, "Yes."

**So why do we do this?**

### Why do we ignore what our gut or heart is trying to tell us?

Why do so many of us sense our instincts and inner knowings, and then just ignore them? And even worse, after reflecting about it, we often *tell* everyone that we knew deep down, but that we'd ignored whatever it was we knew!

**Sometimes, the thing you ignore is small.**

Perhaps it's the instinct to take an alternative route on the way home from work. Maybe you just felt a small tug in the pit of your stomach; and because you ignored it, you're now sitting in a massive traffic jam.

Other times, it's an uneasy feeling about a person. Again, you ignore it only to find it proven right down the track. This is not about judging that person: it's about intuitively recognising the people your values are (and aren't) aligned with.

**And sometimes it's a pivotal moment in your life.**

But because logic (a brain function) disagreed and spoke louder, you pushed your gut instinct and your heart's desire aside.

Or maybe you really *wanted* a situation to turn out a certain way, despite your gut telling you otherwise. So you compromised yourself in some way to get what you want, only to discover once you have it that it's impossible to sustain.

## My heart told me the life I was living wasn't mine

Back when I was 20, I was six months away from being married with the rest of my life pretty well mapped out for me.

My fiancé and I both had great jobs. We had a lovely home, a car, a boat and plenty of savings. I even had my wedding dress. My parents were so proud of me and the life my fiancé and I were creating together.

**Other than a persistent, dull, tugging feeling, I'd created the perfect life.**

Yet I can remember thinking, "What will I do now? Is this it? Is this how my life will look for the next 40 years?" (Back then, of course, I thought 60 was the end of the line!)

The tugging feeling wouldn't go away; the closer the wedding drew, the stronger and more difficult to ignore it became.

I recall thinking that I'd never left Tasmania, much less been outside of Australia. In fact, I'd never even been on a plane. And to make matters worse, I found myself making 'googly eyes' at a forklift driver at work.

**I couldn't shake the deep-down feeling that, however perfect my life seemed, it wasn't actually *my* life.**

I tried to ignore my gut instinct and the constant tugging of my heart, but I couldn't.

At the time, I couldn't understand it or explain it to my fiancé and our families. But I knew that the right choice – the *only* choice for me – was to cancel the wedding.

Not surprisingly, that choice ended the relationship. Luckily, my family, especially my older sister, was incredibly supportive.

However, breaking my engagement impacted many people, not least of all my fiancé. So staying would definitely have been the easier option – much like deciding to let my daughter move to Melbourne in the previous lesson.

But this time, it wouldn't have been the right decision for *me*.

**Had I stayed, it would have been from the fear of not hurting or upsetting anyone.**

Had I stayed, I would have been sacrificing my own desires.

So I left, even though it seemed crazy, scary and against everything society expected me to do.

I listened to my heart and gut and trusted them, even though I had no idea what the next step was or where it would take me.

**And listening and trusting navigated me towards the amazing life that truly WAS mine.**

## Our instincts are just like an inner GPS

We're all born with an 'inner GPS' that is pre-programmed to take us 'home'. And just like an actual GPS, the one inside you doesn't give up the first time you ignore it.

Here's what I mean: have you ever tried to ignore the GPS in your car?

It tells you the route, but you decide you know better, so you turn left instead of right, ignoring the way your GPS tells you to go.

**And what does your GPS do? It reroutes and corrects your course.**

It ensures that you still end up going where you're meant to.

If you miss a turn completely, it tells you the next one to take to get you back on course.

If you overshoot your turn, it tells you (repeatedly) to make a U-turn.

**That's what your internal GPS does too.**

When I broke my engagement to my high school sweetheart, I trusted my gut and my heart.

But here's what life has also taught me.

**You *can* ignore your heart and your gut.**

Two decades later, I was in an on-again/off-again relationship for 11 years, ignoring my gut and not trusting my heart. Or rather, I was trying to override both of them, as we're all prone to do when we're 'in love'.

You can push against it. You can think you know a better way. You can even try to turn it off.

But no matter what you do, your inner GPS will still take you to your final destination, one way or another, no matter how long it takes or how off course you become.

Trusting your heart and your gut just makes the ride a little smoother.

Ignoring them might just mean you take the long way home.

## The Practice – Trust your gut and follow your heart

**That's it! Just those seven words.**

Sorry, but that's really all there is for this one. Whilst this is one of the shortest and simplest practices, it's not always the easiest to master.

So here's a quick tool to help during times when your instincts are trying to communicate with you and you're questioning them.

**Step 1:** First, don't do that! Don't question your instincts. They know the way.

**Step 2:** Second, if you feel uncertain about a decision, try imagining possible outcomes and for each one asking yourself, "Does this make me feel light or does it make me feel heavy?"

Then imagine holding each possible outcome of your decision in your hands. Does it feel light or heavy?

- If it feels light, trust your inner GPS and go in that direction with confidence.

- If it makes you feel heavy (anywhere in your body or mind), go the other way.

# Lesson 7

## STOP TRYING TO FIX PEOPLE

 AKA No one, including you, is broken

### Creating a powerfully peaceful life is an inside job

You may have noticed a common theme running through this book. That theme, of course, is YOU.

**Everything starts, continues and ends with YOU.**

That might sound self-absorbed, but what I've discovered is this. Whenever I'm upset, unhappy, pissed off, sad, annoyed, irritated, wound up, stressed, anxious or in *any* other state that I don't want for myself, there's only one way out.

And that way is through ME.

Transforming my life hasn't resulted from 'fixing' a single person, situation or any other thing externally. And I absolutely know for sure that it will be the same for you.

**If you want your life to look different, YOU have to BE THE CHANGE.**

(And, yes, I *did* just play the Gandhi trump card!)

## Who doesn't want peace and happiness?

Countless surveys and studies around the world have asked people what they want most in life.

**Unsurprisingly, the number one answer is *always* 'happiness'.**

And for a great majority of my life I was no exception. I just wanted to be peaceful and happy – in EVERY area of my life. I mean, who doesn't, right?

I'm sure you'll agree that for the most part our happiness relates to the people and situations around us. It's affected by our work, family, significant others and friends, and by the people and places we interact with daily.

**But when we put our peace and happiness in the hands of the outside world, we can come unstuck.**

Because what happens when things don't go the way you want them to? How do you react when people don't do what you want them to or don't behave as you want them to?

**If you're like most people, you'll probably go into 'fixing' mode.**

To regain your peace and happiness, you'll focus your attention outwardly to see what's making you unhappy. And then, when you *think* you see the problem, you'll put on your little 'fixing' overalls, pick up your 'fixing' tools and start singing, "Heigh-ho, heigh-ho, it's off to work I go!"

## Choose your battles

**The job of parenting comes without any kind of script at the best of times.**

Raising teenagers, however, demands a whole other playbook.

Ironically, we want our kids to spread their wings, become their own people, develop their own personality and be responsible. BUT, on the other hand, we also want them to do as we say (and not always as we do)!

One such 'do as I say' issue happened with my daughter. She was always 'a being of self-expression and personalised chaos' in her bedroom.

**This loosely translates to 'her room was always a pig sty'!**

We'd have so many ding-dong arguments about the state of her room: complete and utter shouting matches. And I was totally self-righteous about it.

Not only was she messing with *my* peace and happiness, but damn it, I was right! It was my house, so she should follow my rules! The truth is that I just wanted her to be a clean freak, even though it was clear that she wasn't.

And this is where the 'fixing merry-go-round ride' can come to an end... or go on forever!

**Either way, the choice was mine.**

I could choose to spend the limited time I had with my daughter trying to fix her and turn her into a clean freak OR I could choose to let it go, allowing myself to be peaceful and happy AND have a daughter who was messy.

And let me tell you what came with choosing to let it go:

- a happy, calm and peaceful relationship
- a happy, calm and peaceful life
- a happy calm and peaceful ME!

Doesn't that sound better than "Hi Jen, how are you?" / "Well, if my daughter would just clean her room, I'd be a lot happier!"

**And honestly, fixing the situation WOULDN'T have made me happy.**

Even if my daughter *had* cleaned her room and I *was* happy for a short time, fixing this wouldn't have created ongoing peace and happiness in my life. Why? Because I'd simply have found some other person or situation in my life that needed fixing so I could be peaceful and happy!

Does this sound familiar?

**NOTE: some things in life are what I call 'deal-breakers'.**

To me, a deal-breaker is something that involves you selling out on your values. For example, if honesty is something you covet, a compromise that involved being dishonest wouldn't work.

The specific situations that are deal-breakers for you will depend on your own personal values. And if the situation you're dealing with truly is a deal-breaker, you may need to place some house rules or boundaries around it.

However, I believe that many of us make everything into a deal-breaker, which then comes at the expense of our peace and happiness.

**So what might you be hanging on to that you could actually let go of?**

## Instead of choosing to be happy, calm and peaceful, we try to fix stuff so that we are

**It's not just about getting our kids to clean their rooms.**

Other things we say to ourselves that base our happiness on fixing other people include:

- "If I could just get my son to stop gaming…"
- "If I could just get my partner to do more around the house…"
- "If I could just get my friend to return the stuff she borrows from me…"
- "If I could just get the person I work with to work as hard as I do…"
- "If I could just get that promotion…"
- "If I could just…"

*Then…* **my life would be calm and peaceful, and I'd be happy!**

But here's the thing: none of these people or situations need fixing *before* you can be peaceful and happy.

When you develop the awareness that you can choose what you're willing to let go of, you realise that you can CHOOSE peace and happiness. And when you can do that, you're literally a single thought away from a powerfully peaceful life.

## The Practice – How to stop fixing and let go

**So what is there to do? How can you be peaceful and happy now?**

First, remind yourself that nobody and nothing needs fixing for you to be peaceful and happy now.

Again: these life lessons aren't about giving in or compromising on the deal-breakers I mentioned above. So this practice is *not* asking you to go against your values. Instead, it's simply asking you to choose what you can let go of in order to be peaceful and happy now.

So open up your journal or a blank document on your computer, and let's work through it.

Step 1:    Recognise whatever is outside of you that's making you upset.

        Write down, "I am upset/irritated because...................."

        [eg. "I am upset/irritated because my daughter won't clean her room."]

Step 2:    Now look at *why* it upsets/irritates you.

        Write down, "I am upset/irritated about this because...................."

        [eg. "I am upset/irritated about this because I like things to be neat and tidy."]

Step 3:    Understanding why the situation upsets/irritates you now makes way for you to look at what you believe about it.

Write down, "This has me believe that........................"

[eg. "This has me believe that she doesn't respect me or my home."]

**Step 4:** Now look at what you've written in Step 3, and honestly ask yourself, "Is this true?" Write the answer down.

- If you answer NO, eg. "No, being neat and tidy is just not important to her. Even though neatness is important to me, being messy doesn't mean she doesn't respect me or my home." – consider whether you can be peaceful with *that* answer.

- Or, if it is YES, eg. "Yes, she really doesn't respect me. If she did, she'd keep her room tidy." – ask whether you can be peaceful even without that respect in the moment.

I want you to consider that most of the things that upset you aren't actually intended to upset you. (You may need to read that sentence again to let it sink in.)

Rather, being upset is something you choose to be because of what you've chosen to believe about a situation.

# Lesson 8

## IN THE FUTURE, YOU'LL LOVE HOW YOU LOOK TODAY

 AKA So why not love how you look today, today?

### Be honest: do you really love how you look?

**Once upon a time, I was a magazine editor.**

Running a magazine was one of the highlights of my entrepreneurial life. It allowed me to combine my knowledge and expertise from the health and fitness industry with my passion for coaching and education. Then it allowed me to share all these things (and more) in a publication specifically about this topic.

I loved creating the magazine and sharing stories of inspiring people. I was not only a part owner but I was also the editor, reporter, photographer, writer and advertising salesperson.

And although I'm not qualified in photography, I discovered a passion for it.

I loved setting up photo shoots to capture just the right shot. And I'm sure it will come as no surprise that the *number one* thing I heard at every photo shoot was, "I hate having my photo taken!"

Every. Single. Time.

## From an early age, we learn to question what we see in the mirror

**My magazine experience prompted me to ask where and HOW we learn this.**

These are, of course, huge questions and ones without a single answer. Personally, I believe I first learnt it from my parents. And it wasn't because they didn't tell me I was beautiful, but because they *did*.

For example, whenever I wore my 'good' clothes, they'd tell me I looked beautiful. And, of course, I then carried that forward, telling my kids the same thing.

Now, I'm sure they didn't mean I *wasn't* beautiful at any other time. However, I can't help but wonder if hearing this planted an unconscious seed of comparison in my mind. Something like 'dressed up equals beautiful, while not dressed up equals not beautiful'.

**Then later, outside influences around me – and all of us – reinforced what was and wasn't seen as beautiful.**

Those influences included:

- our culture
- our environment
- bullying
- sales and marketing within the media.

71

And for many people in the world of social media, body shaming is a sadly out-of-control epidemic that confuses the question of beauty even further.

## I was just as judgemental as everyone else

**For as long as I can remember, I rarely liked photographs of myself.**

Whenever I saw any, I'd inevitably think (and sometimes say out loud where my kids could hear) things like:

- "I hate the crease between my eyebrows!"

- "OMG, I look six months pregnant!"

- "Why didn't someone tell me my bum looks like that from behind?"

- "What's going on with my hair?!"

- "Wait... what?! I have an overbite?"

- "Oh my God! I look so old!"

And believe me... the list could go on.

I'm not sure when those thoughts started or why. But somewhere, somehow, they began to infect my focus.

**Then, in 2008, I decided to enter the world of body sculpting.**

At the time, I thought it would just be another great goal to achieve. Somewhere under the surface, though, I also thought that if I 'sculpted' my body to win a competition, I'd surely start loving the way I looked.

*Then* I might start liking every photograph of myself too.

Logical, right?

**Being an overachiever, of course I won first place at my very first competition.**

So on that day, I was the best of the best. I had an enormous crowd of friends there to cheer me on and my kids were waving a giant banner that read, 'Show us your guns, Mum!'

I walked off stage with a giant gold trophy in my hands, being applauded and celebrated by my family and friends.

**And yet, both in the mirror and in photos from the day, I *still* saw things I didn't like.**

How crazy is that?!

Now, if you knew me at the time, this may have come as a surprise.

After all, for most of my life, I've appeared (at least on the outside) confident, happy, in great shape, fit, healthy... And, yes, I was all of those things!

But my focus wasn't on looking for those things. Instead, it was on looking for flaws.

**I even became bulimic for a brief time following my body sculpting career.**

And here's the thing: I was *never* going to see myself as beautiful, no matter what shape I was in. Not even when I was on stage at a body sculpting competition, holding a first place trophy above my head.

Not yesterday, not today, not tomorrow and not in ten years' time for that matter.

NEVER.

**Now don't get me wrong... I've never _hated_ myself.**

I knew I was intelligent and capable of achieving any goal I set myself. I knew I was a smart, savvy business woman and a great mum.

I was confident in every imaginable way.

But the problem was that when it came to my physical appearance, I had hardwired my mind to see flaws and not beauty.

I thought the body sculpting competition would help in some way but, ironically, it actually exacerbated the problem. However, I'm now grateful that it shone the most illuminating awareness spotlight on this very skewed perception I held of myself.

**I also became aware of what I was teaching my son and daughter about body image.**

At first I was devastated because I'd inadvertently made an impression on them that I couldn't undo. But one of the most powerful things about awareness is that it makes all the difference to what you do/ say/think next.

So with my new awareness, I started to consciously choose the way I spoke to them and myself. And I now have open, honest conversations with them on this topic.

**Ironically, it was social media that gave me this new awareness.**

Look, Facebook has its good points and its not-so-good points; I reckon that one of the best things they ever developed is the 'memories' feature.

At some point after my body sculpting career ended, I began to see photos of myself from two, five and even seven years ago. The funny thing was that I'd look at some of them, especially the body sculpting pictures, and I could actually remember thinking at the time, "Blah! I hate this photo."

Yet years later, when the same photo popped up again, I saw it in a whole different way.

I actually *liked* the me that I saw in all of those photos. Even the one of my daughter and me wearing face masks together!

That really got me thinking about how funny the notion was that in the future, I'd love how I looked today.

And then I thought, "Or I could just love how I look today, today!"

## Beauty is a choice that's available right now

**Something I now know for sure is that beauty is just like happiness.**

It's something we want and something we desire. However, it's something we think exists in the future – something we'll have once we lose weight, get our hair done, remove our wrinkles and so on.

But like happiness, beauty is *also* a choice. It's available to us all right now, in this moment, if we choose it.

No matter how we look today, we can CHOOSE to see ourselves as beautiful right now:

- Not when we lose five, ten or twenty kilos...
- Not when we win a body sculpting competition...
- Not when we're having a good hair day...
- Not after we've had a round of Botox...
- Not if the angle of the camera is just right...
- Not after we delete the 50 selfies we took before we found one that's OK...

RIGHT NOW!

**Now I'm not for one second saying that looking after our health isn't important.**

It is. But if we let beauty define us, then just like with happiness, we'll be chasing it for the rest of our lives!

I also truly believe that our thoughts create our world (more about this in Lesson 27). So if you choose to focus on what's *wrong* with you, you'll see more and more of it. Conversely, if you instead focus on what's right – especially when it comes to things like happiness, beauty, love, gratitude and kindness – you'll see more of that too!

And not just in yourself, but also in the world around you.

(FYI: Whilst I was doing the photo shoot for this book, I never once said, "I hate having my photo taken!" or, "Can you photoshop the images?" or, "Does my bum look big in this?" Because these days, I absolutely LOVE how I look today, today.)

## The Practice – Loving who you are today

For the next seven days I want you to spend each day focusing on a different part of you that you have difficulty loving.

For example, you might choose parts like your smile, boobs, tummy, bum, legs, arms or hair. Only you will know what these parts are.

Step 1:   Begin on Day 1 with, for example, your smile. Write the following letter to that part of you.

"Hello, smile,

I see you and I love you.

Today I notice all of your beauty and magnificence. I especially love................ [insert your own words here].

You are part of the tapestry of my divine uniqueness, and I am forever grateful for you on this day and every other."

Step 2:   Take your letter and stand in front of a mirror. Then, looking into your own eyes, read it out loud.

It's helpful to do this several times during the day, so you may want to stick it on your bathroom mirror.

Step 3:   On Day 2, repeat Steps 1 and 2 with the next part you've chosen. Then do the same on Day 3 with the next part and so on for the entire week.

NOTE: if this seems silly, it's likely even *more* important that you take on the practice.

# Lesson 9

## WHAT PEOPLE THINK OF YOU
## IS NONE OF YOUR BUSINESS

 AKA Don't be a
people-pleaser!

### You've probably heard this phrase before

I first heard the phrase 'What people think of you is none of your business' back in 2004.

It's been attributed to a bunch of people from Wayne Dyer to Gary Oldman, but research suggests it may have originated with Eleanor Roosevelt.

And as it turned out, I'd hear the phrase again in several other conversations with various people over the coming years. It's a very simple concept to understand, but truly applying it to your life requires some practice.

So let's break it down.

## 'People-pleaser syndrome' is one of the biggest blocks to transformation

**People-pleasing and asking for feedback are two different things.**

I think it's important to first clarify the difference between people-pleasing and wanting feedback. Feedback is about helping you to improve. In business, it can be useful for improving products and services. In life, it can help you improve your communication or relationships.

People-pleasing, however, is a mechanism we humans use to boost self-esteem, increase our self-worth and validate that we're 'good people'.

**Put another way, people-pleasing is the *opposite* of knowing that what people think of you is none of your business.**

It essentially means that you do care – far too much – about what people think of you. In turn, that means every decision, thought or action you take hinges on how you think other people see you.

You navigate your decisions in life by constantly asking yourself questions like:

- "What if they think I'm rude?"
- "What if they think I'm selfish?"
- "What if they think I'm lazy?"
- "What if they think I'm a bad person?"
- "What if they think I'm stupid?"
- "What if they think I'm mean?"

What if...? What if...? What if...?

**Psychologists actually believe there's an evolutionary basis for this worry.**

It's the fear that we'll get 'cast out of the tribe' and won't be able to survive on our own.

However, whilst these survival instincts were warranted thousands of years ago, they have very little significance today. What's more, these made-up fears can become a giant block to our awareness of our self-worth and, ultimately, to creating change and transformation.

## The practical difference between seeking feedback and people-pleasing

**I worked for over a decade as a fitness trainer and coach.**

During that time, I conducted thousands of group and one-on-one sessions with all manner of people, both here in Australia and overseas. I was a leader in the industry in my region and went on to receive multiple awards.

However, when I started out, I always worried about what my clients thought of their sessions.

**Loosely translated, I worried about what they thought of me as a trainer.**

I'd even try to dance around the issue by constantly asking, "Was that OK? Did you enjoy that?" I wasn't really asking what they thought about the session, though. Well, OK, I was. But deep down, I really just meant, "Was *I* OK? Did *I* do a good job?"

Now, of course, what my client thought of a session *can* be important information.

However, asking for this information to reassure myself is the polar opposite of asking for it because I want to continuously improve as a trainer.

The first one is the act of a people-pleaser, which I was in the early days of my career. I was always seeking reassurance.

The second is the act of someone who wants to create a high-quality experience and outcome for their client.

It took the support of a mentor to become aware that this approach made my sessions all about me, instead of about my client.

When I realised this, I could let go of my need for approval and validation about being a good trainer.

Because deep down, I already knew that I was.

Then, I could instead focus on asking my clients better questions like, "What would have made that a 10/10 session?"

That way, I'd get the feedback that would help me to become an even better trainer, while also helping them to get the results they wanted.

## What's important is what YOU think of you

So let me ask you another question. What do YOU think about you?

Something I know for sure is that selling your soul for other people's approval is a path to feeling 'not good enough' for the rest of your life!

On top of that, trying to control what other people think about you will keep the authentic, beautiful, shining YOU hidden from the world forever!

The final kicker is that a peaceful heart will constantly elude you. In other words, you'll never feel happy if you're chasing other people's approval.

**But wait, this one comes with a twist!**

The concept that what people think of you is none of your business is in no way a 'get out of jail free card' for being an ass.

So when you ask what you think about yourself, be *honest* about the answer. And I mean be really honest.

If you know you're a good person, own that shit. Give up worrying about what other people think of you: it's none of your business!

**If you know you're being an ass, stop it!**

Because whilst other people's thoughts about you are none of your business, who you're being in this world absolutely is your business. And it's something YOU have complete control over.

At the end of the day, the only things you can control are your own thoughts and actions (see Lesson 28). So acknowledge to yourself whenever you're being awesome, kind and caring, or shining your light on the world.

Don't seek other people's approval to confirm or dispute this, or worry about what they think of you. You know what's in your own heart, so don't question it.

And if you know in your heart that you're being an ass, just stop it.

**Worrying about what other people think is exhausting!**

The crazy thing is that none of us really have any idea what other people are thinking. For example, gym surveys have shown that many people hate walking into a gym because they worry that everyone will be looking at them and talking about them.

The irony is that *everyone* is thinking the exact same thought. So no one is thinking about anyone else: they're all just thinking about themselves!

Which is kind of funny when you think about it.

**Again: it doesn't matter what anyone else thinks about you. It only matters what YOU think of you.**

A great place to start is to notice whenever you find yourself thinking 'What will they think of me?' thoughts.

Noticing when you feel embarrassed to say or do something is another 'pause point' to bring awareness to the possibility that your made-up thoughts are stopping you.

Finally, becoming aware that you're hesitating about making a decision or choice can also tell you that a people-pleasing pattern is present.

## The Practice – Figuring out what YOU think of you

**Give this practice a go to help you switch focus.**

Next time you notice yourself thinking or saying, "What will people think about me?" replace it immediately with, "What do *I* think about me?"

Remember to be really honest with yourself about the answer.

- If you discover you approve of who you're being, keep being it.

- If you discover you're being an ass, stop and choose something you DO approve of instead.

Then acknowledge yourself for being brave enough to ask this question and act on the answer.

# Lesson 10

## FEEL YOUR FEELINGS, BUT DON'T BECOME THEM

 AKA Be OK with not being OK

### Have you ever woken up in a 'funk'?

I call this state a 'funk', but you might describe it as just feeling down, miserable or even depressed.

You sometimes feel as if something bad has happened (or will happen) when there's no real reason for feeling it. Nothing's *actually* happened, but you feel irritated, anxious, annoyed, grumpy or perhaps even sad anyway.

Or maybe something bad has actually happened.

Regardless, whether the reason is perceived or real, you wake up feeling something you don't want to feel.

The next thing you know that little voice we talked about in Lesson 5 jumps to life and asks, "Why am I feeling like this? What's wrong with me?"

Has this ever happened to you?

## Of course, your mind goes to work to find the answer

You'll scan back over the previous days, looking for the thing that set you off.

And the crazy thing is that your mind *will* find something.

Then, after that, the next step is usually trying to stop feeling the feeling. Some people do this by diving into work. Others use exercise, shopping, eating, drugs, sex, drinking... whatever works so long as you don't have to feel the feeling.

You'll do literally anything you can to avoid feeling the funk.

Meanwhile, your thoughts continue to serve up all the reasons you're feeling like this and everything that's wrong with you and your life.

Imagine a fire-hose that's been turned on full bore with nobody holding on to it. Water begins to spray wildly from it in every direction as it twists and turns.

That's pretty much what your mind does with a question like, "What's wrong with me?"

Cue the out-of-control fire-hose!

## Looking for what was wrong never helped me take control of my fire-hose

A couple of drinks is sometimes all it takes for me to feel the effects of alcohol.

Back when I was younger, I definitely drank more than I should on occasion. And, of course, I'd be lying if I said it doesn't still occasionally happen; although now that I'm older and somewhat wiser, it's more rare.

However, the aftermath of alcohol is where I first noticed how any kind of funk I felt was amplified. Truth be told, sometimes alcohol actually created it.

Perhaps you can relate?

**I call this effect 'post-alcohol depression'.**

Just to be clear, 'post-alcohol depression' is *not* an actual condition. It's just the name I made up for what I experience somewhere around two days after too many drinks.

Here's what I've noticed about the effect: a couple of days after drinking too much, I almost always feel down – depressed even.

On that second morning, I wake up feeling like the doom and gloom of the world has set in. Or if I was already dealing with any kind of funk, it now feels ten times as funky.

**Then I immediately start asking myself why I feel like this.**

And then BOOM! Away my out-of-control fire-hose mind goes in search of an answer.

Of course it finds one. Then it finds another and another. And before my feet have even hit the floor, my life is a mess and the world is closing in on me. Tiny problems now seem enormous – like a volcano ready to erupt.

And, of course, I know I'm right about it. My mind has found all the evidence I need to show me I'm right!

**But there are a couple of faults in my mind's logic:**

- **First, in this example, alcohol is a depressant.** Plenty of studies support the negative mood effects of chronic alcohol abuse. Plus, our bodies use mood-balancing nutrients like B-vitamins to help them process alcohol and get it out of our systems. So even a few drinks on rare occasions *will* ultimately affect our moods.

- **Second, as I mentioned above, sometimes we just wake up in a funk.** In my example above, alcohol is a trigger. You might have a different one. But no matter what the reason for the funk is – real, perceived or alcohol-induced – your out-of-control fire-hose will always kick into action. And it will catapult you straight into 'what's wrong with me?' mode.

## Take control of *your* fire-hose

**The first step to taking control, of course, is becoming aware.**

Notice that your automatic response when you're in a funk is to start searching for what's wrong.

Only when you notice that response can you get your hands on your out-of-control hose.

**The next step is to actively direct your thoughts by acknowledging what you're feeling.**

For example, me directing my thoughts may look like me saying to myself, "Hello, funk. I see you there. Looks like we'll be hanging out today."

Then allow yourself to simply feel whatever's there for you.

Can you see the difference between that and letting the fire-hose spray wildly out of control?

If you can become aware that you're just *feeling* a feeling, instead of going off in search of evidence for *why* you are feeling that feeling, you take back control. Then you can allow the feeling to be there without needing to block, fix, avoid or outrun it.

**Now don't get me wrong: it will absolutely take practice to feel your feelings.**

You've been taught to block them by your parents, culture, society and environment.

With practice, however, I've learnt to welcome my feelings – even the ones I once labelled as bad – and I know you can too.

Eckhart Tolle says, *"Whatever you fight, you strengthen, and what you resist, persists."* This is particularly true of feelings.

**Think of your feelings as guides.**

They often come to show you something you may need to pay some attention to.

And whilst feeling them can be a little prickly, avoiding them will only result in them showing up again, often in a much bigger way.

## The Practice – How to feel your feelings

**Give yourself permission to feel ALL your feelings.**

When they come, greet them even if you don't want to feel them. To do this:

**Step 1:**     Acknowledge them.

**Step 2:**     Allow them to be there with you.

**Step 3:**     Ask them what they're here to teach you.

**Step 4:**     Ask yourself what you may be avoiding.

I recommend spending time meditating or journaling about what comes up for you. Don't censor what you write and, above all, don't judge it either.

Just allow whatever wants to pass through you to do so. You may need to repeat this exercise for several days (or even longer in some instances).

Remember: asking powerless questions like, "What's wrong with me?" will simply unleash the crazy out-of-control fire-hose!

# Lesson 11

## BEWARE OF PEDESTALS

 AKA The higher something is, the further it has to fall

### Do you have mentors you admire?

**Are there people in your life you hold in high regard?**

Perhaps you secretly (or openly) model yourself on them. They might be people you follow on social media, people you aspire to be in business, or people you draw inspiration from to continue expanding and growing in your life.

If so, you may have engaged one of them as a mentor, either officially or unofficially. We sometimes have mentors in our lives who have no idea they're even fulfilling that role.

They may be people you work with, members of your family, close friends, community leaders and changemakers, or even celebrities.

In any instance, mentors can be tremendous catalysts for our personal growth.

## Being inspired by someone isn't a reason to place them on a pedestal

**When your self-esteem is low and your confidence is lagging, life can seem to come at you from every direction.**

You can feel tangled up by the thoughts in your own head. In these times, your ability to trust in yourself and your own capabilities can wane. You stop looking within for solutions and start looking outside of yourself.

When this happens, a mentor who'd normally inspire you to tap into your own inner wisdom can instead become a source of comparison.

**In other words, you find yourself putting them on a pedestal.**

When this happens, you might notice thoughts like:

- "They make it look easy."
- "Good stuff always seems to happen to them."
- "They're always lucky."
- "They always make good choices."
- "They always know exactly what to do and say."
- "I wish I were them."

When you place someone on a pedestal, what you're really telling yourself is that they're better than you. (And remember that they didn't put themselves up there: you did.)

## The higher the pedestal, the further someone can fall

**I once had a mentor who impacted my life profoundly.**

They seemed to have ALL their shit together; because I didn't, I revered them. So much so that I often didn't act or make a decision without consulting with them first.

This mentor seemed to be able to instantly pluck from the sky every single answer to every single problem I had – something I didn't believe I could do for myself.

I reached out to them constantly and consulted them about everything.

**In short, they were my go-to at a particularly difficult time of life.**

My adoration grew and grew to the extent that I (unfairly) regarded them as my appointed saviour. And they were completely clueless about the role I'd given them in my life.

Over time, as this person helped me, was patient with me and supported me in a multitude of ways, I began to see myself as 'down here' with them 'up there'.

I want to reinforce here that they *never* asked for this accolade. I didn't even give them a choice in the matter.

They simply extended love and kindness to me during a painful phase in my life.

**I realise now that I'd placed them on a pedestal.**

Then, one day, a misunderstanding occurred between us: one that resulted in a heated exchange with completely opposing viewpoints.

At the time, we were both under some pressure and, in hindsight, the misunderstanding could have been easily resolved. But in one fell swoop, my 'revered saviour' plummeted from the pedestal I had placed them atop.

I became their judge, jury and executioner – even though I'd once held them in the highest regard and they had no idea of what had occurred inside my mind.

**The thing about pedestals is that they're often very tall and very wobbly.**

Not only that, but whatever we put on the top of them is usually something we adore. So this precious thing precariously balances there, until one day, with only the tiniest of bumps, the pedestal begins to wobble.

Before we can steady it, the precious thing on top falls, smashing into a million – often irreparable – pieces.

Which begs the question: if it was so precious, why did we put it up there where it could so easily fall in the first place?

**Fortunately, my friendship with this person *wasn't* irreparably broken.**

Once I became aware of my pedestal-placing tendency, I didn't require all the king's horses and all the king's men to put the friendship back together again.

And these days, we have a beautiful relationship – one where we draw inspiration from each other.

# We all have something to teach and something to learn

**Placing someone you admire on a pedestal only ever has one outcome.**

It doesn't matter whether this person is a friend, family member, mentor or celebrity. They inevitably fall, usually with only the tiniest bump.

It's also important to understand that putting someone you admire on a pedestal actually sets them up for failure and sets you up for disappointment.

There is absolutely no other possible outcome.

**Then consider that you created this, not them.**

And when they fall – which they will, just like Humpty Dumpty – you may not be able to put the relationship back together again.

In Lesson 20, we'll dive deeper into the topic of people making mistakes. However, for now, realise that making mistakes is inevitable for any human being. And one of those inevitable mistakes *will* be the bump that overturns your pedestal.

We are all students. We are all teachers. We are all mentors.

And most importantly, we are all *equal*.

**That means we all have much to teach and much to learn from each other.**

## The Practice – Bringing awareness to other people's positive traits

This lesson has established the benefits of mentors, whilst also highlighting the danger of putting them on pedestals.

So how can you identify and begin to embody the traits you admire in others in a way that will inspire you?

Step 1: Write down what it was about the person that first caught your attention. What did you notice that piqued your admiration?

eg. "What I noticed about Bill was his can-do approach to life."

Step 2: Now write down three or four traits that you admire about this person.

eg. "Bill is humorous and positive. He offers support and seeks solutions."

Step 3: Choose the one trait that you'd most like to embody in your own life.

eg. "I'd like to embody Bill's ability to offer support."

Step 4: Now make a list of three or four ways in which you could practise expanding more of this trait in your own life.

Step 5: For the next seven days, set the intention each day to embody this trait – eg. offer support to other people – throughout your day.

When you choose to embody what you admire in others, you potentially create a ripple effect in your home, community and, eventually, the world.

# Lesson 12

## LOOK FOR 'WHAT'S SO RIGHT'

 AKA Don't get stuck
in the shit cycle

### Do you know someone that 'shit' always happens to?

**We all know that person whose life is one big 'my life is shit' story, don't we?**

You're almost too scared to ask this person about their day, because you know they'll just respond with, "My life is shit, and here are all the reasons why!"

And then they'll tell you:

- "This is the shit that happened yesterday."

- "This is the shit that happened today."

- "This is the shit that will probably happen tomorrow."

- "These are the shitty things that happened 20 years ago."

- "And while I'm at it, let's take a look at all the shitty things in your life too!"

Before you know it, you're both knee-deep in a shitty conversation about how shitty both your lives are!

## What if you focused on what is going right instead?

**OK, let's be real, focusing on 'what's so right' in your life does not stop shit from happening.**

So I'm not suggesting you skip through life pretending that it does: smelling wildflowers, wearing rose-coloured glasses, singing Kumbaya and chanting 'Om'.

Looking for 'what's so right' in your life absolutely begins with acknowledging the shit and taking action, if necessary, to deal with it. But then, once you've dealt with it, STOP FOCUSING ON IT!

**Instead, switch your focus to what's actually going *well* in your life.**

At the heart of this lesson is the practice of honing your awareness to notice what's going right in your life as your new default way of seeing the world.

It's not about being 'right' (or making others 'wrong'). Instead, it's about harnessing your awareness to see 'what's so right' in *your* life for you.

Yes, sometimes shit will happen. And when it does, you'll need to deal with it swiftly and powerfully. But after you've dealt with it, this practice will show you why it's necessary to get the hell out of shitsville and bring your focus back to 'what's so right'.

# Focusing on 'what's so right' in practice

**I used to get stuck in the shit cycle a lot!**

Then I got the idea of looking for 'what's so right' from an incredible friend and business partner back in 2013. I'd wander into their office almost daily to tell them all about the shitty things that were going on in my life at the time.

Of course, that focus only increased the number of shitty things I saw. (See Lesson 43, which shows how easy it is to spiral into this way of thinking.)

**One day, they responded by telling me to write a list of 100 things that were so *right* about my life.**

I wasn't to return to the office until my list was complete.

The only rule was that I had to write every statement positively, without using the words 'not' or 'don't'. For example, I couldn't write, "What's so right about my life is that I'm not broke." Instead, I had to write, "What's so right about my life is that my bank account has money in it."

**Challenge accepted.**

I agreed to write the list; although truthfully speaking, I couldn't see how it would make one iota of difference!

I went home, sat down with my pen and paper in hand, and began to write.

And I have to be honest, it wasn't easy: the first ten things took me more than half an hour to come up with. My mind had become so attuned to only seeing what was wrong that seeing anything right had become a challenge.

But I persevered.

Four hours later, I had 50 things.

**And finally, five hours later, I had my 100 things.**

As I continued with the practice, something shifted in me. My mind seemed to become unstuck. Where my thoughts had once been trapped in doom and gloom, they now somehow floated into light and bright.

I was dumbfounded and ridiculously happy!

**So I decided to go one step further and type out my list on a sheet of paper.**

I wanted to carry it with me. That way, if I found my thoughts creeping back into 'what's wrong', I could pull out my list and read it in its entirety.

I began making this a night-time practice as well.

Before I went to sleep, I'd make a mental list in my head of what had been so right in my day. I'd find myself drifting off to sleep while re-enacting the highlights of my day.

This not only helped me to sleep more peacefully but it was also like a complete reset for my mind.

**I passed this practice on to my children, friends and family.**

I even created a free Facebook group called *What's So Right?* (www. facebook.com/groups/whatssoright) to help others make this a daily practice. And the practice *needs* to be daily to shift gears on your focus, rewire your neural pathways, and ultimately transform the way you see yourself, your life and the people in it.

(Incidentally, the scientific word for your brain's ability to create new neural pathways is 'neuroplasticity'. For more information on how this works, try googling the term.)

Today, I find it almost impossible to focus on what's wrong. On the rare occasions where I do, the new neural pathways in my brain kick in and I flip my perspective in an instant.

All because I've made this practice a consistent daily habit.

## We all have the power to focus on 'what's so right'

**Does this practice just sound too simple to you?**

I've been questioned many times about the simplicity of my 'what's so right' practice.

People tell me that it couldn't possibly change the way their world shows up. That just thinking happy thoughts is naïve and that being positive can't possibly change their life.

And, in part, that's accurate.

**Because remember: in life, shit happens.**

It will always happen. And there's no real way of *stopping* it from happening.

We can't control the uncontrollable, and what happens outside of ourselves is 100% uncontrollable. (Sorry to all the control freaks out there – I know that's hard to hear because I used to be one of you.)

**But there's far more to this practice than imagined positivity.**

I'm not suggesting you just think positive thoughts about the shit that happens.

Instead, I recommend that you sift through your day and extract the good stuff to focus your thoughts on.

In doing so, over time you'll literally increase your brain's ability to notice the good things in your life. You'll start to see opportunities that were maybe always there, but were previously shrouded in shit.

**You can even practise this when people around you are having a shitty day.**

Here's how: first, resist the urge to get caught up in their 'my life is shit' story.

NOTE: that doesn't mean being all hard-ass and refusing to listen. Sometimes all people need is to be heard.

But when you're trying to be a good friend/partner/mother/father, etc., it's easy to inadvertently become caught up in the other person's shitty day.

Instead, I'm suggesting that you refuse to join in the 'my life is shit' conversation (or tell them to 'just get over it' or try to 'fix it' for them). This will only lead to creating more shit – for them *and* you.

Rather, try to listen with empathy, and perhaps steer them towards either dealing with the situation or letting it go.

This may be a bit tricky at first, and you'll probably need to set your own 'shit shield' to maximum. The person you're talking to may also get angry that you don't agree with them or that you don't seem to support them.

If so, it may be better to walk away for the moment. And yes, sometimes that won't feel easy. But by staying and getting drawn into their shit, you're actually allowing your energy to feed it.

**Seek out people who'll do this for you too.**

As you go through life, try to surround yourself with people who will do the same thing for you. Because what I know for certain is that while shitty things do happen in life (which is outside your control), the length of time you stay in your shit cycle depends upon you (which is 100% within your control).

Will this happen overnight?

NO! Of course not. It takes practice... lots of practice.

But again, if you want your world to change, you have to 'be that change'.

## The Practice – What's so right?

**Take out your journal and make a list of 100 things that are going right in your life.**

Make sure that every item on your list is worded positively (see above for examples).

You don't have to complete the whole list all in one go. Take breaks if you need to, but keep coming back to it until you have 100 items.

**Bonus ideas:**

- Consider typing your list up as I did, so you can carry it around with you and take it out to re-read when things *aren't* going right.

- Consider creating a morning or evening ritual like I did that involves either writing down or just mentally reviewing 'what's so right' in your life.

- Join our FREE Facebook Group - *What's So Right?* - at www.facebook.com/groups/whatssoright.

# Stage 2:
# Acceptance

"I am a lover of what is,
not because I'm a spiritual
person, but because it hurts
when I argue with reality."
- Byron Katie

## The second stage of experiential transformation is acceptance

**If you google the word 'acceptance', you'll find various definitions.**

But if I had to try to sum up the general consensus, I'd say it's about 'being OK' with something. However, in the context of transformation, acceptance is about more than just being OK.

Instead, the true potency of this superpower lies in letting go of *not* being OK.

**Acceptance is about letting go of resistance.**

Acceptance will open you to what life has to offer, whilst resistance will keep you blocked from it.

Acceptance is about moving from a place of avoidance and the feeling that something is wrong to a neutral, peaceful place of allowing 'what is'.

In Buddhism, acceptance is fundamental to happiness and it shows up in many Buddhist teachings. In fact, the premise of the second of the Four Noble Truths of Buddhism is that desire is the root of all suffering.

Translated, 'desire' means 'desiring reality to be anything but what it is'. In other words, in Buddhism, our suffering happens when we resist something.

Acceptance is also one of the foundations of the 12-Step addiction recovery program.

So if acceptance can literally make our suffering disappear, why aren't we all living in a permanent state of blissed-out peace and harmony?

# Resistance: the 'kryptonite' of transformation

**Remember in the comics how Superman had just one thing that could stop him in his tracks?**

For the most part, there was nothing that could keep him from his purpose of having good prevail over evil. Nothing, that is, except for that one pesky green substance: kryptonite.

I want you to think of resistance as your kryptonite. As I mentioned above, resistance is the opposite of acceptance. And as soon as it shows up, it can completely derail your efforts to live happily and peacefully. Luckily, you've already gained access to your first superpower, awareness, so being able to spot this fiendish villain will now be a lot easier.

**Ironically, even the mere suggestion of acceptance can create resistance.**

This is particularly true if you're a control freak (as I used to be). We tend to see acceptance as requiring us to compromise our principles, back down, show weakness, be a doormat or not speak our truth.

How many times have we uttered words like, "That's just unacceptable!" or, "I will not accept this/that"?

In fact, resisting is where most of us exist on a daily basis. It's no wonder we're all in a constant state of struggle and suffering.

**So let me make this crystal clear.**

Acceptance is in no way an act of submission. It's not about giving in, tolerating or passively resigning yourself. It's not about biting your tongue or giving up any of your principles or values.

Nor is it about asking anyone else to do this either.

Rather, acceptance brings YOU inner peace. It will untether you from anything that weighs you down, keeps you stuck in repeated patterns or prevents you from moving forwards in your relationships, business or life.

## Join me on a journey to – and through – acceptance

**By the end of this stage, my intention is for you to willingly embrace the power of acceptance.**

The following practices will show you how to harness the power of acceptance and bring it into all areas of your life.

By mastering acceptance of 'what is' and letting go of your resistance to how things 'should be', you'll unleash your capacity to 'just be' with life. You'll also understand that letting go of resistance is in no way submissive. Instead, it's a superpower that helps you to defuse the angst of life's dramas and curveballs.

Accessing your awareness and embracing acceptance are integral to preparing you for the third stage of transformation, which is understanding your Area of Control.

# Lesson 13

## HUMAN FIRST, ENLIGHTENED SECOND

 AKA Goodbye disturbance, hello peace

### You've probably heard the saying 'Nobody's perfect'

**So let me ask you. Have you ever done any of the following?**

- lied, cheated or stolen

- yelled at your kids or your partner

- had a meltdown or thrown a tantrum

- made a mistake, made the wrong choice or let someone down

- said YES when you meant NO (or said NO when you meant YES)

- been jealous of someone or something, or given someone the silent treatment

- made someone feel guilty or enacted revenge

- judged someone unfairly (or fairly)

- broken your word (or even broken the law).

I could keep going, but I'm pretty sure that – if you're conscious and have a heart beating in your chest – you've answered YES to at least one of these.

If so, I'm going to go out on a limb and say, "Welcome."

**Welcome to the Human Club.**

Currently, the membership stands at around 7.5 billion.

## It's easy to love who you're being when you're nailing life

**Here's what I mean by 'nailing life':**

- when you're being a good friend
- when you're being a good partner
- when you're being a good parent
- when you're being a good human.

You love who you are in those moments. You love how the world sees you. You feel powerful and in control of yourself, your responses and your reactions.

**In other words, you feel 'enlightened'.**

I use the word 'enlightened' here, but you could also use the words 'peaceful', 'happy' or 'light'. It's that feeling you get when you're in the zone and just know you've truly 'got' this thing called life.

*Nothing* troubles or triggers you when you're in this space.

**And then... something happens and you feel all-too-human again.**

- You get an unexpected bill and the emergency fund is empty.
- Your partner lets you down, again.
- You get dumped.
- Your friends organise a party and don't invite you.
- You find out one of your kids is taking drugs.
- You have a full-blown five-year-old tantrum at the front of the room in a self-development seminar with 250 sets of eyes watching (yes, I actually did this).

Again, I could go on, but by now, you're probably thinking about some of your own all-too-human moments.

Life has a way of completely derailing us all. Often.

**The good news is that you now have the tools to help switch you to being enlightened.**

This book is *filled* with tools for you to pick up and use.

And if you choose to do this (and then practise, practise, practise using them), the space of time between being human and being enlightened will become shorter and shorter.

**But make no mistake: you will *always* be human first.**

Your initial reaction or response will always be a human one.

Because... newsflash! Human is what you are.

So unless you crack yourself open and remove your 'emotion centre' (which would render you a robot), you will always be human first.

**The only thing you can control is how long it takes you to notice your humanness and switch to being enlightened instead.**

Just remember that your default is always human, so you *will* revert back to this. But that's OK, so long as you're aware of it and accept it.

(Side note: it's important to understand that I'm not giving you a 'get out of jail free card' for the whole human thing.

Being human comes with consequences. You're 100% responsible for whatever you think, say, do or create from your human perspective. You're equally responsible for cleaning up any mistakes – intentional or unintentional – you make too. In fact, this is part of the process of moving yourself into an enlightened state.)

## This may be the most important life lesson I've learnt

I only grasped this lesson later in my life, but it's one of the most important ones to practise. That's why I made it the first lesson in this section about Acceptance.

**However, there was a time when I judged myself harshly for being human.**

Whilst my humanness showed up everywhere, the place I noticed it hitting me hardest was in my role as a solo mum. And if you've ever thought, "I suck at being a mother!" or muttered, "Why is parenting so hard?" you'll understand what I'm about to share.

What so often happened when my kids did something 'wrong' was that I'd react like a crazy person.

Then I'd beat myself up for not handling the situation very well, and for saying or doing something that might have negatively impacted them. And *then* I'd feel like a crappy mum for days.

**One day, my son told me he'd left his mobile phone on the school bus.**

I went nuts. "What?! How could you do that?! Why can't you be responsible with your things? If it's gone, I don't have the money to replace it!"

And on and on and on: crazy mum gone wild.

But for any sleep-deprived parent who'd already put out 20 other fires that day *and* was juggling a household and a budget, it was a normal human reaction.

After a few phone calls and some ranting on my part (ie. yelling at my son, slamming doors, and then more yelling), the mobile phone was eventually located.

**And although I was relieved to find it, I was furious at myself for the way I'd handled the situation.**

I was angry that I'd levelled so many judgements at my son, all of which were untrue.

The reality is that it was a simple mistake that could have happened to *anyone,* including me.

**Now, I could have left it there.**

I could have continued to beat myself up for days for the way I'd handled it.

I could have stayed feeling angry, annoyed, stupid and embarrassed about what had happened. Even worse, I could have let a great big, ugly black cloud stay sitting between my son and me.

**Or I could step into a place of acceptance.**

I could accept that the 'human me' had run the show in that moment.

Then, with the same acceptance, I could acknowledge my own humanness and invite the 'enlightened me' to step forwards.

**I chose the latter.**

I apologised to my son.

I explained that I'd been under pressure that day and had feared him being without his phone. I reminded him that I relied on him having one so we could always communicate with each other. Finally, I shared that I was concerned about how we'd replace it.

And then I acknowledged that none of this justified how I'd spoken to him or what I'd said.

**Now, on this occasion, he accepted my apology, which I was grateful for.**

However, he could also have stayed angry at me.

This isn't about what he chose to do next: it's about what I chose to do for myself.

I created my human 'mess', so it was my responsibility to clean it up. And in doing so, I restored my own inner peace. In other words, I chose to switch my state to an enlightened one.

**I've made peace with the fact that I'm human first.**

I'm completely aware that I can transform myself to being enlightened in any situation or experience. And I can do it as quickly or as slowly as it takes me to engage with this practice or any of the other practices in this book.

There are days when picking up and practising the tools in this book is effortless. And there are also times when I know a tool's available, but I stubbornly choose to stay stuck in my humanness. (That's also a very human thing to do, by the way.)

But if I'm upset in any way, I know I can transform that feeling if I choose to. Byron Katie, creator of *The Work,* tells us that suffering is optional. I wholeheartedly agree; I know I can restore peace, calm, joy and love to my life in an instant.

I also know that it can sometimes take me a few hours, days, weeks, months or even years to make that choice. However long it takes, though, it's 100% within my control.

**What I no longer do is beat myself up for being human.**

I know it will always be my default reaction or response to life.

Because that's what I am: I'm human.

And so are you.

But with awareness, you can begin to catch it more quickly and flip to being enlightened if you choose to.

## Knowing when you're being human is a bit like playing a rattle drum

**I've come to think about the 'human first, enlightened second' concept as being like a Chinese rattle drum.**

This drum has a long history, but it's mostly known in modern China and around the world today as a children's toy.

The drum has two small balls attached to a string on either side of it and, in turn, is itself attached to a stick. When you roll the stick backwards and forwards between the palms of your hands, the balls swing on their strings and bang the drum.

As you play the drum, you first see one side of it, then the other. The faster you go, the quicker the beat and the more the front and back of the drum blur into one image.

**Imagine now that *you're* a Chinese rattle drum.**

On one side of you is the word 'human' and on the other side is 'enlightened'.

When you wake up each day, you know that your default is to be human. So it makes sense that you'll see the 'human' side of the drum first.

To turn the drum so you can see the side that says 'enlightened', you must pick it up and play it.

**But how do you play an instrument that you've never learnt to play?**

It starts with awareness, which you learnt about in Stage 1.

In this example, building awareness is like picking up a musical instrument for the first time. You can see it, you know what it does and you know what it's capable of creating.

The lessons in this book are like music lessons for that instrument. They'll show you exactly how to play it. They'll give you *access* to mastering it.

**But, like with any instrument, mastery comes from practice.**

So it's up to you whether you choose to practise playing the instrument with the intention to master it.

You can also choose not to.

Of course, if you don't, the drum doesn't move. That means you stay 'human' side up with your 'enlightened' side forever hidden from view.

## The Practice – Becoming OK with being human

**It's important to recognise that being human is normal and it is our default setting.**

It's how our brains operate and how we process the world coming at us. And, as we discussed in Stage 1, only by first noticing this can we choose a different response.

The simplest way to bring acceptance to being human is to follow this three-step process. I call it 'Notice, Accept, Choose'.

Step 1: *Notice* when you're reacting to a person or situation that has upset or disturbed you in any way.

Step 2: *Accept* that your initial response was a human one. Because you *are* human.

Step 3: *Choose* to bring love, kindness, compassion, empathy and an open heart to the person or situation. And, most importantly, bring it to yourself, either directly or indirectly (eg. in your mind or journaling).

Finally, to reiterate the fundamental ingredient in all of the practices in this book, you – and only you – have the power to do this.

# Lesson 14

## FRONT OF HAND, BACK OF HAND

 AKA The Universal
Law of Polarity

## Sometimes, our perceptions can mislead us

In her spiritual guide *A Return to Love: Reflections on the Principles of 'A Course in Miracles'*, Marianne Williamson defines a miracle as "a shift in perception from fear to love".

That shift can be easily accessible, but often, it's not.

It can be particularly difficult to access when your perception has been cemented into place through a lifetime of programming from belief systems, experiences, community values and cultural influences.

So unless we're encouraged to question our perceptions, we often walk around with a one-dimensional point of view: our own.

## The Law of Polarity

To understand how perceptions can lead you astray, it helps to understand the Universal Law of Polarity.

This is one of seven universal laws according to *The Kybalion*, a book first published in 1908 by a group of authors known only as 'The Three Initiates'. These laws, also known as the Seven Hermetic Principles, are believed to be derived from sacred writings that date back over 5000 years from Ancient Greece and Egypt.

I highly recommend googling these seven universal laws. They've been significant in cracking open many aspects of my life and have brought much clarity to areas I hadn't previously completely understood.

They've also brought me an even greater awareness of many of the practices in this book – including this one.

**Everything has its opposite.**

In summary, the Universal Law of Polarity states that, just as every hand has a front and a back, everything is dual and has two poles. In other words, everything has, and is, its own opposite.

As *The Kybalion* states, *"Everything 'is' and 'isn't' at the same time, all truths are but half truths and every truth is half false, there are two sides to everything, opposites are identical in nature yet different in degree, extremes meet, and all paradoxes may be reconciled."*

**And if that's too woo-woo for you, let's not dismiss the scientific version.**

Remember: Sir Isaac Newton stated that any action has an equal and opposite reaction, and that forces come in pairs.

## My lesson in polarity came through my parents

**To really explain the power of this life lesson, I need to go back.**

*All* the way back to the dairy farm I grew up on in the Derwent Valley in Tasmania.

It was the 1960s and my parents, who were unable to have children of their own, adopted my older brother, older sister and me. Then before I turned five, a miracle blessed our home.

Despite the medical experts' prediction and a prior miscarriage, my mum carried a red-haired, blue-eyed daughter to term. We were a family of six: all loved, all wanted and all special.

**Sometime in 1968, Dad left a secure mill job to move us all to a farm.**

His love affair with the land and animals lasted until his death in 2003. I went with him to 'work' every chance I got. His love of wide-open spaces, the outdoors and all creatures great and small became part of my soul too.

I'd describe my dad as a strong, kind, peaceful man of very few words who was completely selfless. He had very few personal possessions and even when he received a new jumper or shirt for his birthday, he'd always put it aside and go back to one of his old, worn-out favourites.

He didn't farm for money or to grow a business. He did so because it was what he loved to do.

**If opposites attract, my mum and dad were *definitely* Exhibit A.**

For many years, I thought of Mum as weak, lazy, anxious and selfish. She carried many troubles inside her, some of which stemmed from witnessing tragedy at a young age. I also suspect, having experienced this in my own life, that the sorrow of a miscarriage played a role.

So nerve medication was a part of her daily life. And when I was 15, the nerve medication and her slowly increasing daily alcohol consumption collided.

She entered rehab and, with love, help and support from her family, she recovered. She never drank or took any kind of anxiety medication again for the rest of her life, but other addictions like cigarettes, sugar and gambling were ever-present.

**I grieved so much when Dad passed away in 2003.**

When Mum passed away in 2008, though, it was different. I carried a *lot* of resentment and anger towards her. So although I knew I was supposed to be sad (and I was on some level), it just wasn't the same sense of loss that I felt with Dad.

I aspired to embody my dad's traits in life, while I was determined to never, *ever* be like Mum.

**Following her death in 2008, and later as part of my own self-development, I did many exercises to make peace with Mum.**

I wrote letters and did Reiki, NLP (Neuro Linguistic Programming), EFT (Emotional Freedom Technique, also known as tapping) and other modalities.

But whilst I could *intellectually* make peace with her, I never managed to fully open my heart to her.

**Then I discovered The Law of Polarity.**

For the first time, this law introduced me to the idea that both Mum and Dad had had the *exact* same traits. And I mean all of them: the good, the bad and even the ones I'd decided were ugly.

I started to consider the idea that all the traits that I deemed worthy, as well as the ones I deemed unworthy, had existed in them both. These traits, and every other trait you can think of, actually exist simultaneously in all of us.

But back then, I'd always seen my dad as strong, brave, peaceful and selfless (good), and my mum as weak, lazy, anxious and selfish (bad).

**So I put The Law of Polarity to the test.**

First, I looked back at Dad and searched for times where he might have been weak, lazy, anxious or selfish. Then I did the same for Mum, looking for times where she may have been strong, brave, peaceful or selfless.

I tried to look with an open mind and ask questions like:

- Had Dad's desire to be a farmer really been selfish?
- Had Mum been a city girl who'd selflessly made this sacrifice for Dad?
- Had Dad's inability to address and handle Mum's illness been weak and anxiety-ridden?
- Had Mum in fact been incredibly strong to endure the inner torment she'd clearly been living for as long as she had?
- Had Mum been incredibly brave to come back home and face the small-town people who knew of her breakdown and probably gossiped relentlessly?

**This new observation left me speechless.**

For the first time in my life, I could recognise that both Mum and Dad had shared the same traits. Neither of them were good, and neither were bad.

Understanding this also allowed me to accept that I too have all of these traits, along with many others. We all do.

This practice has opened my mind to the simple but powerfully profound capacity I have to transform the way I see myself and others – especially my mum.

I no longer see people as having good or bad traits that I either covet or reject. Rather, I now view myself – and others – as whole, complete, multi-dimensional works of art.

## Are you prepared to give up your one-dimensional point of view?

**Accepting the idea that everything has – and is – its opposite is life-changing.**

When you can truly do this for yourself and for those around you, you'll instantly be able to bring a loving, open-hearted perspective to everyone. With that will come an inner sense of peace. Resentment, grudges, angst and hurt will begin to fall away.

Think about all the people in your life who you've described over and over and over again in a certain way. What if the equal and opposite is also true?

**You might think that I can't know your situation.**

Perhaps you're thinking, "Oh, but you don't *know* this person!" or, "You have no idea of the crappy things they did to me."

And it's true. I don't.

But what I *can* tell you is that this lesson isn't about bringing peace to their life. It's about bringing peace to yours.

If you're holding on to a viewpoint about someone that triggers any kind of negative emotion in you, then *you're* the one who's suffering – not them. That negative emotion will keep your heart closed.

**Wouldn't you love to have a heart full of peace, rather than one with even the tiniest bit of anger or resentment in it?**

## The Practice – Seeing more than one perspective

Discovering this wisdom helped me to understand that everything was both how I saw it and also how I *couldn't* yet see it.

So for every trait or experience I could see or feel, the equal and opposite was also present. Of course, this understanding was only available if I chose to look for it and, more importantly, was open to accepting whatever I saw.

So how can you practise seeing more than one perspective of yourself and others? Let's first look at how you see another person.

Step 1: Focus on a particular person in your life who has any kind of trait that you deem wrong or bad, or that you never want to embody.

Step 2: Make a list of all the traits you can identify in them. Then go ahead and circle the three that irritate you the most.

Step 3: Look at the three traits you've chosen, and write down next to each of them a word that means its opposite to *you*.

This is important because, to some people, the opposite of angry might be calm, but to someone else, it might be happy.

The word you associate as the opposite will also come from your experiences of this person.

Step 4: Next, try to put aside how you currently see this person. I realise that this may be harder than it sounds, because it will likely be an ingrained opinion that you've collected plenty of examples to support over time.

Step 5: Look at the opposite traits you wrote down, and scan back over this person's life to see if you can find examples of those too. If you really do this exercise objectively, you *will* find those examples.

Now, to really complete this practice, I want you to repeat Steps 1–5 while looking at yourself.

But this time, begin with the traits you really like about yourself and move on to finding the opposites of those.

Doing this will help you to accept every facet of every trait that exists in us all.

**BONUS: using the Universal Law of Polarity can also create a shift in your day-to-day thoughts and feelings.**

For example, let's say you receive an unexpected bill and hear yourself saying something like, "I'll never be able to save money!" If so, notice that this response could be described as a thought of 'poverty'.

Next, identify the opposite thought – perhaps it might be one of 'prosperity' – and now look for where in your life you're experiencing that.

Because what you focus on grows (see Lesson 43), shifting your thoughts from poverty to prosperity can actually help to create more prosperity in your life.

# Lesson 15

## ACCEPTING YOUR S.E.L.F.

 AKA Meet your four
"new best friends"

## The four elements of being human are Soul, Ego, Love and Fear (S.E.L.F.)

**It's easy(ish) to listen to Love and Soul.**

As we navigate our way through life, many teachings from around the world tell us to lean into the love in our hearts and the guidance from our souls.

In general, I believe that's a great practice to get into. However, many of those teachings also tell us that we need to separate ourselves from our egos and manage our fears at all costs.

**The misconception here is that Ego and Fear are our enemies.**

Some spiritual traditions often see these elements of our selves as things to be fought and overcome at best, and completely extricated at worst.

However, I believe that Fear and Ego both hold immense amounts of wisdom. And that wisdom can be integral to not only seeing the complete picture in any situation but also to peacefully accepting that picture.

**This lesson focuses on accepting ALL four elements of being human: Soul, Ego, Love and Fear.**

It shows you how to see them as your 'new best friends' and how to harness the power of their wisdom.

## The four stages of a story

As a coach, I've had thousands of conversations, covering all manner of problems and challenges.

**But regardless of the issue, my clients inevitably experienced it as a four-stage story: one stage each for Soul, Ego, Love and Fear.**

And while the elements sometimes showed up in a different order, they were invariably all there.

Sometimes a client's story began from the perspective of their ego. Then their fears might have bubbled up. Eventually, they may have moved into a more loving viewpoint. And finally, they might have seen (almost) everything from a deep-down soul-based perspective.

Other times, they might have started from a different element and taken a completely different path through the stages. Occasionally, they passed through all of the elements in a single session but, in my experience, the process most often took more time.

**Here's how one of those stories might play out:**

- [Ego] "I just found out my boyfriend is cheating on me. I feel so betrayed. I can't believe he's being such jerk. Mum was right; all men are the same."

- **[Fear]** "What will I do? I don't want to be alone. What if I never meet anyone else? There are so few good men out there."

- **[Love]** "In time, I know I can fill my own heart with love and joy. I can surround myself with people who love me and fill my time with things that light me up."

- **[Soul]** "Deep down, I know he's not the one for me. I also know that it's up to ME to fulfil me, with or without the love of my life being present."

**It's interesting how Ego and Fear always seem to shout the loudest.**

Raise your hand if this is familiar: maybe you've listened to a friend work through a similar story. Or perhaps you've even seen it in yourself.

Either way, you might have noticed the same thing I have. In any kind of upset or challenge, Ego and Fear are *always* the loudest voices and their stages last the longest.

Sometimes, these two elements seem to play a never-ending game of ping pong!

**At some point, I discovered that the quickest way to quiet them is to listen.**

It sounds strange, but if you turn *towards* the yelling voices of Fear and Ego and actually listen to them, they'll quieten down. Not only that, but you may also learn something from them.

Then, once the shouting dies down, you'll be able to hear the soft whispers of Love and the calming voice of Soul more clearly.

**All four elements have something they want you to know.**

You just have to be willing to listen to all of them.

The grid below summarises what you can expect to experience when each element is trying to communicate with you.

Right/Wrong, Good/Bad, Yes/No, Judgement of self and others, Comparison, Jealousy, Hurt, Feeling Unheard, Blame

Trust, Abundance, Joy, Happiness, Wonder, Compassion, Empathy, Respect, Peace, Gratitude

EGO

LOVE

YOU

SOUL

FEAR

Truth, Spirit, Higher Self, Surrender, Reverence, Expansion, Grace, Hope, Faith

Lack, Scarcity, Not Enough, Missing out (FOMO), Anxiety, Procrastination, Uncertainty, Abandonment

**It's time to connect with your four new best friends.**

Listening to each voice will help you begin to build a relationship with *all* four elements of yourself: your new best friends. By giving them all a chance to be heard and absorbing all of their wisdom, you'll get a more complete picture of whatever disturbance you're dealing with.

That will allow you to move effortlessly into accepting 'what is' rather than grappling with what you wish it was (or wasn't).

Acknowledging the elements, rather than ignoring them, is your fast track to peace and calm.

# The wisdom of my S.E.L.F.

Back in August of 2015, an opportunity to pioneer a health and fitness program in Saudi Arabia fell into my lap.

I'd always wanted to work overseas, so I was ecstatic about this opportunity. They asked me to be there on 1 September so I resigned my existing position immediately in order to be ready.

What I *didn't* know was that not only would I have to get my ducks in a row but I'd also need to place them in a holding pattern for four months.

**1 September came and went with no approved visa in sight.**

So did 1 October; at which point, a hint of panic entered my thoughts.

Then so did 1 December. Money was getting incredibly tight and my meagre savings were running out fast. And still no visa was in sight.

**Finally, just like in the movies, a Christmas Eve miracle occurred.**

On 24 December, my visa arrived in the mail.

I felt an immense wave of relief flow through me: four months of nervous waiting had come to an end. My decision to take up this position hadn't just affected me: it had affected my entire family and the responsibility of that had been weighing heavily on me.

**Things moved quickly at that point, and I departed a few days later.**

My first day on the job was filled with paperwork, orientation activities and getting to know the other teachers.

But in amongst the practicalities of meeting my dean and filling out forms, I also discovered that I'd be paid monthly in arrears.

**This meant I wouldn't receive my first month's salary for another _four weeks_.**

I was already two months behind on my mortgage, and my savings had almost completely run out.

And _then_, around the middle of January, I started hearing rumours in the teachers' room. It seemed that nobody had received their December salary, which was now two weeks overdue.

**I could barely comprehend what I was hearing.**

For almost four and a half months, I'd put my life (and my family's lives) into a holding pattern. I'd placed all my trust in this job. And now, not only was I broke and in debt but it also looked like I wouldn't be paid.

I didn't even know how I'd get back to Australia.

What had I done?

**These thoughts began to spiral around in my head.**

The anxiety of losing everything began to consume me.

My ego and fears were _screaming_ at me. And instead of listening to what they were trying to tell me, I put my hands over my ears and screamed, "La la la la la la la, I can't hear you!" right back.

Not surprisingly, that didn't help my inner peace in the slightest.

So that night, I went home to my apartment and intuitively began a visualisation process that would bring me face to face with my own ego, fear, love and soul. It also helped me to get my first peaceful night's sleep in Saudi.

**I don't know how I knew what to do or where the guidance came from.**

What I do know is that, at the time, I felt guided to this practice. And I now know that it allowed me to meet all four elements of my humanness – my four new best friends (S.E.L.F.) – and invite each of them to be seen and heard.

Listening to each of their perspectives in turn took me from a state of distorted drama to a place of peace and calm and into the acceptance of 'what is'. It also helped me realise that the only thing that had prevented me doing this before was *me*.

**As it happened, despite the rumours, a couple of days later the teachers were paid.**

Then, as the month ended, so was I.

And I realised that although my inner turmoil had been based on unfounded rumours, if the worst-case scenario *had* transpired, I could still be at peace in that circumstance.

**That wasn't the first time (nor the last) that the voices of my ego and fear drowned out everything else.**

It certainly wasn't the first time the dulcet tones of my loving heart and peaceful soul had to struggle to be heard.

But for the first time, I discovered that giving into their yelling – or trying to block it out – just made them scream louder.

So if I wanted them to quiet down, I had to start listening. Only then could I hear the voices of my heart and soul.

And when I truly listened, I knew without question that I was and would always be OK.

## Who am I being in this moment, and who do I *want* to be?

Oprah Winfrey once said that every human being just wants three things: to be seen, to be heard and to know that what they say matters.

And I believe this is true.

I *also* believe that your four new best friends want exactly the same thing.

Your ego and fear may be loud talkers, while your love and soul probably speak softly. But they each want to be seen and heard, and to know that their voice matters.

Of course, when you ignore a loud talker, they tend to get louder. And when you ignore someone who's softly spoken, they eventually stop speaking and become silent.

**When this happens, you only see half of the picture and hear half of the story.**

Accepting your S.E.L.F. (Soul, Ego, Love and Fear) is like accepting the counsel and guidance of four best friends. And just like any true friend, they each only want the very best for you.

But each one is limited in their perspective. So the true power of their counsel comes when you listen to each of them separately.

Only then can you embrace their perspectives, which will reconnect you to your inner peaceful power and the 'you' that you know you're here to be in this world.

## The Practice – Connecting with who you are

**So how do you bring balance to the noise in your head?**

**And how do you connect to your S.E.L.F. and reconnect to 'who you are' in this world?**

Step 1:    First, notice the 'noise' of your anxiety, upset or disturbance. Try to see it as though you were standing beside it and watching it.

        For example, imagine you can see four people standing in a closed circle. Two of them (Ego and Fear) are yelling, arms flailing wildly, whilst the other two (Love and Soul) roll their eyes and stand silently.

        Imagine that you're walking around the outside of the group – not involved, but simply watching the argument.

Step 2:    Once you can visualise this, see each person turning to face you one at a time, starting with Ego. As they do, ask each of them what they want you to know.

Step 3:    Spend time with each element, and allow it to share what's bothering it and what it wants you to know.

        For example, imagine Ego replying with...

        "Hi, I'm your ego.

        Finally, I have your undivided attention! This is what I want you to know and why it's important that I tell you..."

Write down everything it has to say, unscripted and unedited. Simply allow that part of you to express all it wants to tell you.

Step 4: Once you've finished with Ego, repeat Step 3 for Fear, then for Love and finally for Soul.

Step 5: After you've written all that you can from each element, you'll have four very different perspectives.

Read over them in the same order you wrote them down, and acknowledge and thank each element for its love and wisdom. After all, they really just want you to be OK.

**Doing this exercise allows you to move outside of the disturbance and reconnect peacefully to 'you'.**

Completing this practice helps you to discover that, despite what's going on around you and inside you, you ARE always OK.

Accepting 'what is' connects you to your peaceful power. Listening to your four new best friends is how you access that power.

# Lesson 16

## DO YOU WANT TO BE RIGHT OR DO YOU WANT LOVE?

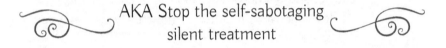 AKA Stop the self-sabotaging silent treatment

### Three life lessons, one concept – 'being right'

**This life lesson is a part of a big overall concept: the idea of being right.**

Call it a trilogy, with each lesson being Parts I, II and III: a bit like *The Lord of the Rings*. In this case, though, you won't have to wade through hundreds of pages or sit through hours and hours of film before you discover the outcome.

However, I'll place a warning here. This trilogy is easy to grasp in theory, but it can be difficult to master. It *will* take practice.

So, like everything else in this book, accessing the power of this lesson (and the next two) will take more than intellectual understanding. You'll need to practically experience it – possibly repeatedly – before you see transformation happening.

That's why the common denominator over the next three lessons is the word 'right'.

Over the trilogy, we're going to cover the ideas that:

- You can be right or you can have love, but you can't have both.
- Giving up being right, even when you know you are, is your fast track to restoring love and peace.
- Giving up being right does not make you a pushover.

It's time to bring your four new best friends into the conversation.

Before you begin, I suggest you invite your ego, fear, love and soul back into your mind. Yep, all four of them. The concept of being right will likely trigger them *all* in some way.

(And before you begin the next three lessons, it may help to re-read Lesson 15 if you need to.)

## How long can you stay angry?

Have you ever had a fight with a loved one?

Maybe it was your partner, parent, child, sibling or bestie?

Silly question, right? We all have!

And, let's face it, you don't argue about anything unless you truly believe you're 100% right!

But if you believe you're right and the other person believes they're right too, how does that work out?

**Often it ends in angry silence.**

Because, dammit, you were right. And they were wrong!

And how long have you refused to speak to someone after an argument?

- An hour?
- A day?
- A week?
- A month?
- A year?
- A lifetime?

What I can tell you is that however long you weren't speaking to them – an hour or a lifetime – love *wasn't* present during that time.

**So how long are you prepared to be right?**

How long are you prepared to forsake love?

Time may be infinite (at least according to the science-y dudes) but OUR time isn't. Remember Lesson 3 about asking for one more week?

So think about it: NEWSFLASH! You don't get all that time you spend 'not speaking' to someone back. Nor are you guaranteed one more moment, much less one more week, to get over it!

**Let's for just one moment consider that tragedy struck.**

Imagine the last words you spoke to someone were about being right.

I have no doubt that you'd give up being right in an instant to have them back for just a moment so you could tell them you loved them.

**And here's another NEWSFLASH!**

Any time you spend tapping your toes, waiting for an apology (because you were right!) is also time where love isn't present. And it's *also* time you can't get back.

Finally, let me ask you: how often can you recall arguing and later completely forgetting what the argument had even been about or what started it?

Unfortunately, even though most of us know this intellectually, in the heat of the moment we choose to be right.

## I lost so much time to being right

**I was so guilty of this in the past.**

I used to give the silent treatment to everyone: my partners, my kids and sometimes even my friends.

If they challenged me or disagreed with me in any way, I'd simply shut myself off from them and become silent.

**I wasted SO much time not speaking to people I loved.**

And, although I don't know this for certain, I may have even taught them through my actions to do the same thing to me.

As one anonymous relationship expert put it, *"When two people give each other the silent treatment, the winner is always the one that cares the least."*

For example, following an argument with my daughter where I'd given her the silent treatment for days, she asked me, "Why do you do that? Why do you shut me out because I don't agree with you?"

**I honestly didn't have an answer for her.**

However, what occurred to me in that moment was just how much of my life I'd wasted giving people I loved the silent treatment. Once I could accept that holding on to being right was costing me precious, precious time with those people, my new awareness let me choose a different action.

Then, when I chose differently, love became present. And when love was present, finding solutions, reaching common ground, and either making new agreements or just agreeing to disagree was effortless.

So what will you choose?

## Anger closes your heart, while love opens it

When you're upset (or angry, sad, jealous, annoyed, frustrated, etc.), love isn't present.

If I asked whether you could feel the difference between love being present and absent, I'm sure you could.

**But how do you shift from one state to the other, especially in the heat of the moment?**

Start by noticing the blocked, heavy feeling that being upset inevitably brings. This will move you towards recognising that any time you're caught up in being right, your heart is closed. And as soon as you let yourself choose love over being right, you'll feel your heart open again.

Once you accept that you *always* have this choice available to you, staying angry and giving someone the silent treatment can become a thing of the past.

**Remember: this isn't about being right or being wrong.**

It's not about what they did or didn't say.

Nor is it about what they did or didn't do.

It's about deciding how you want to spend your time on this planet: with a closed, angry heart or an open, loving one.

**Giving up being right doesn't necessarily mean you were wrong.**

It just reflects that having love present is far more important to you. It takes your closed, angry heart and reopens it, allowing love both out and in.

Then, with a loving, open heart, you can actually 'hear' one another. That makes a peaceful outcome possible.

Mastering this life lesson will make it difficult to hold out for the other person to give in. They might not know how to instantly restore love to the relationship, but you will.

And you'll know you can, at any moment, decide that restoring love is more important to you than being right.

**If you find you have some 'Yeah, buts' coming up (and I suspect you will), I suggest two things.**

First, do the practice below. Second, read the next two lessons in this trilogy (and then do the practice below AGAIN).

## The Practice – Restoring love to your relationships

When you find yourself arguing with a loved one, especially when you're certain that you're right, try these steps:

Step 1: Ask yourself, "In this moment, am I choosing to be right over having a loving relationship?"

Step 2: Next, ask yourself, "Can I give up being right in order to allow love in?"

Step 3: Then ask yourself, "What would love do right now?"

Step 4: Finally, ask yourself, "What action can I take right now to restore love to this relationship?"

And, of course, do your best to actually *take* that action, open your heart and restore love to the relationship.

# Lesson 17

## GIVE UP BEING RIGHT, EVEN WHEN YOU KNOW YOU ARE

 AKA Get on the fast track to peace and love

### You can be right without making others wrong

In the previous lesson, we discussed the concept of choosing to have love present over being right.

We also established that you have the power to flip from one state to the other instantaneously if you want to.

The next part of this process is to begin to give up being right (yes, even when you absolutely, categorically, *know* you are) everywhere in your life.

Let me explain.

## It's time to quit your job as 'Judge of the World'

**It might sound extreme for me to describe you as the Judge of the World.**

After all, you're not that judgemental, are you? Well, you might be surprised.

For example, think of something you wholeheartedly believe in. It might be a belief about:

- **Religion:** perhaps whether it's necessary to go to church regularly.

- **Politics:** maybe who should be taxed and at what level.

- **Parenting:** should you smack or not smack?

- **Nourishing your body:** is vegan or paleo healthier?

- **Business models:** should a new business owner sell retail or through a co-op?

- **Generational differences:** eg. 'the young/old folk have no idea!'

The specifics really don't matter.

What does matter is that we all have our own 'ways of being' in this world. And most of them have been handed to us by our parents, environment, teachers, friends, etc.

**This life lesson isn't asking you to give up your beliefs.**

Instead, it simply suggests that you give up needing to be right about them. In doing so, you'll be able to stop making other people wrong for theirs.

## Who's right and who's wrong?

**Is it right or wrong to have a tattoo?**

I once witnessed someone ask on Facebook, "What's with tattoos? I don't get it. Why would you want one?"

It triggered a colourful debate over whether having tattoos was right or wrong according to each individual. Over one hundred comments later, the debate was still going. And unfortunately, as is often the case on social media, it was becoming ugly and personal.

**Now, I have many tattoos.**

So I could have easily jumped into the debate and expressed at length why I thought they were 'right'.

But one of my sisters doesn't have any tattoos. And her view is completely opposite to mine.

So she could have also chosen to jump in and express why, actually, they were wrong (because she was sure that *she* was right).

**Which one of us is right?**

The answer is neither. Or both. The truth is, we can both be right. But what we *don't* have to do is to make each other wrong to prove this.

## Can you *be* the change instead of forcing the change?

**Trying to change someone else always causes problems.**

It's normal to feel upset when you feel you have to prove your position on something to someone else. And if they still don't share your opinion, it can make the associated feelings flare up even further.

But what if you can be 'right' about your place, space and beliefs in the world AND accept that the person standing next to you doesn't share them? What if you can let them have their *own* place, space and beliefs in the world, and accept that that's right for them?

**This acceptance will give you a calm, peaceful, love-fuelled life.**

Now imagine a world filled with calm, peaceful people, all standing side by side and accepting each other. It's hard to imagine, isn't it? And it probably won't occur in my lifetime, although one of my intentions in writing this book is to contribute to creating that world.

Of course, this life lesson (like all the others in this book) isn't about changing the outside world. It's about shifting your thoughts and subsequent actions, which – with practice – will change both the way you see the world and how it sees you.

**And that, collectively, WILL change the world, one person at a time.**

I truly believe that the world will change when we all begin to take responsibility for our own changes.

(And I can give up being right about that and be completely calm and peaceful if you disagree!)

## The Practice – Giving up being right, even when you know you are

Remember that this practice is not about figuring out whether you're right, how many people agree with you or whether you can prove your point.

Instead, it's about letting go of the need to make others wrong.

**Step 1:** Make a list of five things you feel strongly about (refer to the first section of this lesson for ideas).

**Step 2:** Beside each thing, write down the opposite viewpoint.

For example, your viewpoint might be 'eating vegan is ethical' while the opposing one might be 'eating meat is fine'.

**Step 3:** Take a look at each viewpoint and see whether you can find a way to peacefully accept *both* of them.

For example, you might say, "This is right for me, that's right for them, and neither viewpoint is right or wrong in itself."

**Step 4:** If you're having difficulty with this practice, whenever you come upon something you're opposed to, try using the phrase, "That's an interesting point of view."

Then genuinely look for how the viewpoint *is* an interesting one. Get curious about why the other person might see things that way. Maybe even do some unbiased research. You might actually be surprised with what your curiosity uncovers.

# Lesson 18

## GIVING UP BEING RIGHT DOES NOT MAKE YOU A PUSHOVER

 AKA The power of peacefulness

### Becoming a powerful peacemaker

This is the final part of our trilogy about 'being right'.

And if I'm being honest, it's the part that I need to *consciously* practise daily.

As we talked about in Lesson 15, Ego is one of the four elements of being human and, if we choose to allow it, one of our four new best friends. We know we can't separate ourselves from our egos – and nor would we want to, knowing the wisdom they can share with us.

However, paying attention to Ego, rather than remaining blindly unaware of it, is also integral to this life lesson. Ultimately, it's also essential to become peaceful in all areas of your life.

## Your ego really wants you to be right

**Let's bring in the key player in 'being right': enter Ego, stage left.**

Your ego doesn't want to have *any* part in you giving up being right.

It will have you believing that the only way to survive is to constantly assert your 'rightness'.

It will convince you that if you aren't right, you're therefore wrong. If you're wrong, you're not intelligent or valuable, which means you'll probably be 'cast out from the tribe' and be all alone.

And if you're all alone, you'll die.

**You see, being right is a primal survival mechanism that exists in all humans.**

It was absolutely necessary in our caveman days, back when being part of a tribe grossly increased our chances of survival.

But times have changed, and being wrong very rarely means being cast out of the tribe anymore (at least in Western culture).

However, your ego doesn't know it's 2019. As far as it's concerned, letting other people think that they're right makes you wrong, which means letting them walk all over you.

Your ego won't have any part of that either!

## Mother doesn't *always* know best

**To bring this trilogy together, let me tell you a story about my son.**

He's a young man now and we have an amazing relationship.

But during his mid-teen years, with all my self-imposed pressure to 'get it right' as a solo mum, things could easily have ended with us becoming estranged.

**You see, halfway through Year 11, my son stopped going to school.**

He went from being happy and social and planning his future pathway to being a reclusive hermit. And although I couldn't accept it then, I can now acknowledge that he was possibly experiencing depression.

Initially, all *I* saw was a defiant, lazy, disrespectful young man.

And no one, and I mean NO ONE, was going to treat me that way. After all, I was busting myself in half most days to give my kids a good life and good opportunities.

**After discovering that he hadn't gotten up and gone to school most days for several weeks, I was at my wits' end.**

I can remember standing at his door and *screaming* at him to get up and either get to school or get out of my house.

I'd tell him that if he didn't get an education, he'd have no chance of getting a job. And once he left school, he'd be out on his own and I'd no longer support him. Then I'd ask how he'd support himself without a job.

Of course, on reflection, this was not helpful. Nor was it going to earn me the title of 'Mother of the Year'.

Some days he'd just outright ignore me. Other days he'd scream back that I didn't understand a thing and that he hated me.

Then I'd try to wield my 'I'm your mother and you don't get to speak to me this way' power. I'm not sure now why I thought that would get him to school; of course, it didn't.

**The 'I'm right and you're wrong' battle went on for months.**

So did the yelling, screaming, guilt-tripping and fearmongering.

I knew there had to be another way, so I searched for the wisdom to figure out what I couldn't see.

Then, one evening, I attended a personal development seminar about 'being right'. Feeling completely vulnerable, I raised my hand and spoke at the front of the room about what I was experiencing at home.

**The feedback I received that evening showed me that what was going on was actually a deeply ingrained story.**

I realised that I needed to be right about my son's behaviour. If I wasn't, I believed he'd think he was getting away with treating me like I was stupid.

Of course, that wasn't what was actually happening. It was just what the story I was telling myself had me believe.

So in my subconscious mind, my ego (and now my fear of being treated like I was stupid) stood between my son and me having a loving relationship. I *had* to be right, because the alternative would make me a pushover and allow my son to be right.

**The next step was to give up being right, even though I thought I was.**

It took a while and several more fights with my son. But eventually, now aware of my story, I went to him for the first time and asked, "What's really going on for you? What is it that you're feeling? What can't I see? If this isn't about school, what *is* it about?"

And then I sat and listened.

I offered nothing back. No fixing. No "You're wrong." No "I'm right." No "Try this." No "Try not doing that."

I offered nothing but listening.

**You see that's what's really at the heart of this lesson.**

Whenever you assert that you're right about something, you equally assert that the other person is wrong. And I don't know about you, but when someone tells me I'm wrong, my automatic response is to defend my position.

That's *exactly* what my son had been doing, which is why he and I hadn't 'heard' each other for months.

I eventually shared my own vulnerability with him. I shared my fears, my concerns and my worries.

And for the first time, he finally opened up about what was going on for him.

**As parents, we often need to be right.**

It's how we keep our kids safe.

But if you choose being right over having a loving relationship, you need to prepare for having *no* relationship.

So did I believe I was right to try to get my son to school? Absolutely.

And did I only want the best for him? For sure.

Did I do what I did and say what I said because I loved him? Without question.

But do you think that's what my son was experiencing from me? Definitely not!

By making him wrong, I (unconsciously) implied that he couldn't handle himself and his life. I took away his capacity to be responsible. I disabled him with guilt, rather than enabled him with love.

My words literally reinforced everything he was already thinking and feeling.

It wasn't until I stopped asserting my rightness and started *listening* that he could open up and we could find a way forward together.

## The choice is yours

So what do you do when you're locked in this kind of battle with someone?

You choose love over being right, even when you know you are.

You choose to enable that person with your love, rather than disable them with guilt.

You choose to be OK with whatever the outcome may be.

You give up the idea that you're being a pushover.

You let go of the concept that they 'win' or that you're allowing them to walk all over you.

I almost lost my son because my ego needed to be right.

Neither your ego nor mine is interested in love. It's *only* interested in surviving.

Yes, as we discussed in Lesson 15, Ego can be a powerful teacher if you choose to let it. But to truly find peace, you *must* listen to what it's telling you, rather than blindly letting it run the show.

And when you listen, you'll be able to peacefully and powerfully put aside your need to be right. Only then can you make way for an outcome that's for everyone's highest good.

## The Practice – Trusting the outcome

This practice is about moving away from your *need* to be right, and rather, making way for love, peace and a positive outcome for everyone.

Step 1: Ask yourself, "In this moment, what's in the way of me choosing to give up being right and trust in the outcome?"

Step 2: Next, consider first the outcome you want and then the one you don't want.

Step 3: Now make two lists on a single piece of paper. On one side write 4–5 benefits of the outcome you want. On the other side write 4–5 benefits of the outcome you don't want.

When you can feel peaceful about both lists, your ego will relax and stop trying to survive. When you no longer need to be right (even though you think you are), you create space for new possibilities, solutions and outcomes.

# Lesson 19

## PEOPLE JUST DO WHAT
## PEOPLE JUST DO

 AKA WTF? Why would they DO that?!

### Why do we get so annoyed with other people?

**People just do what people just do, and they just say what they just say.**

And let me tell you a secret: so do you.

So why do people's words and actions sometimes piss us off so much?

They press our buttons. They irritate the shit out of us.

**Why do we get so wound up?**

Why do we get upset?

And why do we complain about it over and over to anyone who's willing to listen (sometimes for days)?

# People – including you – do things because they can

**Have you ever noticed yourself saying or thinking:**

- "Why would they do that"?
- "Why would they say that"?
- "How could they behave that way"?
- "Why would they think such a thing"?
- "Surely they must know that's wrong"?

The answer to all of these questions is 'because they can'.

And so can you (and I).

**Let's start with Facebook.**

Have you ever read a post and had all the above questions come rushing at you?

*Especially* when the post is from someone you know!

You find yourself face-palming and thinking, "WTF?! Why would they say that? What were they thinking?"

And then the bigger question becomes whether you comment, PM them your opinions, or even unfollow or unfriend them.

**Plus, there's that person you work with.**

You know, the one who comes in late, leaves early, contributes nothing at the meetings and never even washes up their own coffee cup!

**And then, what about your business?**

Copying may be the highest form of flattery, but not when they're copying *your* ideas, right?

**Then there's:**

- the person who jumps the queue
- that driver who cut you off on the road
- that kid who talked all the way through the movie
- that friend who keeps talking over the top of everyone (oh wait, that last one might be me... oops! I don't do it consciously or to upset anyone – I just do it!)

You see that's just it.

**People just do what people just do... AND SO DO YOU.**

Look at all of the examples I've given you above, and turn your awareness spotlight on yourself for a moment. Now ask yourself, "Have I ever done ANY of these things?"

Really? You've *never* done any of them? It's just me then?

No, I figured I wasn't alone.

The good news is that answering YES to any – or all – of these things doesn't make you a bad person. It just makes you a human being, which we already talked about in Lesson 13.

That's why this lesson isn't actually about *what* people do.

It's about *how* you respond to it.

## This really wound me up!

During my fitness business owner days, I created some really progressive, forward-thinking programs.

One of these was a 12-week beginner triathlon program to help women train for the National Breast Cancer Foundation's Triathlon Pink fundraiser.

It wasn't intended to create champion triathletes – just to build confidence in women who'd never have otherwise thought it possible to complete a triathlon.

Some of these women were scared of water. Some hadn't ridden a bike for decades (most didn't even own one!) And many of them had only a basic level of fitness.

So when my program achieved a 100% success rate, it gathered plenty of attention.

A 100% success rate meant that every single woman who took part crossed the finish line of the Triathlon Pink.

Every single one punched the air with jubilation and felt an immense sense of achievement as their families cheered them on.

And I repeated this program many more times, always with the same 100% success rate.

One day, another fitness business owner asked if she could pick my brain.

Their business was in the startup stage, and they really admired the success I'd created for my clients. Of course, I was more than happy to support a colleague.

So we chatted on the phone for more than an hour, and I openly shared everything about my business and programs. (To be clear, I'm still an open book and am happy to share anything I know with anyone if it will help them).

**The next day, I discovered with shock that this person had replicated my program *exactly*.**

What I mean by 'exactly' is that they'd copied my program information from my social media event word for word. The name of the program was exactly the same. Even the pricing was identical.

I was gobsmacked and totally lost my shit!

That little voice inside me immediately started with the questions:

- "Really? How could they?"
- "Why would they do that?"
- "Do they have no conscience?"
- "Who would do such a thing?"

And, of course, every other question you can think of went through my head!

**So I sat with the situation.**

I chatted about it to people close to me.

I wanted to call this person, tear strips from them and *demand* they shut down their program.

But what I didn't consider doing was calling them to perhaps take the time to understand what had motivated them to copy me. For example, they could have been inexperienced and lacking confidence in the early stages of their business. Perhaps they'd inadvertently taken our open phone call as permission to use my content.

The truth is that there were plenty of possibilities. I'd only considered one: that they were ripping off my program.

**That's how I learnt this life lesson.**

I had to ask myself where I'd ever done that. Where had *I* copied something from someone and taken credit for it?

Of course, at first, I said I'd NEVER done that!

But as I sat with it and parked my righteousness for a moment, I took a deeper, more honest look.

**And yes, I found a few examples.**

I *had* often copied social media posts – you know, those funny, inspirational or thought-provoking memes. And in almost no instances did I give any credit to the places I'd found them.

I'd also copied various exercises that I'd seen other trainers doing.

I'd copied outfits that I'd seen other people wearing.

And I'd copied ideas that I'd found in all kinds of places.

I'd never consciously done these things to negatively impact anyone in any way.

**In fact, it hadn't occurred to me that I was doing anything wrong.**

So I chose to acknowledge the possibility that this other trainer hadn't considered that *they* might be doing anything wrong either.

A few days later, I emailed them to say that I was glad they'd found our chat helpful and that I'd seen their program. I suggested that, in future, they might put their own twist on it as that would enhance the program to make it more unique to them and their business.

And again, they were grateful for my advice and took it on willingly.

## Try asking yourself whether YOU'VE ever done 'that thing'

**As humans, we walk around with our judgement caps on, passing opinions on everything we see.**

And mostly, we do it without ever taking the time to consider any other perspective or possibility.

I once heard a story that really helped me understand this. I'm not sure whether it's true or not, as I've since heard it repeated in various places with slightly different twists each time. In any case, it is great for showing us how we judge and how there's almost always another perspective.

*The story is about two men on a train.*

*One man sat on his own reading the paper. The other man was also sitting quietly while his three young sons ran amok. The boys were loud, climbing over the seats and running up and down the aisles.*

*Meanwhile, the dad just sat there, doing nothing to rein them in.*

*The man reading the paper was getting very annoyed, thinking that the other man was the most terrible parent.*

*Finally, a couple of stops later, the man with the paper got up to disembark.*

*Before he did, however, he went up to the father and said, "You really need to get your kids under control!"*

*The other man turned to him slowly with a blank look on his face. "I'm so sorry," he said. "We've just come from the hospital. Their mum just passed away."*

**Now, before you say, "Yeah, but that's different," consider that no, it's not!**

Because in any situation, at any point in time, people just do what people just do. So do you, and so do I.

And before your ego (which – as we've said – loves to be right) kicks in, consider as well that this is NOT about the actions of any other person. Yes, of course, certain actions create consequences in life.

However, this lesson isn't about what happened.

It's about what you make the thing that happened mean and the judgement you attach to it. Because the one thing I know for sure is that the ONLY person you have any control over is you (see Lesson 28 for more on this topic).

**So when people just do what they just do, it's not personal!**

It's not about you (or me). It's about them!

And the moment you can let go of it being personal... BOOM! You suddenly have access to a calm heart, a peaceful mind and, often, completely transformed relationships – potentially even a transformed life!

At the very least, you have the capacity to have a powerful conversation, instead of one that's laden down with being 'all about me'.

This lesson is about freeing yourself from judgement, both of others and of situations. And ultimately, with practice, it will help you to accept the world and the people in it, just as they are and just as they aren't.

## The Practice – Accepting that people just do what people just do

This practice is not about what people do; it's about letting go of the judgements you are making.

Step 1:   When you feel yourself being pressed by something someone says or does, stop and just breathe.

Then, in the next moment, remind yourself that people just do what people just do (and so do you).

Step 2:   Next, take a moment to ask yourself, "Could there be another perspective here that I can't yet see?"

You may need some time before you are ready to look for one, but when you do, I invite you to be radically honest with your answer.

Step 3:   When you come up with an answer (maybe more than one!), ask yourself, "Can I accept these perspectives as actual possibilities?"

Step 4:   After you've honestly explored this, begin to notice any changes in how you feel about the situation.

Whilst you don't ever have to agree with *what* people do, you do have complete control over whether you let go of your judgement about it.

And when you're judgement-free about what you see outside yourself, you'll free yourself from the judgements you carry within yourself too.

# Lesson 20

## PEOPLE MAKE MISTAKES (AND SO DO YOU)

 AKA Forgiveness isn't for them: it's for you

### Everybody makes mistakes

**The fact is that people make mistakes.**

People lie, cheat and steal. They betray other people. They make choices they regret, and they don't make choices that they wish they had.

And another fact is that so do you (and I!)

**But like so many previous life lessons, this one isn't about the mistake itself.**

After all, mistakes are subjective. They don't always look like mistakes to the person making them. Sometimes they just look that way to you.

Instead, this lesson is about how you *react* to the mistake. It's about what you hold on to when you decide someone has made a mistake and what you do next.

And, ultimately, it's about how to instantly (at least with practice) restore a sense of peace and calm for yourself.

## What do YOU do when someone makes a mistake?

**Believe it or not, 99% of people don't wake up and think, "Hmmm, what mistake can I make today?"**

Most of us just navigate our way through life doing the best we can with what we know in any given moment.

Then (mostly), when we know better, we do better.

**But, as humans, we're *experts* at noticing other people's mistakes long before we notice our own.**

And, of course, when we notice a mistake, we like to point it out. Usually with every intention of staying calm and reasonable about it.

Unfortunately, that intention can so easily evaporate when they stare back at us blankly with no idea of what we're talking about... Arghhhhh!

**Luckily, there's a part of every mistake that you do have a say in: your reaction to it.**

And since this is a powerful lesson in acceptance, I want to share a more specific version of a mistake that you may have experienced.

That version is lying.

Lying can be a small mistake in itself, but it can also play a part in some of life's biggest mistakes.

# Has someone ever lied to you?

I can't imagine a single person on this planet who *hasn't* experienced a lie at some point.

**In my own life, there was a situation where I suspected my daughter was lying to me about smoking.**

I confronted her about it, and she insisted that she didn't smoke.

Being lied to always made me feel betrayed, hurt and let down. But most of all, it made me feel unloved.

And on this occasion, it felt even worse because my daughter had looked me straight in the eye and still lied. So when I busted her (because parents have an uncanny knack for this), I lost the plot with her completely!

**I yelled, screamed and unloaded every guilt-inducing accusation I could think of at her:**

- "How could you lie to my face?"
- "You must really hate me to do that!"
- "You must think I'm completely stupid."
- "I'm so disappointed in you."
- "You've broken my heart. I'll never be able to trust you again."

**Ouch to all of these! And I say that for us both.**

Because where do comments like those leave our relationship? Where do they leave ANY relationship?

In a shit pile, that's where!

Luckily, that day I truly took this life lesson on.

After I'd had my meltdown and confined her to her room, I sat crying in my own room. Then, using the practice I shared in Lesson 4, I stopped and asked myself whether I'd ever lied.

And of course I had.

**For example, I know for a fact that I also lied to my parents when I was a kid.**

(In fact – can you believe the irony here – I even lied to them about *smoking*.)

It wasn't because I didn't love or respect them. Nor was it to upset or hurt them. In fact, sometimes I thought not upsetting them was actually protecting them.

When I lied, it wasn't about them at all. It was 100% about me being a young girl who was surviving in the world of 'being a teenager'.

Just like my daughter was doing now.

Just like we're *all* doing at any stage in our lives.

**When I 'got' this, I realised that I love my children, my children love me AND sometimes they make mistakes (and so do I).**

Now, you might feel your blood boiling right now. You might be thinking, "I'll NEVER accept being lied to!"

I hear you.

But I want you to consider that that's *exactly* the same as saying you won't accept that people make mistakes.

**You see, I want to suggest that it's not the mistake itself that upsets you.**

Rather, it's the judgement and expectation you place on whoever made the mistake that leaves you feeling let down, betrayed and hurt.

Similarly, when people make a mistake, it's important to understand that you didn't cause it – even if it impacts you.

**It's OK if this life lesson takes a while to sink in.**

I've personally grappled with it for the majority of my life.

Before I truly 'got' this life lesson, if someone made a mistake, I'd ask myself, "Why would they do that?" And if it was someone I loved and trusted, I'd ask, "Why would they do that *to me?*"

However, the moment I switched my mindset to one of accepting that everyone makes mistakes (and so do I), I felt an incredible sense of peace.

And then I noticed for the first time the ridiculous expectations I was placing on the people in my life – and the world – to never make mistakes.

## You can't control people

**Let's talk about the things you can and can't control.**

We'll dive deeper into this in Lesson 28, but for now, I'll just say that you have no control over a mistake someone else has made.

You also have no control over the person who made it.

The ONLY thing you can control is your own reaction.

**Just understanding this will often bring you closer to peace and calm.**

Of course, you may still dig in your heels and internally scream, "But I'm right! They did make a mistake and it did upset me!"

If so, you may want to go back and re-read Lessons 16–18: the 'being right' trilogy.

Now don't get me wrong. There are sometimes (irrevocable) consequences to mistakes, which may determine what you do and don't allow in your life

I get that. I really do.

BUT, at the same time, your peace and calm around any mistake rely solely on your reaction to it. It depends on your ability to acknowledge that the mistake wasn't deliberately done to spite you, hurt you or make your life a living hell.

That's *why* it's called a mistake.

**Now, just for a moment, turn the spotlight on yourself.**

Just as you did in Lesson 19, turn your awareness spotlight inwards and ask yourself whether you've ever made a mistake.

And when you discover that you have (because we all have), ask yourself whether you did it to deliberately unleash hell on someone.

No?

Of course not.

You made a mistake because you made a mistake. And, quite possibly, there was a consequence.

Look, I make mistakes. You make mistakes. Everyone makes mistakes. (Now, read that again in the voice of Oprah!)

**The important thing is that YOU get to decide what happens next.**

You get to decide whether you can acknowledge to yourself that people will make mistakes. You get to decide whether to be right about someone making a mistake. Or, you to get to decide to exercise forgiveness and get on with your life calmly, peacefully and with an open heart.

And before you fire up your keyboard to email me that some things are unforgivable, I'd ask you to remember this. As I mentioned above, this life lesson is NOT about the mistake itself. Instead, it's about whether you choose to stay attached to the mistake or to forgive it and let it go.

**Forgiveness isn't *for* the other person. Forgiveness is completely for you.**

As the famous quote that's attributed to everyone from Anne Lamott to Marianne Williamson says, *"Not forgiving someone is like swallowing poison and expecting the other person to die."*

So you're not letting anyone get away with anything.

Instead, you're letting YOU get away with a peaceful, open heart.

# The Practice – Letting go of other people's mistakes

So here it is: three steps to letting go of other people's mistakes:

Step 1: Recognise that the mistake may only *be* a mistake in your mind and not in the mind of the other person.

Step 2: Acknowledge that the mistake is not about you (even if it feels like it is).

Step 3: Write an 'Open Letter of Forgiveness'.

To do this, take out your journal or a blank piece of paper, and write a letter that starts with 'Dear Forgiveness'.

Express what, in your mind, the mistake was about, what you made it mean and why you're now choosing to let it go.

Refer back to Lesson 4 for the Ho'oponopono practice if you need to.

Reminder: forgiveness is a gift of peace that only you can give to yourself.

# Lesson 21

## GOOD TIMES DON'T LAST AND NEITHER DO BAD TIMES

 AKA Trust in the process

### We all experience good times and bad times

As with previous life lessons, despite the title, this one isn't really about the good times *or* the bad times.

Because I know for certain that I'll experience both until the day that they're shovelling sand onto my face. And so will you.

Life is just like that.

It's made up of a series of moments, days, weeks, months and years. And in each of these time frames, we'll *all* have good times and bad times.

The key is to realise that neither the good times nor the bad times will last.

## Life is full of unknowns

**The truth: things will happen in your life that will throw you for a loop.**

Some of those things will be within your control and some won't. Either way, you simply don't know what tomorrow will bring:

- Something amazing could happen or you could have the rug pulled out from under you.

- There could be a beautiful sunrise or there could be floodwaters.

- You could have your best 'Mum moment' or have your worst.

- You could land your dream job or be made redundant.

- You could meet your soulmate or feel your heart break.

**A couple of years ago I came upon a story about a farmer and his horse.**

This story really made a light bulb flash on in my head! The way I've told it below may not be exactly how it was originally written, but it's how I remember it:

*A farmer had only one horse; and one day, it ran away.*

*His neighbour said, "I'm so sorry. This is such bad news. You must be so upset."*

*The man just said, "We'll see."*

*A few days later, his horse came back with 20 wild horses following.*

*So the man and his son corralled all 21 horses.*

*His neighbour said, "Congratulations! This is such good news. You must be so happy!"*

*The man just said, "We'll see."*

*Then one of the wild horses kicked the man's only son, breaking both his legs.*

*His neighbour again said, "I'm so sorry. This is such bad news. You must be so upset."*

*The man just said, "We'll see."*

*The country went to war, and every able-bodied young man was drafted to fight.*

*The war was terrible, killing everyone who fought. But the farmer's son was spared since his broken legs had prevented him from being drafted.*

*Once more, his neighbour said, "Congratulations! This is such good news. You must be so happy!"*

*And as always, the man just said, "We'll see."*

**Just like the farmer in this story, we never know what's coming at us.**

We do, however, get to decide whether we'll see something as good news, bad news or 'we'll see' news.

And, most importantly, we can trust that *whatever* we're facing right now will be totally different tomorrow (or at least at some point soon).

In other words, we can – if we choose to – trust in the process.

# I used to spend SO much time worrying about bad times

**I used to miss a lot of the good times in my life.**

Why? Because I was busy worrying about the bad times. I often worried about things that hadn't yet happened (and that quite often *never* happened).

For example, I worried that:

- I was a bad mum.
- I might go broke.
- I'd fail in business.
- I'd grow old alone.
- I might make the wrong decisions (often!)

**My mind was a constant whir of all of those worries and so many others.**

So much so that even though my life was filled with good times too, I completely missed them. They were there, but I simply wasn't present for them.

And even when I knew things were going great, I'd tell myself to make the most of them while they lasted... because good times *never* last.

Sound familiar?

**I noticed this pattern recently when I was selling my house.**

I've mentioned before that transformation is experiential, not intellectual. I've also said that it's ongoing – not something you do once and then, ta-dah, you're done.

That means the opportunity to transform any part of ourselves or our lives is available to all of us. And it's there in every moment, which is kind of cool when you think about it. In fact, I *even* got to do some transforming while I was writing this book.

You see, during the writing process, I put my house on the market. And being 'human first, enlightened second' (see Lesson 13), I found myself getting sucked into worrying about it selling.

**I'd become really attached to the outcome that the house had to sell by a certain date.**

At the same time, I completely resisted the idea of it not selling by that date... because I had no idea what I'd do if it didn't.

You see, part of my plan was to self-publish this book using some of the money from the house sale.

**I wondered whether I'd made a big mistake in taking the leap to write this book.**

What if I ran out of money before the house sold?

What if no offers came for the house?

I also noticed how being stuck in the 'bad times' impacted my creativity.

And, as a result, I missed out on multiple chances to be happy, calm and peaceful in the positive 'what is' of each moment. For example, I found myself discounting the numerous people who attended my open homes each weekend.

Instead, I spent my days either worrying about everything that might go wrong or worrying that the outcome I wanted to happen wouldn't.

**Then one day, my awareness finally kicked in. I noticed where my thoughts were taking me.**

As soon as I did, I knew I had the tools to bring myself back to a neutral place.

And, just like the farmer, once I assumed that neutral position where neither outcome was good or bad, I could get back to enjoying writing this book. I even started to remember why I wanted to write it in the first place – such a twist of irony when you think about it.

(Interestingly, the moment I made peace with both outcomes and accepted that whatever would happen would happen, the house actually sold.)

## Instead of worrying, allow and accept

**The farmer in the story was an expert at accepting 'what is'.**

He realised that 'good' and 'bad' are simply definitions that our human minds construct. I realised exactly the same thing with my worries about my house selling.

If you can do the same thing – allowing and accepting, rather than resisting or avoiding – you can peacefully and calmly flow with the natural rhythm of life.

And that rhythm will include the human definition of both good times and bad times.

**When you're struggling to make peace with a situation, ask yourself, "What's the worst-case scenario here?"**

Although you may not want that outcome to eventuate, accepting that it's possible and that you'll be OK if it occurs is your fast track to a powerfully peaceful life.

Joy and happiness may only appear to be there in the good times, but you can access *peace* on all days, in all ways. You just need to choose to allow and accept every moment and every outcome just as it is or isn't.

I've previously mentioned the Eckhart Tolle quote: *"What we fight, we strengthen and what we resist, persists."* Accepting and allowing gives you a far greater capacity to trust in the outcome.

With practice, it will allow you to see the gift in every situation.

Just like the farmer did.

And just like I did with my house.

## The Practice – Accepting 'what is' right now

**Accepting 'what is' will allow you to detach from resisting the 'bad' and clinging to the 'good'.**

In turn, that detachment will bring you to a place of peace and calm in *this* moment.

To practise acceptance:

**Step 1:** Write down the situation that's worrying you.

eg. "I really need my house to sell by xx/xx/xx."

**Step 2:** Describe the negative outcome that you don't want.

**Step 3:** Make a list of actions you can take if this eventuates.

**Step 4:** Describe the positive outcome that you do want.

Now that you've given yourself the knowledge that you'll be OK in either instance, let it go and trust in the process.

# Lesson 22

## KIDS TURN OUT

 AKA I grew up and
so did you

### Nothing prepares you for parenting

**Becoming a parent is something that I believe no one can prepare you for.**

It doesn't matter how many books you read, how many gurus you consult or how many conversations you have with other parents. Until you actually walk out into the world holding a baby in your arms, the magnitude of the task ahead just doesn't register.

And this job called parenting doesn't come with any entitlements.

There's no clocking on and off, no working nine to five, no sick leave, no annual leave, no long service leave and definitely no retirement.

It's just 24/7 for the rest of your life. You're always on duty.

**And here's the kicker: there's no bloody instruction manual!**

NOTE: before I go any further into this lesson, I want to stress that I'm not a child psychologist. I'm also not in *any* way dismissing tragic or traumatic events that break laws relating to parenting.

Nor am I making any specific assumptions about your individual circumstances.

Support with healing from these kinds of events is beyond the scope of this book. So if you're dealing with them, I strongly recommend reaching out for professional help.

These are simply my own observations and information that's helped me personally.

OK? Let's move on then.

## So how do you know whether you're getting it right?

**How do you know if you're doing a good job as a parent?**

How do you know you're not completely screwing your kids up?

How do you know that the decisions you're making on their behalf are the best ones for them?

How do you know that saying, "No," to them is the right thing in any situation?

And how do you know when saying, "Yes," to them is the right thing?

**The truth is that we don't know. And nor did our parents...**

Personally, my doubts often showed up after the "I hate you!"s, the "You've ruined everything!"s, and of course the "You just don't care about me, do you?"s.

And there were many other situations where my doubts arose too. You might relate to some of these – like when your kids:

- sneak out or aren't where they said they'd be

- take up smoking (dope even) or get drunk

- pierce their septum (or something else)

- steal something

- start hanging out with kids or start doing activities that you don't relate to

- throw a public tantrum that would measure 5.0 on the Richter scale.

It would be totally understandable if your reaction to any of this was a 'Showdown at the "I'm the parent, do as I say!" Corral'.

But if this rings a bell, you'll know that reaction isn't super-effective.

## I used to worry about screwing my kids up. A lot.

**I especially worried when I became a solo parent.**

The need to get it right suddenly weighed even more heavily on me. I fought a desperate inner battle to make the right decisions for my kids.

I wanted so much to make sure that I was doing everything I could and *teaching* them everything I could, so they'd have an amazing life.

I wanted to shield them from the hurt and pain in life, and just expose them to all the good, happy stuff. I wanted to sort out all their problems for them so their lives would be easier.

**Now, there's no question that I loved my kids.**

But what drove all this crazy thinking was guilt.

In my mind, if they grew up to have amazing lives, it would be because I'd loved them and had been an awesome parent. So if they *didn't* have amazing lives, it could only be because I'd somehow screwed up as a parent and screwed up their lives in the process.

What crazy thinking!

**Why did I think my version of an amazing life was even what they wanted?**

Now don't get me wrong, my kids weren't spoilt brats.

We had house rules, which they mostly hated. We had agreements around chores like unstacking and stacking the dishwasher, taking out the garbage and folding washing. And, of course, manners and respect were a big part of growing up in our home too.

I'm sure if you asked them, they'd tell you we had a whole lot of other rules as well. Like if they wanted to have a sleepover, it would only happen if the parent of the sleepover friend called me directly to confirm the details. (They really hated this rule.)

And like most families, we fought over all manner of things. We yelled and sometimes screamed at each other. We said things we didn't mean in the heat of the moment. Plus, like I said above, I received my fair share of "I hate you, Mum!"s too.

So on the crappy days (and there were a few), I'd say to myself, "I must be the worst mother in the world!"

Then, when my kids were young teenagers, we went to a seminar about families together.

It was led by one of the coolest, wisest, noblest gentlemen I'd ever met (except for my dad of course). He spoke about families, parenting, children, rules, boundaries and love.

He believed that our only job as parents is to love our kids: purely, openly and honestly. And then we had to be prepared to get back whatever came, without reacting to it.

Because, he said, sometimes love doesn't look like love to a kid. *Especially* when they don't get what they want. And kids are very, very good at making their parents wrong about everything!

But his words that I took the most inspiration from were these:

*"Kids turn out. I did and so did you.*

*In spite of you and despite you, kids turn out!"*

You could actually *see* the lightbulbs flashing on around the room from over 200 families. Wow! Such a simple yet profound statement.

This somehow lifted the pressure I'd placed on myself to be a good mum.

It dissolved my constant inner worry that my actions might screw my kids up.

For the *first* time in my parenting life, I knew I was doing my very best and that this was always going to be enough.

# Think back to the parenting job YOUR parents did

I invite you to look at the whole parenting thing through the eyes of a kid. (Because, let's face it, we were all kids at some point.)

**Think about your own parents for a moment.**

Sometimes they made mistakes, right? Mine sure did. Not just as parents, but in their adult lives too. Now, despite those mistakes, I invite you to consider that they loved you:

- even though sometimes you got what you wanted and sometimes you didn't
- even though sometimes you liked their decisions and sometimes you didn't
- even though sometimes there were consequences to your actions
- even though sometimes they didn't appear to see, hear or listen to you
- even though, looking back, you may know that you wouldn't make the same parenting choices.

Consider too that most parents don't wake up every day and think, "Hmmm, how can I screw up my kid's life today?"

**Now flip it back to you as the parent.**

Can you feel some of the burden to get it right all the time and never get it wrong begin to fade? Even just a little?

This is a big lesson to take on, but it can bring so much peace to your home.

## The Practice – Accepting yourself as a parent

**Going forward, the practice is to trust in yourself.**

Trust in your love for your kids, no matter whether you're nailing the parenting gig or throwing your hands in the air.

Your love for your kids is the pathway for them 'turning out' – in spite of you and despite you!

And on the crappy days (and there will be some), when all your parenting strategies, house rules, agreements and well-laid plans go out the window, do two things:

1.  Tell your kids you love THEM (and that this is separate to their behaviour).

2.  Tell yourself YOU are a loving parent (and that this is separate to *your* behaviour).

And guess what? Your kids WILL turn out.

I did, and so did you...

# Lesson 23

## THERE'S THE 'TRUTH' FOR YOU AND MILLIONS OF OTHERS

 AKA The truth about the "truth"

### Do your beliefs belong to you?

**Our beliefs (including our opinions, preferences, values and habits) aren't actually our own.**

Well, they are today, but they've been passed on to us over time. They come from our parents, families, environments, cultures, friends, communities, spiritualities... and the list goes on.

Then our day-to-day experiences enhance those beliefs.

And from our experiences, we create 'stories' that further support the strength of each belief, cementing them into our thoughts, minds and psyches.

**Eventually, these beliefs become our truths.**

They become what we believe to be true about ourselves and the world around us.

So if you have your truth (from your beliefs) and I have mine (from my beliefs) and everyone around you has their truth (from their beliefs), which truth is true?

Which truth is real?

Which truth is right?

What if they all are?

## All beliefs are true for the person who believes them

In psychology, there's a concept known as the false-consensus effect or false-consensus bias.

Basically, this is a cognitive bias in which people overestimate how often others share their opinions, beliefs, preferences, values and habits. This means they generalise what *they* think is 'normal' and assume it's shared by others far more than is actually true.

Additionally, I mentioned back in Lesson 18 that the idea of 'right and wrong' is a survival mechanism that we humans use to align with large groups. Agreeing with the general consensus is often preferable today, because thousands of years ago, it kept us safest!

In other words, assuming that your beliefs mesh with everyone else's (and vice versa) is just another way for you to feel safe.

Of course, we all hold very different beliefs. Strap yourself in for some examples here:

- **My truth:** I eat meat (because I believe it's OK to do so).

- **A vegan's truth:** they don't (because they believe that eating animals isn't OK).

- **My truth:** I love tattoos (because I believe they're beautiful).

- **My sister's truth:** she doesn't (because she believes they aren't).

- **My truth:** I love to be active outdoors (because I believe it's good for my health).

- **My son's truth:** he loves online gaming (because he believes it's social and fun).

- **My truth:** I don't smoke anymore (because I believe it creates disease in my body).

- **My mum's truth:** she smoked until the day she died (because she enjoyed smoking).

- **My truth:** I occasionally drink alcohol (because I believe it's OK to enjoy a glass of wine socially).

- **My mum's truth:** she didn't (because she was an alcoholic, and she believed it negatively impacted her life).

Of course, I have many truths around a multitude of other things too. And so does every other human in the world.

**Now, before I go on, I'm not condoning breaking any laws.**

Every state, territory and country has a clear set of laws. And, as a condition of living in that place, you agree to abide by its laws. That, or you agree to accept the consequences of breaking them and/or get involved in trying to officially change them.

Either way, your responsibility to abide by a law doesn't depend on whether it's 'true' for you.

**In fact, beliefs often both come from and shape the laws of a country.**

For example, in 2017 here in Australia, a change in our laws enabled same-sex couples to marry. This created an enormous debate, largely because of the differing cultural and religious beliefs embedded in our community and society:

- The earlier law was shaped by the belief that same-sex marriage was wrong.
- The changed law was shaped by the growing belief that it was actually OK.

And the fact that same-sex marriage is now legal will no doubt also shape the belief of future generations that it's OK.

The key point for this lesson is that many people (including me) wanted the law updated, and many people didn't. Either way, we all held opinions about what the law should be, based on our beliefs.

This lesson is NOT about giving up your truth.

Instead, it's about giving up that YOUR truth is right and THEIR truth is wrong.

## My truths are my truths

**It took me some time to realise that my truths weren't right or wrong – they were just mine.**

Some people share some of those truths with me and others don't.

My truths have also changed over time as new experiences have opened me to other people's truths. And I hope that they keep changing as I continue to live, learn, expand and grow as a human.

For example, my time in Saudi Arabia changed many – but not all – of my truths.

**One that *didn't* change was that killing people under any circumstances went against my beliefs.**

Yet the day I arrived in Saudi Arabia, I learnt there'd been 47 beheadings.

Did I have an opinion about these beheadings based on my beliefs? Absolutely.

But did that make me right that beheading was objectively wrong? NO.

For Saudis, the act of beheading a criminal as a form of punishment is 'right' based on their beliefs.

You see, things aren't objectively right or wrong in themselves. Rather, our beliefs about them *make* them right or wrong for us.

## Ask yourself whether your truths are true for everyone in the Universe

**For the most part, other people's little truths won't trigger us.**

If you only drink tea and I drink coffee, who cares, right?

But it's our big truths that we'll ultimately step up on a soapbox about and defend in a 'battle to the death'.

Respectful, healthy discussions can add value to the world – immense value. These kinds of conversations can be the catalyst for problem-solving, are solution-focused and can bring about change in our world.

But arguing over whose truth is right or wrong will cripple any opportunity for change.

**I see this on Facebook all the time (and I'm sure you do too).**

First, someone shares their truth. Then someone else takes offence at that person's truth and attempts to put their own truth forward as the 'real' truth.

And then on it goes, backwards and forwards – usually until it ends up becoming personal.

The Facebook community grabs their virtual popcorn, unable to stop watching the train wreck. All because two people with different beliefs each believe their own truth is right.

**But here's the thing: we don't have to agree, but we don't have to disagree either.**

We could just choose to accept there are millions of truths in the world, none of which are right and none of which are wrong. They're simply not the same as our own truths.

And that's actually OK.

The first step is always simply to notice (ie. become aware) when something is triggering you. You may also notice when this happens that your ego is running the 'you' show.

Then remind yourself that what's true for someone else may just not be for you – and that's OK.

And, of course, what's true for you may also not be true for someone else – and that's *also* OK.

## The Practice – Accepting other people's truths

This practice is designed to help you peacefully accept other people's truths.

It will assist you in navigating this world where differing beliefs aren't inherently right or wrong. And it will help you to see opportunities for powerful, solution-focused communication that may then lead to growth or change.

Step 1: Identify something you're certain that you're right about regarding something or someone.

Step 2: Ask yourself, "Is this thing I believe about the person or situation true for me AND the entire universe?"

If the answer is that it's only true for you and not universally true, then it's a belief that belongs to you.

This means the rest of the universe may not share it.

And this, in turn, gives you an opening to shift your perception around the person or situation. This doesn't necessarily mean giving it up, but rather seeing it from another perspective.

Step 3: Let's test the example belief that 'you need oxygen to survive'.

- Is this true for you? Yes.

- Is it true for the rest of the world? Yes.

That means it's a universal truth.

**Step 4:** Now let's test the belief that 'people who have tattoos are dangerous and belong to biker gangs'.

- Is this true for you? Yes (well, actually it might not be – but this is just an example, so you get my point, right?)

- Is this true for the rest of the world? No.

**That means it's a belief/experience of yours (that likely came from your culture or community) and not a universal truth.**

Being able to identify your personal truths and separate them from universal truths will open the door to a greater acceptance of the truths of others.

# Lesson 24

## COMPARISON IS THE THIEF OF JOY

 AKA What do Kurt Cobain, Oprah Winfrey and Bruce Williams have in common?

### The plain or the floral?

**Comparing one thing with another is a useful tool – one we often use for making choices.**

For example, I'll sometimes take my daughter clothes shopping with me to help me choose. I'll hold up two dresses and ask her, "What do you think? The plain or the floral?"

Comparing the two options helps her – and me – to make a decision. (Although, let's be honest, many women would prefer to just buy both dresses, right?)

And whilst comparing one dress with another is about choosing the most fabulous one, comparing *ourselves* with others will make us feel anything BUT fabulous!

## Ever wanted 'what she's having'?

**Do you remember the movie *When Harry Met Sally*?**

It contains the infamous coffee shop scene where Sally (Meg Ryan) proves to Harry (Billy Crystal) that women can fake orgasms without men knowing the difference. Search for it on YouTube if you haven't seen it... just not while you're at work!

As the scene unfolds, Sally demonstrates her ability to 'fake it' in full view of all the coffee shop customers. And she's so convincing that when she's done and Harry is sitting there in stunned silence, a lady at another table tells the waitress, "I'll have what she's having!"

It's very funny, and it makes this life lesson that much easier to explain.

You see, Sally's performance was good enough to make this other woman compare her own apparently boring sex life to Sally's.

**Now, how often have you 'wanted what she's having'?**

And no, it doesn't have to be an orgasm... Well, OK, it could be, but let's just treat the word 'orgasm' as a metaphor in this instance!

It could be anything that you see (or think you see) someone else enjoying or seeming to do easily.

**These days, it's all too easy for social media to lure us into falsely believing that our lives just don't measure up.**

Scrolling through the millions of 'perfect life' images on Instagram or Pinterest can instantly bring us down.

And that can then trigger us into believing that 'we want what they're having' too, metaphorically speaking.

## I've had 'comparison-itis' too many times to count

I can recall many, many times in my life where I 'wanted what she's having'.

I wanted to:

- run as fast as her
- be as organised as her
- be as strong as her
- have as much money as her
- have her body
- be as pretty as her
- be as smart as her
- have her career
- have her relationship
- have her patience
- have her life.

And the list could go on...

**Now, none of these comparisons have ever truly ground me down.**

They haven't affected my self-esteem or stopped me being driven and determined to create my own life. But I'd be lying by omission if I didn't admit that all these thoughts and more have popped into my head at one time or another during my life.

And making peace with these types of thoughts is what this life lesson is about.

There are several quotes that I remind myself of when these thoughts appear:

- *"Wanting to be someone else is a waste of the person you are."* – thanks, Kurt Cobain.

- *"Be thankful for what you have; you'll end up having more. If you concentrate on what you don't have, you will never, ever have enough." – thanks, Oprah Winfrey.*

- And, of course... *"Comparison is the thief of joy."* – thanks, Theodore Roosevelt and thank you also to my friend Bruce Williams who I first heard say this.

Once I started to become aware of my 'comparison-itis', I could shift through it. The thing I finally understood was that I could actually have a 'Sally' moment any time I wanted to. (And not the 'fake' kind of Sally moment either!)

## Comparison steals more than just joy

**Wanting to be something else robs both you and the world of who you are right now.**

That's because comparison doesn't just steal your joy. It also steals the magnificence of YOU from the world, because while you're comparing yourself, the person that you're here on this earth to be isn't present.

And it's not just the world that misses out on the YOU that you're here to be. So do the people you love. You see, when you're being yourself, you're actually putting something unique and brilliant into the world that wasn't there before. This, I believe, is what we're all here to do.

Now, can you improve upon the current version of yourself? Of course you can! But doing this starts with who YOU are and not who someone else is.

**This really shows up in fitness training and sporting events.**

Imagine being in a running race with ten thousand other people. There will be people faster than you and people slower than you. Agreed?

So is everyone – the people faster than you, slower than you and you yourself – all doing the best they can? I would say, in most instances, the answer to that is YES!

Now, your mind might be whirring away thinking, "But what if I came last? I'd be at the end of the line then!"

And yes, that's true if that's how you want to think about it. But consider that there are millions of people who didn't make it to the start line of that race.

The same goes if you come first. There are over seven billion people in this world, so the ten thousand in this race only represent a tiny, tiny percentage of people who can run.

**Now, imagine that you're standing in a long line that contains *every* person in the world.**

Are there people ahead of you? Yes.

Are there people behind you? Yes.

And if you swapped places with anyone in that line, would there be still people ahead of you and behind you? YES!

In life, this will *always* be the case. While you're busy wanting to be someone or somewhere else in the great line of life, someone else will want to be where YOU are!

So instead, imagine that there is no line.

Who you are and where you are is exactly where you're meant to be.

**This life lesson is *not* about staying where you are.**

Instead, it's about how to be PRESENT to where you are right now and acknowledge the awesomeness of that.

It's about making friends with who you are and being peaceful in the knowledge of *where* you are right now!

And, most importantly, it's about not comparing that person to anyone or anything else.

Because the thing I know for sure is that the only person you can be right now, in this moment, is YOU.

As Dr Seuss said, *"Today you are you, that is truer than true. There is no one alive who is you-er than you!"*

## The Practice – Letting go of comparison

When you notice you're comparing yourself to others, try these steps below.

Step 1:   First, express gratitude to yourself for who you are and where you are right now.

Step 2:   Next ask yourself, "On a scale of 1–10, how important to me is the situation/person I'm comparing myself to right now?"

Step 3:   If your answer rates low, send some love to the person or situation you're comparing yourself to, and then to yourself.

Or, if your answer rates high, make a list of actionable steps you could take to embody more of the traits of that person/situation in the magnificent person you already are.

Step 4:   Stop comparing yourself! It's a waste of the talented, smart, funny, beautiful person you are right now!

Note: this practice may reveal that the comparison-itis you're experiencing is actually an unconscious habit, possibly brought on by social media scrolling.

# Stage 3:
# Area of Control

"Don't let people pull you into their
storm. Pull them into your peace."

– Kimberly Jones

# The only thing you can control is 'you'

**In almost all situations, there are two distinct areas.**

The first area, where you're most powerful, is the one that contains the things you CAN control. The second area, where you're completely powerless, contains everything you CANNOT control.

However, most people spend their lives trying to manage everything in that second area. Then they get bent out of shape, frustrated, upset and derailed because they're trying to control the uncontrollable.

**So what's actually within your area of control?**

The things you can control include:

- your thoughts
- your actions
- your feelings
- your reactions
- your responses.

**And the only person who can access all these things is you.**

What's outside your area of control and which you have no influence over, however, are *other people's* thoughts, actions, feelings, reactions and responses.

So anything you think or do is completely within your area of control. What other people think or do, however, is completely outside your area of control.

## Life is for living, not for juggling

**Trying to control the uncontrollable is like a never-ending juggling act of personalities, situations, rules, wants and desires.**

Just when you think everything's cruising along and life is behaving itself and doing what you want, one of these variables will do a 180-degree flip. And suddenly, you'll be left feeling upset, disappointed, frustrated and let down.

IMPORTANT: this is not about *avoiding responsibility*.

When you truly understand that all you can control is within you, you realise that this isn't permission to shrug your shoulders and avoid controlling anything.

Life is happening all around you all the time. But if you find yourself thinking, "I have no control over what's happening out there, so there's nothing I can do," you've likely missed the point. (Although if you have, that's OK. By the end of this section, you'll 'get it'.)

**As you'll discover, there's ALWAYS something *you* can do.**

And that 'something' starts – and ends – with you.

Mastering this stage of experiential transformation will show you how easy it can be to defuse almost any drama in your life. And you'll discover you can do it WITHOUT getting into a control jousting match with anyone or anything else.

## Focusing on what you CAN control is your next step

In this next stage, you'll learn some surprising things about control.

You'll discover that being in control actually requires you to loosen your grip – sometimes to the point of eating chocolate for breakfast. You'll find out how choosing to be right can create a cascade of drama that's completely within your control to defuse.

Plus, you'll also discover the three phrases in the English language that almost always set a disappointment trap both for you and the people around you. (And, surprise, surprise: you'll learn that whether or not you use those phrases is also ALWAYS within your area of control.)

**Throughout this book, you've been building your transformation superpowers.**

You've dialled up your awareness and invited acceptance to the table. Now, you're ready to dive into the third stage of experiential transformation, which is controlling your controllables. As I mentioned above, it's a practice that starts and ends with *you*.

Bringing mastery to these lessons will prepare you for the final stage, which is Actualisation.

# Lesson 25

## TODAY IS THE FIRST DAY OF THE REST OF YOUR LIFE

 AKA You can start a new day every single day

### Have you ever had a really bad day?

**Sounds like a silly question, right?**

And on those days:

- Have you ever wanted to crawl into a hole and never come out?

- Have you ever done or said things you wish you could undo or unsay?

- Have you ever wished you could go back in time and make a different decision?

- Have you ever asked, "Why is this happening to me?"

- Have you ever woken up feeling like everything is crashing down around you (and whilst that feeling makes you want to stay in bed, you're equally scared of not getting up)?

Yep, me too. I've personally experienced them all.

# You don't have to keep carrying those days with you

**Most of us carry our bad days around in something that feels like a heavy, oversized backpack.**

Every messed-up day that ever happened to us is inside that backpack.

Every.

Single.

Bad.

Day.

Ever.

We carry them all, and we *never* take it off. We don't dare put it down. It's ours and ours alone to carry.

Then, as if the bad days in the backpack weren't heavy enough, we weigh it down further with our despair, anger, sadness, shame, guilt or embarrassment too.

**There was a time in my life that I carried a backpack just like this one.**

I experienced many bad days and, although I soldiered on (as women are prone to doing), those days were always there with me in my backpack.

I sometimes wonder if I did this as some kind of penance or punishment for the things that happened on those days. They were a constant reminder of the crap that had happened in my life.

As you read this, you may be feeling the weight of your own backpack.

But here's the thing: when we hang on to bad days after they've happened, we're actually punishing ourselves. We're suffering in the present moment for things that happened in the past – things we can't change or undo.

Buddha said, "*Suffering is not holding you. You are holding suffering.*"

## Here are just a *handful* of my 'bad days'

I don't know anyone who hasn't had a bad day. Below are just a few of mine:

- I lost my virginity when I was 13.
- I was caught shoplifting when I was 16.
- I've borrowed money for food.
- I miscarried my second child.
- I've been on the verge of bankruptcy more than once.
- I've detected more than one breast lump.
- I've had my heart broken into a million pieces.
- People I love have wished me dead.
- I've said goodbye to both of my parents and to close friends way sooner than I wanted to.
- I've made countless poor choices, broken my word, let people down, lied and failed many times.

**And there've been many more.**

You may have experienced similar or possibly far worse days. In fact, you may be having one right now.

This isn't about the scale of the bad days: it's about what you do with them.

At some point, I learnt that having a bad day doesn't make me a bad person. It just makes me human, which we talked about back in Lesson 13.

I also learnt that only I can choose to drop my backpack of bad days. What I mean is that only I can choose to leave my bad days behind in the past where they belong. And when I do that, I get to let go of my own suffering and stop punishing myself or other people.

## I've learnt how to put the backpack down (and so can you)

When I was struggling with the guilt of ending my marriage and breaking our family apart, Fran wrote something in my *Recipe for Life* book.

**She said, "Today is the first day of the rest of your life."**

I really didn't understand how powerful this single statement was back then. Now, however, I live by it.

I've long since learnt that we're not what we've done or what's been done to us. Instead, we're what we do *now*.

The practice below will show you how to not only take off your backpack of bad days but also how to find the gifts that are hidden inside it. This is important because gratitude for the gifts of each day – good or bad – is one of the keys to a happy and peaceful life.

So put down your backpack, open it up and take everything out. You no longer need to keep anything hidden, and you have nothing to be ashamed of. Then, once you've done that, close it and throw it away. You'll never need it again.

Everything in there will have something to teach you. But you can take the learning and leave the backpack behind. You no longer need to carry it with you.

**Because today really is the first day of the rest of YOUR life.**

## The Practice – Putting down the backpack

**When you are feeling the weight of a bad day upon you, try these five steps.**

**Step 1:** When you wake up, remind yourself that TODAY is the first day of the rest of your life.

**Step 2:** Give thanks for both the gifts of the past and the gifts of the future that you've yet to receive. Then give thanks to yourself for being open to receive all the gifts.

**Step 3:** Spend a few minutes reflecting on yesterday (or previous days), and ask yourself, "What is there for me to learn from that day?"

If you feel drawn to, journal whatever you notice (this is a great awareness practice).

**Step 4:** Then, when you've finished reflecting (either in your mind or in your journal), ask yourself, "If today were the first day of the rest of my life, what could I choose to do and who could I choose to be?"

**Step 5:** Become aware of at least one thing that comes to mind as an answer, then try to find a way to enact that during your day.

**It may be helpful to anchor this practice as a seven-day ritual.**

This can be particularly useful if you're feeling stuck on a problem, or if there's a situation you're finding difficult to forgive or let go of.

To do this, keep a notebook beside your bed and complete this practice for seven consecutive days.

# Lesson 26

## IT'S OK TO EAT CHOCOLATE FOR BREAKFAST (OCCASIONALLY)

 AKA You don't have to be perfect to create moments of perfection

### Eating a nutritious breakfast IS important

This is a profoundly simple life lesson, and it's one of the shortest in this book.

But it's still an important one to remember.

Now, before I launch into it, I want to preface it by saying that I'm not condoning (or condemning) any particular nutritional practice, diet or food choices.

And yes, I almost always eat a balanced, wholefood diet – both for breakfast and every other meal.

But this life lesson isn't actually about what anyone eats or when they eat it.

So whilst I do believe it's OK to *actually* eat chocolate for breakfast occasionally, the phrase is really a metaphor to remind myself (and you) to enjoy life.

And I discovered this life lesson during a time that I literally ate chocolate for breakfast.

## Enjoying ALL the moments in life

**Throughout my life, I've been prone to get caught up in 'doing'.**

In fact, I'm a very good 'do-er', as you discovered in Lesson 1.

But I've come to understand that it's important to notice when I'm caught in the grip of 'doing my life', rather than 'being *in* my life'.

**Kids are great role models for simply enjoying the moment.**

If you ask a kid whether they want chocolate for breakfast, what do you suppose they'll say? Of course, they'll answer, "YES!"

Why? Because they not only live in the moment but they also *enjoy* the moment. They haven't yet forgotten how to do this. As a result:

- They know how to have fun for the sake of having fun.
- They know how to play for the sake of playing.
- They know how to do nothing for the sake of doing nothing.
- They don't live by any rules (except the rules we teach them).
- They know it's perfectly OK to eat chocolate for breakfast (or at any time of the day, for that matter!)

Now, of course I'm not suggesting we just throw all the rules out the window.

The 1954 bestseller *Lord of the Flies* by Nobel prize-winner William Golding gave a pretty good account of what would happen if kids made the rules.

However, I *am* suggesting that as adults we remember to question the rules occasionally. Especially the ones that won't end the world if we bend or even break them.

Most mums are insanely busy keeping it all together so they can actually get into bed before midnight.

So even just the thought of deviating from the schedule or bending the rules can cause mental pandemonium and possible household chaos.

But that's exactly why it's so important to take this lesson on.

Because, sometimes, our 'keeping it all together' blinkers can keep us blinded to the lighter side of life.

## A moment of complete perfection

I was a 'keep it all together' blinker-wearing mum most days.

Growing up, I never ate chocolate for breakfast, and nor did my kids. Well, never except on *one* day of the year: Easter Sunday!

And not surprisingly, when I scan back over the memories that fill my heart and soul to the brim, this is one of my favourites.

The night before Easter, the kids' dad and I would hide the chocolate eggs. We'd leave notes with clues from the Easter Bunny himself hinting at where the kids might find them.

And the next morning, the excitement was electrifying!

When the kids eventually found their stash, they'd look at me and ask, "Can we eat one now?"

And just for this brief moment, once a year, I'd bend the rules and say, "Yes!"

Their absolute joy, infectious giggles and giddy discussion over which one they'd eat first was pure bliss to watch. So was the intense delight on their faces as they took that first bite.

Then they'd bring some of their chocolate to me to eat too; I'd hear more fits of giggles as I also ate chocolate for breakfast.

**That moment in my life was complete perfection.**

Nobody can go back in time. However, if I could, I'd go back to the 'me' in that perfect moment and whisper in her ear, "Do this more often, not just once a year."

I can't go back in time, but these days, I can at least make sure I remember that moments of perfection don't always come from being perfect.

## Let go of being perfect to embrace moments of perfection

**Sometimes, there's little difference between being controlled and being controlling.**

For example, society will tell you that eating chocolate for breakfast breaks all the rules, which is society controlling you. Then you unconsciously enforce that rule in both your life and your kids' lives, which is you being controlled.

Letting go of enforcing and abiding by those rules, however, neutralises the control. And when you neutralise control, what can open up is a light, carefree space and an energy that allows for life to occur 'in the moment'.

**So let me ask you: where does the need for perfectionism and control show up in your life?**

What effect could this be having on your level of fun and joy? What rules have you created for yourself? What rules have you taken on – either from society or family traditions? And what would it look like if, just for one day, you threw those rules out the window?

Maybe you might:

- have a makeup-free day
- go barefoot to the supermarket
- post a selfie you'd normally delete
- let the kids choose their own dinner
- let the kids choose your outfit.

Or maybe, like me, you might eat chocolate for breakfast.

Regardless, when you can occasionally let go of being perfect and perhaps break a rule or two, who knows what might show up? You might be surprised, like I was, by a moment of pure perfection.

## The Practice – Allowing yourself to break your rules

This may be about chocolate for you or it may be something else. Regardless, the practice is still the same.

Step 1:   Grab a piece of paper and write down the numbers 1 through 10. Now beside each number write down a rule you've created in your life.

          For example: "Not eating chocolate for breakfast."

Step 2:   Now, for the next ten weeks go through your list and – focusing on one rule per week – break every single one of them.

Step 3:   Optional: in your journal, describe what you felt. What memories came up for you (if any)? And who could you share the experience with next time?

# Lesson 27

## YOUR THOUGHTS CREATE YOUR REALITY

 AKA You can think yourself down or think yourself up

### It's easy to be positive when things are going great

**But have you ever wanted to punch a 'positive person' in the face?**

Or have all the cringeworthy 'inspirational' quotes and motivational hashtags made you want to blow up Facebook or Instagram?

Of course, you don't feel like that when your life is in flow and humming along, right?

When things are going great, it's *easy* to be positive and not become upset or irritated by anything. In fact, on the good days, you're happy – even bursting – to tell everyone just how much you're loving your life!

**On those days, all the positive quotes on social media just make sense.**

So of course you share them because you really *get* it. You're 'in the zone, baby', and you just can't wipe the smile off your face!

But what about when you're having a crappy day? Now *that's* when you really want to punch every positive person in the face.

## I used to get stuck on wondering which days were 'real'

**Here's where it gets confusing.**

You're happy because everything's going great. And that's real, right?

But then along comes a shitty day. And you feel like crap, and that's also real.

Now, just thinking happy thoughts doesn't magically turn a shitty day into a great day. The shitty day is still real. And no number of positive quotes or inspiring hashtags will change it.

So why do I say that your thoughts create your reality?

And how can your thoughts possibly change a shitty day into a good day?

## It's amazing how differently two people can experience the same situation

**I truly discovered this when I lived in Saudi Arabia.**

I've mentioned that I spent time in Saudi Arabia teaching fitness, health and wellness at a women's college. During my time there, the phrase, "We're not in Kansas anymore, Toto!" was constantly in my thoughts.

In fact, whenever I reacted in shock or surprise at day-to-day occurrences, the response would always be, "Welcome to Saudi!" with a winky face. Life there definitely took some adjusting to.

It was, to this day, one of the most challenging places I've ever lived.

But it was also one of the most amazing and hugely rewarding experiences of my life.

**Around the same time I arrived in Saudi, so did another teacher.**

The two of us got on brilliantly. In fact, due to some accommodation challenges, we ended up as roommates. And believe me, I scooped the pool here: sharing with her was easy and comfortable.

We lived together, travelled to and from the college together, worked together and did our grocery shopping together too. And, as there were limited opportunities to do things on the weekends, we also spent most of our downtime together. Much like all of the other teachers, we existed as a collective – either in our apartments or at the college.

**Our day-to-day lives were identical.**

We shared the same environment, the same conditions and the same challenges. We also shared the same good stuff and the same shitty stuff.

We basically shared the same everything.

**Then after two months she resigned, saying life in Saudi just wasn't for her.**

I was really sad to lose a great friend and an awesome roommate; although I totally understood her decision and respected that it was the right one for her.

But here's the interesting part.

**When she left, she told me it had been the worst experience of her life.**

Wow! The worst? Really?

Her words shocked me at first. How could we have been exposed to *exactly* the same situations, but had two totally different experiences?

Now I'm not for one second saying that we didn't deal with difficulties. We did: we dealt with some crazy challenges and situations.

But when I think about it, I recall the most amazing, hugely rewarding experiences that I've ever been privileged to have.

Yes, sure, there were days when I cried. Days when I threw tantrums and told the dean, "It's all shit!" And yes, that was all real. But during that same time, I also:

- laughed out loud a lot and made lifelong friendships
- learnt about and immersed myself in an incredible culture
- saw some truly breathtaking sites and more stars in the sky than I'd ever seen before
- watched students play their first games and run their first 500 metres
- discovered that I'm an excellent teacher

- attended a Saudi wedding as the guest of honour
- grew as a person and shared hugs, food, personal stories and jokes with extraordinary women.

... and the list goes on and on.

**And all this was also real.**

## For every bad thing, there are at least ten good things

**For every (real) shitty thing in your life, you can also find at least ten (real) amazing things.**

There's no magic. No pretending. It's not about 'peace, love and mung beans' positivity.

And it's definitely not fake.

Both my experience and my roommate's experience were real. However, our thoughts created very different realities from our experiences (neither of which were right or wrong).

**In fact, just the other day, I found my thoughts pulling me into a shitty reality.**

My daughter and I were returning from a weekend away, and we struck some really bad traffic.

I'd also hurt my foot the day before, so I was grumpy with pain and could feel myself becoming irritated. In that moment, I'd forgotten that I could see the traffic as shitty or I could just see it as traffic.

Sensing my irritability, my daughter turned to me and asked, "What's great about being stuck in traffic?"

**We shared more than ten great things in a matter of minutes!**

Your thoughts about any situation are ultimately what you believe to be true about it. They're what your mind believes too. And so your reality (consciously or unconsciously) comes from your thoughts.

So it's not about having only great days and no shitty ones. As you learnt in Lesson 21, you *will* have both.

Instead, it's about choosing which thoughts you'll apply to each of those days. Because, whether you apply shitty thoughts or happy ones, both will be true and *both* will create your reality.

## The Practice – Turning a bad situation around

Next time you're in a situation that feels unpleasant, irritating or uncomfortable, try this practice.

Step 1: Acknowledge what's occurring that's upsetting you. This really helps in letting the upset go.

Step 2: Then, notice the part of the situation that's outside of your control.

Step 3: Now, look all around at the rest of the situation. What else is going on that being upset has distracted you from seeing?

Step 4: See if you can come up with at least ten things that are great about where you are right now.

# Lesson 28

## YOUR THOUGHTS AND ACTIONS ARE ALL YOU CAN CONTROL

 AKA How to stop seeing arseholes

### I practise this lesson every day

**The lessons in this book have become fundamental to the way I live my life.**

I didn't just learn them, however. I *practise* them. Daily.

Some days I practise all of them, and some days I only practise a few. But every second of every day, while my mind lives in this skinsuit, there's an opportunity to practise the lessons in this book.

Because that's what experiential transformation *is*. It's not something you learn. It's something you do.

And the lesson that 'My thoughts and actions are all I can control' is one I get to practise every single day.

## We only have access to our own thoughts and actions, not other people's

**You can't control the world around you.**

So often, people try to manage their lives by managing what (and especially who) is outside of them – the other people, situations and their immediate surroundings.

And they get *incredibly* bent out of shape when any of these things clash with what makes them comfortable.

**For example, when someone cuts you off in traffic, you might shake your fist at them.**

Or maybe you flip them the bird or read them the 'Road Rules According to You' sermon.

Regardless, it's almost like you think that loudly expressing your thoughts in your own car will actually make a difference to the other person's driving. Like it will somehow ensure the same thing doesn't happen again to you or anyone else!

That's kind of funny when you realise that the only person who *actually* saw or heard you was your three-year-old in the back seat. And, as a bonus, that three-year-old now knows how to flip the bird and say, "What a bloody idiot!"

**The other interesting thing is that, in the moment, you assume you're 100% right and they're 100% wrong.**

More than that, you often assume that they did whatever they did deliberately – just to make your life harder! (For more about the traps of being right and why people actually make mistakes, see Lessons 16–18 and 20.)

So this lesson has nothing to do with transforming what someone else does in their life. Instead, it's about transforming what you see and how you respond in yours.

## Enter my 'modern family'!

**This is probably the most personal story I will share in this book, but it's an important one.**

NOTE: this lesson is not about 'what happened' or 'who did what'. It's about removing blame, leaning into love and compassion, and transforming my relationship by taking radical responsibility for what my thoughts and actions had created.

In other words, it was about controlling my controllables – and how doing so gifted me my 'modern family' (whom I love and adore).

**Remember in the introduction I talked about the eve of my 50th birthday?**

I was sleeping on a mattress on the floor of the spare room of my own home, whilst my ex-husband and his fiancée slept in my bed in the master bedroom. And I realised in that moment that I was the happiest and most peaceful I'd ever been.

Now, this would NOT be the 'dream scene' that most women would wish for their 50th birthday!

So here's how this situation ended up happening.

**Ten years earlier, we'd just separated.**

And although I'd once loved and adored my ex-husband, I began to judge him. I'd judge his choices, his actions and his words.

No matter what he did or didn't do, I'd make myself right and him wrong. In my mind, I was the 'martyr mum' and he was the 'arsehole ex-husband'. That's exactly how I thought about him so, of course, my actions matched.

We communicated only when necessary. Our only common ground was loving our two beautiful kids, where we were unified in our parenting decisions.

**Then at one point, due to health reasons, he relocated to another state.**

And all I could think was, "How could you do that!? How could you leave your kids and only see them on school holidays? I would *never* do that – what an arsehole!"

All my thoughts ever showed me was that he continually made the worst choices ever – choices I'd *never* make. And those thoughts would eat me up day and night. I complained to my closest friends constantly about him.

Every time I even thought about it, I'd feel myself getting wound up like a spring.

My thoughts and actions had created a totally dysfunctional and distorted view of my ex-husband. More than that, they'd created a completely fractured family. But I was still absolutely sure that I was right about it.

**Now, how likely do you think my thoughts and actions were to change this man?**

What do you think the outcome was every time I told him how wrong his choices and behaviours were, or that he wasn't trying hard enough?

Would you be surprised to discover that constantly telling someone that they're an arsehole doesn't make any difference – in your life or in theirs?

**Yes, when he moved states, it did create all manner of challenges for all of us.**

But I'd never been able to see the challenges it created for him too. And if I'm being honest (which is critical to finding peace), I hadn't allowed myself to see the challenges that *my* decision to separate had created either.

It wasn't until I understood that my own thoughts and actions had created my fractured family that I could start accepting responsibility for the outcome. And that meant I understood that, if I chose to, I could also create a 'modern family' that was filled with love, compassion, empathy and kindness to one another.

**I'd actually learnt this piece of wisdom several years earlier.**

However, as I've said before in this book, intellectually understanding how to create change doesn't actually create that change. Transformation requires action and applying the principles of the wisdom experientially.

This wisdom was still in my 'grey matter', but it had started to seep into my conscious thoughts, which meant all I had to do was apply it.

**So one day, I began by calling him, just to ask how he was doing.**

That was it. I can still recall the shock in his voice when he realised that was all I was calling for. And going forward, when the kids ended their calls with him, I'd always ask them, "How's your dad?"

I also stopped badgering him in my mind and began exercising compassion and empathy in my actions instead.

I continued to make this my focus.

No matter what he said or did, I chose thoughts that were kind and compassionate.

And over time, the energy between us completely shifted. It went from angry, bitter and judgemental to one of two human beings who genuinely cared for each other's wellbeing and, of course, that of our kids.

**Now, do you think HE actually changed at all during this?**

No, of course he didn't: he was exactly the same person he'd been from the day we'd first met!

He was the same person I'd married, the same person I'd separated from and the same person I'd divorced. The same person I'd self-righteously blamed for making choices I'd never make and then treated like an arsehole. The same person I'd been unable to find an ounce of empathy, compassion or understanding for.

What had changed were my thoughts and my actions around him. And by changing these, EVERYTHING about him changed to me!

**The Christmas of 2013 was a landmark change in our relationship.**

For the first time ever, I travelled interstate *with* my kids to spend the holidays in the home of my ex-husband and his fiancée.

Those were truly some of the happiest days of my life, as they were for all of us. The holidays were filled with love, laughter, fun and a sense of complete and total joy.

Had I been unable or unwilling to take control of my thoughts and actions, this would never have been possible. And the last five years we've all shared – me, him, our kids' stepmum and our kids – would never have happened.

So I ask you: how many potential relationships might *you* have missed out on by insisting that people change to fit how you think they should be?

**This practice is like a magic wand for transforming every 'arsehole' in your life.**

You'll no longer be able to think of them as 'arseholes', because you'll view the world around you with eyes of empathy, compassion, understanding and love. You'll believe two things without question:

- First, every person on this planet is doing the best they can with what they know in any given moment (yes, even you).

- Second, when any of us (yes, even you) knows better, we do better.

## What if you took radical responsibility for YOUR thoughts and actions?

**You may think that you can just cut people out of your life if they piss you off.**

And yes, I agree that you can absolutely do this. In fact, if your physical or emotional wellbeing (or that of your kids) is threatened in any way, you need to create safe boundaries.

However, have you ever noticed that the people who drive you the craziest are often members of your family? And have you also noticed how many families have members who, sadly, no longer speak to each other?

**It's all too easy to stop speaking to a relative simply because they drive you crazy or make different choices to you.**

That's why this lesson is about taking radical responsibility for what *is* in your area of control, which are your thoughts and your actions.

Because what I know for sure is this: if you can change your thoughts and actions around *one* person, you can do it for every single person on the planet. So if you can have that one person show up differently because you've changed your thoughts, you can have your entire world show up differently.

**And what *that* means is that you'll simply no longer see arseholes around you.**

Instead, you'll see good people – people who are doing their very best in life, just like you are – everywhere!

## The Practice – Releasing what you can't control

**Is there a relationship in your life that's anything but peaceful?**

If so, try this.

**Step 1:** Get a clear picture of the person in your mind.

**Step 2:** Write down all of the things that drive you crazy about them. Especially all the things they do that you'd *never* do.

**Step 3:** Now, set that list aside and make a new list. Write down 3–5 things about this person that you see as admirable.

You may need to look at them in all areas of *their* life, not just how they show up in yours, to find these qualities.

**Step 4:** For the next week, take action by sharing the good stuff about them with someone else. If you're up for a challenge, see if you can find a way to compliment the person directly too.

When you consciously begin to change your thoughts and actions, don't be surprised if they start showing up differently in your life.

And when what you regularly think and do takes a new direction, don't be surprised if you can no longer see 'arseholes' either!

# Lesson 29

## DON'T MAKE THEIR ACTIONS YOUR ACTIONS

 AKA If you want different, you need to be different

### If you do what you've always done...

You've probably heard the definition of insanity as *"Doing the same thing over and over and expecting something different."*

Another way of putting this that shows up regularly in self-development circles is *"If you do what you've always done, you'll get what you've always got."*

Either way, nowhere is the concept more applicable than when you react to someone else's behaviour with exactly the same behaviour. For example, when someone's rude to you, your automatic response is often a knee-jerk reaction. Before you know it, you've been rude back to them – even though you know it often just makes the situation worse.

**Does this sometimes happen to you?**

Of course, you can replace 'being rude' with being angry, mean, abrupt, standoffish, cold, hurtful, arrogant or anything else for that matter. Regardless, the behaviour that comes at you is something you take exception to – and then you respond in kind.

(NOTE: in some instances, they might not have *actually* been deliberately rude to you. Instead, it might just be your perception or their general personality.)

## Have you ever made someone else's actions your actions?

**The only person you can change is you.**

In the moment, responding in kind can seem to be the most obvious solution for creating change in our immediate world. But long-term, it often creates our biggest obstacles, barriers and difficulties.

We all want change.

The problem is that we're often not prepared to do what's required to create that change ourselves. Instead, we pass off the responsibility to people around us. For example, we might say, "I'll be nice to them if they're nice to me... but otherwise, it's game on!"

I see this most often in relationships: in partnerships and families, amongst siblings and friends, and even in business.

**For example, imagine hubby has pulled a double shift while you've been at home with two sick kids.**

Then, when he finally arrives home, he heads straight to the shower without responding when you ask him about his day.

You hear him turn on the taps, and even though you don't know whether he actually heard you or not, it doesn't matter. You've already decided that he did and that he deliberately ignored you. So you mutter to yourself, "What a rude bastard! Fine – if he won't talk to me, I won't talk to him."

You keep that silent treatment going for a couple of days, before you eventually begin talking to him again in one-word sentences. Finally, at some point, you tell him, "I was so mad at you the other night for ignoring me!"

And he just looks at you, confused, because he has no idea what you're talking about.

Meanwhile, you've spent two full days bagging him to your girlfriends and sleeping so close to the edge of the bed you think you might actually fall out. Not to mention feeling completely and totally miserable.

Does this ring any kind of bell? Maybe your situation's not exactly like this, but something similar.

**The thing is that it doesn't matter whether he heard you or not.**

Let's just say that he genuinely didn't hear you: two full days have gone down the gurgler for absolutely no reason.

Or let's say that you were right and that he *did* ignore you for whatever reason. Two full days have still gone down the gurgler. (And if you think being right is more important than losing two whole days with someone you love, try rereading Lesson 3 about the Angel of Death.)

**Either way, the outcome is still the same, right?**

All because, in either instance, you made his actions your actions.

# A beautiful friendship that almost didn't happen

I've done *exactly* what I described above many times.

I've done it with my partners, my kids, my friends, my workmates and sometimes even strangers. However, the story I want to share with you now is where 'making their actions my actions' almost cost me an amazing friendship.

**Many years ago, when I was very new to business, I joined the local business women's network.**

I was pretty outgoing, and I enjoyed going along to the events and meeting like-minded people. I was also in awe of the incredible business women who made up the committee. They were hugely successful and had received all kinds of accolades for their business achievements.

I struck a rapport with all of them. Well, all of them except one woman.

Everyone spoke so highly of her and said how lovely she was. However, this wasn't my experience of her at all: I found her to be cold, standoffish and unfriendly.

And I was pretty damn sure she had no interest in knowing me.

**So I made no effort to get to know her.**

It wasn't because I didn't *want* to know her – she just intimidated me. And so I made her (perceived) actions my actions.

A few years went by (yes, years!) and then one day, she joined a partnered fitness program that I ran through my business. I was initially surprised because, by that point, I'd completely turned my earlier perceptions into the 'truth' that she didn't like me. I sat with this whole crazy notion and only then I realised what I'd been doing.

**So I began to just be 'me' with her: friendly, outgoing and kind.**

And what do you know? She was actually all those things too. However, she was also naturally shy and introverted – and I'd made that mean that she didn't like me.

Today, this woman is one of my closest friends and we've shared so many incredible experiences together. But that never would have happened if I hadn't become aware that I was 'making her actions my actions'.

Needless to say, I'm much more aware of this lesson these days.

## What about the ripple effect?

**Making someone's actions your actions blocks all possibility of creating anything positive.**

It just creates more of the same negative stuff. Nor will it change anything in the world around you for the better.

Just for a moment, think about the ripple effect. This is the concept that every action we take has the potential to send out a ripple of something similar into the world.

**When you make someone else's actions your actions, you're sending out a ripple of the same thing into the world.**

So instead:

- If you want more love, be loving.
- If you want more kindness, be kind.
- If you want more honesty, be honest.
- If you want more happiness, be happy.

- If you want more peace, be peaceful.

- If you want more friends, be friendly.

But if you want more arseholes, well... you know what to do!

## The Practice – Taking responsibility for your actions

**The first aspect of this practice is to recognise what lies in your area of control.**

The other person's actions *aren't* within that area, so let's look at the steps to change the things that are.

**Step 1:** Notice the behaviour that's upsetting you.

**Step 2:** Give it a name, eg. 'rude', 'arrogant', 'mean', 'nasty'.

**Step 3:** Ask yourself whether you want more or less of this in your life.

**Step 4:** Now ask yourself, "Is this who I am or who I want to be in the world?" If not, who DO you want to be in this world?

**Step 5:** Choose to respond from that place instead of responding in kind.

# Lesson 30

## YOUR PAST MEMORIES CREATE YOUR REALITY TODAY

 AKA What happens and what you make it mean are two different things

### As kids, we learn through our experiences

When you were a child, your experiences very quickly taught you what you wanted to repeat and what you didn't.

If you learnt to do as your parents said, followed their house rules and kept away from danger, your life was good.

Mostly, you were guided by what made you feel good and what didn't. That taught you right from wrong and good from bad. It also taught you how to stay safe, avoid dangers and survive.

Then, as you grew up, the experiences from your environment, parents, family, culture and society helped you to formulate your own personalised map for navigating life.

However, your map is *only* readable to you – because only you know what each road, landmark, detour, highway, town and river on it means.

## Sometimes, we're very creative about what we make our experiences mean

**It makes sense that every kid's experiences are different right?**

For one kid, being late to the dinner table might mean not getting dessert. For another, it might mean getting all the leftovers as *well* as their own dinner. The first kid will probably grow up never being late and get annoyed when someone else is. The second will probably see being late as perfectly OK.

Or, as another example, you might have grown up in a home that was always clean and tidy. So you made this mean something good, especially if you saw that tidiness made your mum happy. Meanwhile, the opposite might be true for another kid who had a slightly messier home, but an equally happy mother.

**In other words, for some people clean means happy; while for others, happiness goes with mess.**

So let me ask you:

- Is being late (for dinner or otherwise) good or bad?
- Is a clean house good or bad?
- Is a messy house good or bad?

The answers will always depend on what you made each thing mean as a kid. You'll have memories around each thing that made you feel good and others that made you feel uncomfortable.

So which patterns do you think you'll repeat or avoid (either unconsciously or consciously) in your adult life?

## What I made a childish trick mean in my adult life

**When I was a little girl, we'd sometimes go to my aunty and uncle's place for Sunday lunch.**

Afternoon tea would follow in the 'good' lounge room, using the 'good' china, and then the 'good' children would play outside.

Sometimes the adults would invite me to share something to impress them. It might be spelling some big word, singing a song I'd made up or reciting a rhyme. (I think all parents love to show off their kids' latest 'party tricks'.) I loved doing this because it seemed to make everyone happy, especially my parents.

One day, one of the adults in that room was my cousin's fiancé. He was incredibly handsome, and I had a giant 'little girl' crush on him.

**On that day, I was playing outside with my brother who called me aside.**

Out of the blue, he told me that I should go inside and tell this man that he was a big 'c\*\*t'. Yep! 'That' word. No doubt my brother had either heard the term on the farm or in the schoolyard.

Now, of course, I understand just how heavy-hitting that swear word is (so much so that I've chosen to not write it in full without the asterisks). Back then, though, I'd never heard the term before. And because my brother knew I loved to entertain the adults and I looked up to my cousin's fiancé, I thought it must be something good to say.

**So in I ran into the 'good' lounge room, where the adults sipped tea from the 'good' china.**

I can remember putting my hands on my hips and smiling my biggest smile as I turned to this man and exclaimed, "You're a big c**t!"

Of course, I truly didn't expect the reaction I got.

Instead of getting a round of applause, I felt the sting of a hand across my bottom. I can still feel the embarrassment that rose inside my tiny body and the tears on my cheeks.

**And more than that, I can feel the shock of not understanding what had happened.**

I recall running from the room and out to our car. I was so small that I could stand on the back seat. My parents tried to coax me out, but I was so ashamed that I couldn't even look at them.

I've since asked my brother if he remembers this and, interestingly, he has absolutely no memory of it.

**Here's why: his mind didn't make it mean anything.**

My brother never intended to hurt me or treat me like I was stupid. He didn't *intend* anything. And because it meant nothing to him, he has no memory of it.

Of course, he went on to make other meanings from other memories from his childhood. We all do. But he didn't remember this one.

I, on the other hand, made the memory mean something huge.

I made it mean that if someone treated me like I was stupid, they were trying to hurt me. Of course, that's completely untrue. It was simply an experience I had as a child.

**But from that experience, I decided something that day.**

My child's mind made up a life-changing story that remained hidden in my unconscious mind. And from that story, I decided no one would *ever* treat me like I was stupid again.

So then, as I grew into an adult, I avoided looking or feeling stupid as an unconscious protection mechanism. That meant:

- If someone laughed at me, I'd feel anger rising inside me.
- If I didn't understand something, I'd pretend I did (and try to figure it out later).
- I'd avoid any situations where I didn't know how to do something.
- If I couldn't avoid those situations, I'd get irritable.

And perhaps the worst thing: I'd compare myself to people who seemed smarter than me, and avoid both them and their knowledge. Because if they were smarter than me, they'd undoubtedly discover that I was, in fact, stupid.

## What meanings have you made from your memories?

**Imagine how much I missed out on to avoid feeling stupid!**

How many opportunities, connections, friendships, knowledge and wisdom did I unconsciously hold myself back from? And until I unpacked this story of my memory much later in my life, I didn't even realise I was doing it.

Your child's mind creates these unconscious patterns and behaviours to protect you from something that impacted you negatively.

This doesn't have to be a big trauma. It can be something that seems insignificant when you remember it as an adult. However, if you can recall specific details of *any* memory you probably made up a meaning about it as a child.

**Why do we react the way we do to certain situations, people or experiences?**

It's because we've put a self-protection mechanism in place to avoid some kind of pain.

So then, as adults, the words we both speak and hear pass through filters that we've created from the 'meaning-making moments' in our memories.

When you think about it, it's surprising that we *ever* truly hear each other.

**Unpacking a memory takes some practice.**

It's easy to start with your memories and look around for something that feels traumatic.

However, doing so may be misleading. Instead, the best way to unpack a 'meaning-making memory' is to begin with whatever upsets you as an adult.

In my example, I recognised a pattern around 'feeling stupid' and then realised that my first reaction was always to get angry.

**You might notice that you react similarly to certain situations and lose control.**

However, it's also important to be aware of times that you go out of your way to *avoid* feeling something, eg. certain kinds of people, situations or experiences. Avoiding is just another way in which we try to be 'in control'.

Throughout this book, I've repeated that transformation begins within – not without. So, like all the other practices, this one requires self-reflection, complete honesty and radical responsibility (see Lesson 40).

Unpacking your memories requires your full, honest inward attention.

## The Practice – Unpacking memories

**How do you unpack the meaning you've given to a memory?**

**Step 1:** Start by noticing when you feel most annoyed or upset by something. Journal what the situation was and, most importantly, note down how it made you feel.

**Step 2:** Now think of other similar situations that have upset you recently. Again, note down what each one was and how it made you feel. You may start to notice a pattern here.

**Step 3:** Try to remember the first time you ever felt that way. Ask yourself:

- What actually happened back then?

- What did you make it mean back then?

- How did creating that meaning protect you in some way?

**Step 4:** All there is to do now is notice when that feeling of being upset occurs again.

This time, however, as soon as you notice it (you may not notice in the heat of the moment, but it may occur to you after), remind yourself that whatever you're feeling now comes from a memory you made as a child.

**What's in your area of control here is to notice that *whatever* you're making the situation mean about you isn't true.**

Then, from this new awareness, you'll be able (with practice) to remind yourself that it isn't true.

And from there, you can see the situation differently, which gives you a new-found ability to choose a different response.

# Lesson 31

## ELIMINATE THE WORDS 'EXPECT', 'SHOULD' AND 'SUPPOSED TO' FROM YOUR LANGUAGE

 AKA Keep clear of the disappointment trap

### When things don't go to plan...

Have you ever 'expected' something to happen and then been disappointed when it didn't (or sometimes did) pan out?

Or, as an alternative, do you tell yourself you 'should' do something, then beat yourself up when you don't? Perhaps you tell other people what they 'should' do and then get annoyed when they do the opposite?

Maybe something wasn't 'supposed to' happen, but it did? Or was something 'supposed to' happen that didn't?

Regardless of what actually happened, the disappointment and frustration are the same.

The language we use, whether internally or outwardly to others, can often be the difference between being OK with an outcome or experiencing a 'smack in the head' let-down.

And it's the words we choose (and how we use them) that determine which feeling we experience.

## Beware of disappointment traps!

**When we place *our* expectations on a situation, we almost always set a 'disappointment trap'.**

What I mean by our expectations are any unexpressed, unnegotiated 'shoulds' or 'supposed tos' that we assume apply to the situation, person or even ourselves.

In other words, we set an outcome that we internally think 'should' happen, without clearly expressing it outwardly.

**For example, you might expect that:**

- Everyone in the office will wash up their own coffee cup.
- Your kids will notice the garbage bin overflowing and take it out to the wheelie bin.
- Your partner will just bring you flowers for no reason.
- Your in-laws will call first rather than surprising you with a visit.

And, of course, expectations are at play in any other situation where you find yourself muttering, "Really? WTF?!" either inwardly or outwardly.

**Remember the trappers in the old Tarzan movies?**

They'd dig a big hole and put some sticks, grasses and leaves over the top. Then they'd wait for their unsuspecting prey to step on the grass, thinking it was solid ground.

And BOOM! Down the prey would go, into the dark hole of (at least, in our example) disappointment!

**The words 'expect', 'should' and 'supposed to' do exactly the same thing.**

They're a concealed trap with guaranteed disappointment.

But instead of just our 'prey' falling into the pit of disappointment, we often spiral down along with them. Not only do *we* experience disappointment but they also experience our disappointment along with us.

You see, there's no way out for either of us once the trap is set.

And what almost always results is either a loud, immediate argument or, worse, an inward seething that builds up over time, eventually exploding – again, into an argument.

**And often it's exactly the same argument over and over again.**

## I used to *expect* my best friends to remember things that were important to me

For example, on one occasion, I needed to get a biopsy for a lump I'd detected.

I reached out to a friend and shared my news; they were, of course, concerned, supportive and loving in response. I let them know that I hadn't told anyone else at this stage and told them when my test was booked in. Then I automatically just *expected* that they'd call or send some kind of message of support right before my scheduled appointment.

On the day of the test, I awoke nervously. I showered, had breakfast and did a few things around the house. Despite me checking my phone continually, however, no missed call notifications or messages came through.

**So then my mind went to work to set my disappointment trap, covering it with grass like:**

- "Isn't your bestie 'supposed to' remember important stuff like the fact that you're having a biopsy?"

- "I 'should' have known they'd forget, which obviously means I'm not important to them!"

- "Why did I 'expect' anything else?"

And these thoughts wouldn't stop bombarding my brain.

Now, remember that I had no idea why they hadn't messaged or called. And remember too that I'd put this expectation on them without their knowledge or consent.

## I CANNOT control other people

**I can only control what *I* do.**

So here's the thing: I could have started my day and sent them a message that said, "Hi, I'm off for my biopsy this morning. I'm a little nervous, but I'm sure everything will be OK. I'll give you a call later on. So grateful for all your support."

I knew I could have sent that message, but at the time, my reaction was, "Why 'should' I? After all, if they cared, they'd message me, right?"

And so they inadvertently fell into my 'trap of disappointment'.

**The truth is that I set disappointment traps all the time.**

For example, I knew that – just like me – they were juggling, work, kids and a family of their own.

But if I knew that, why would I set them up in my disappointment trap?

Was it so that I could be right that they didn't care?

That I wasn't important?

Of course, neither of these were true. They simply didn't message.

But every time I did this, we both ended up in the disappointment trap – and so did our friendship.

You may have noticed that you do this too. Perhaps with your partner, kids, work colleagues or your family? You may even do it with yourself.

**It's up to YOU to communicate your expectations.**

If you want everyone in the office to wash their own coffee cups, establish this clearly with them during your next team meeting.

If you want your kids to take out the garbage, ask them to. Or leave them a written list of chores you'd like them to do.

Buy *yourself* flowers if you love them. And tell your in-laws that you'd love to know when they're coming so you can have the kettle on.

Be the friend you want your friends to be.

**The point here is not to stop any of this stuff from happening.**

Instead, it's to let go of the disappointment you're holding on to because of your unexpressed expectations. Instead of placing silent 'shoulds' or 'supposed tos' onto someone (especially someone you love) and setting a disappointment trap, TELL them what you want. Perhaps even create the expectation together.

Remember that you can only control what *you* think, do and say.

Being clear about your expectations is firmly within your area of control and will help you to avoid repetitive arguments and bruised relationships.

## The Practice – Communicating what you want and don't want

Here's how to identify when you might be unconsciously setting a disappointment trap in your life.

Step 1: Notice when you're feeling let down or disappointed by someone or a situation. What was the expectation in your mind that wasn't met?

Step 2: Next, ask yourself how you can take responsibility for clearly expressing your expectation.

Step 3: Finally, have a conversation *directly* with the person concerned. Without blaming or becoming angry, clearly verbalise your previously unexpressed expectation.

(NOTE: resist asking someone else to have the conversation for you, eg. "Tell your sister I said she has to..." This shifts the control away from you and may still result in disappointment.)

# Lesson 32

## LOOSEN YOUR GRIP

 AKA Let go of what you think you know

### What if you stopped knowing everything you know right now?

**There's a principle that psychologists call the functional fixedness cognitive bias.**

This bias relates to our human tendency to see everyday things like chairs, trees or pens in a fixed way. Then, once we learn what these things are 'meant for', we can *only* see them in terms of that function going forward.

And, sometimes, that principle can be a useful timesaver.

But what if, for one day, your current mind was erased? What if you suddenly didn't know everything you know now?

**What would be possible?**

Anything? Everything!

## Letting go of what you know makes room for new insights

**As you practise the tools in this book, they'll embed themselves into your thought process.**

And once they do, you may find that you're much more open to the pieces of wisdom that fall into your lap every second of every day. At least, you may if you're open to noticing.

One of my favourite quotes is: *"When the student is ready the teacher appears."*

To me, this translates to the idea that wisdom, information and knowledge are swirling around us all of the time.

Our job is simply to see it, hear it and notice it.

**In short, we need to pay attention.**

I don't believe the wisdom vanishes if we don't notice it. Rather, I think it's always there in some form, waiting for *us*.

Our 'teachers' can arrive in the form of a random conversation or a flyaway comment from a stranger. We can discover their wisdom in books, podcasts, seminars, conferences, workshops, nature or even dreams. It can also come from our children (mine have been my greatest teachers) and, of course, mentors.

And that list is in no way definitive.

**My point is that, just like the student in the quote, we can only recognise the wisdom, knowledge and information when we're ready to.**

Meanwhile, it just keeps swirling around us.

Then, when it *does* penetrate our thoughts, it kind of hits us with a great big WOAH! We find ourselves thinking, "I've never seen it that way before."

Oprah Winfrey calls these 'a-ha' or 'bing bing' moments.

But if we're going to make room for those kinds of moments, we need to first let go of our functional fixedness and loosen our grip on how things are 'meant' to be.

**We need to let go of the need to know the outcome and trust in the process.**

Now I know it's easy to trust the process when you already know the outcome. But knowing the outcome means there's no space for a new teacher to appear.

I've personally found that loosening my grip on how things are 'meant' to be has opened me up to some mind-bending, heart-opening, life-changing new perspectives.

I just had to trust and let go first.

## That time I stopped knowing that I hated swimming...

One morning, I was working away at my job when a friend who worked in self-development came by.

What ensued was a quick, almost insignificant five-minute conversation about life, business, and shifting societal norms and values. We had plenty of questions, but no real answers.

Out of the blue, my friend asked, "What if we gave up knowing *everything* we know about life and business? What do you think we'd choose then?"

I don't recall my answer in that moment.

**I do know, however, that for the rest of the day, I couldn't stop replaying the question over and over in my mind.**

- I looked at my lunch and asked myself, "What if I didn't know whether I liked tuna salad or not?"

- I looked at people and asked myself, "What if I didn't know whether I admired them or not?"

- I looked at my clothes and asked myself, "What if I didn't know whether I liked what I'd dressed in that day or not?"

I was in a complete state of perplexed-ness.

(And yes, I'm pretty sure I just made that word up.)

**I decided that I'd use the question as a challenge for the next week.**

I'd begin each day simply by becoming aware of it. And I'd come back to it during the day to remind myself to let go of everything I 'knew'.

So that's what I did.

I loosened my grip on what I knew to make way for what I didn't.

**A few days later, I was about to get in the shower before work.**

And without warning, the thought, "I want to dive into the ocean!" came crashing into my mind.

Now this isn't really anything life-shattering, except for the fact that I DID NOT like being in the water. I loved to see it and be near it. I loved to walk along beaches and hike around lakes.

But I NEVER voluntarily went in.

As they grew up, my kids would beg me to swim with them, but I'd just wave and keep reading my book. And growing up myself in rural Tasmania, the only water around me had been icy cold rivers and dams – so I'd been almost ten before I'd even learnt to swim.

It's safe to say that water had never been a love in my life.

Yet there I was, in the doorway of my bathroom, with this thought about diving into the ocean repeating itself louder and louder each time.

**I asked myself, "What if I didn't *know* that I didn't like the water?"**

As I did, the desire to immerse myself in the sea became overpowering. Compelling even.

So I drove down to the ocean wearing only my togs and, without hesitation, I ran into the waves.

And it was the most amazing experience I'd felt in a long time. I felt light, happy, peaceful and free. What a way to start my day!

**This continued every day for the next 166 days.**

Every morning, I was drawn back to the water. And, as I immersed myself and floated around, I realised how much sheer joy and delight I'd missed out on from avoiding this simple, pleasurable experience.

It occurred to me that sometimes we can be so certain in our convictions about how stuff is 'meant' to be (or not be) in our life. We know what we want and don't want. We know what we like and don't like. We trust only in what we think we know for certain.

But what happens when we trust in what we don't know?

**When that happens, anything's possible. Even 166 days in the water.**

Now, you may be thinking, "So what? It's only water!"

And initially I didn't see the profoundness of what had happened either.

But then I considered replacing the water in my experience with a person I didn't like. I imagined giving up my fixed perspective of that person.

And then I imagined what might be possible if I gave up my fixed belief of what my strengths and weaknesses were.

Who (or what) might *you* be inadvertently blocking from your life because you already 'know' what you know?

## What if you could trust in the process?

When we loosen our grip we make way for ALL possibilities.

We make way for the possibilities we think we want, the ones we think we don't want and the ones we haven't even considered.

**A fun way to practise trusting the process and flexing your mind muscle is to play the 'colour game'.**

You can do it on your own; or for even more fun, do it with a friend or a child.

First, choose something to focus on. For example, it might be the ocean.

Now, if you didn't know the ocean was blue, how would you describe its colour? Your answer might be, "The ocean is soothing liquid metal." Or perhaps it might be 'rippled bottle glass' or 'angry storm cloud'.

There's no right or wrong answer here. It's just about the practice of giving up your default 'knowing of colour' and asking your mind to consider other possibilities.

**Another version of this game is to look at an object and describe it as if you didn't know what it was.**

For example, you might choose a tree. If you didn't know what a tree was, how would you describe it? You might see it as 'a living protrusion from the earth', or perhaps 'a hard, brown cylinder topped with shiny, fluttering green blades'.

These are both mindfulness practices that interrupt your default of 'knowing' what you know.

In other words, they interrupt functional fixedness.

## The Practice – How to loosen your grip

**Letting go of what you think you know makes way for what you don't know.**

These are the steps that have helped me to practise loosening my grip.

Step 1: Start by noticing whenever a fixed perspective, desired outcome, habit or repeated way of being comes up for you.

Step 2: Then ask yourself, "What if I didn't know what I *think* I know about this?" What do you notice?

Step 3: Make a list of what you notice: try to come up with three new possibilities that you haven't previously considered.

Step 4: 'Try on' the new possibilities. Notice any resistance that comes up in your mind or body.

Step 5: Note down at least three benefits of allowing those new possibilities to occur.

When you can loosen your grip and trust in the process, you make space for those new possibilities to show up. You may even choose one of those possibilities to act on.

# Lesson 33

## THE PEACEFUL POWER OF MAKING DECISIONS

 AKA Get out of the "hell in the hallway" of life

### Choose a door – any door

**How do you feel about making decisions?**

Do you make them swiftly or do you procrastinate over them? Do you like to be in control of the decision-making or do you prefer to pass it off to someone else? Or do your answers to those questions depend on what the decision is about?

On any day, you'll be faced with decisions – sometimes hundreds of them.

Some are easy, some are difficult and some go into the 'too hard basket' and stay there (procrastination). Others get passed off to someone else (avoidance) or just don't get made at all (resistance).

Of course, when you don't make a decision and then don't like the outcome of someone else's decision, you get to blame whoever made it. You get to claim that it's not your fault. But the end result is that you've still gone in a direction you didn't want to go because of a decision YOU didn't make.

**Sure, it can be scary to make decisions.**

The good news is that, as the old saying goes, *"When one door closes, another one opens."* It's a reminder that if you don't like the results of a decision you make, you can always make a different one.

But when you hesitate for too long about the decision – or worse, avoid deciding at all – life becomes 'hell in the hallway'!

## Decision-making is just direction-taking

**This life lesson is NOT about lurching from decision to decision without any care for consequences.**

Putting some research, education, mentoring and forethought into your decision-making is highly advisable. But even if you do, life is a funny thing: there are no guarantees that anything will go as planned.

Instead, it's about noticing when you've become *stuck* in the process of deciding.

Sometimes having to make a decision can fill you with paralysing dread.

**The problem is that *not* making a decision will simply keep you stuck in a place you don't want to be.**

It will keep you doing things you don't want to do and wondering how you're living a life that's so far from the one you want.

The biggest obstacle to decision-making is often the fear of making the wrong decision, because so often we relate the 'wrong decision' to failure. However, as Oprah said in one of her speeches, *"There is no such thing as failure. Failure is just life trying to move us in another direction."*

Imagine if you took the pressure off your decision-making and instead saw it as direction-taking?

Feels better already, right?!

So what direction would you head in for things like:

- what to have for breakfast?
- whether to accept an event invitation?
- whether to take that job offer?
- which school is best for your kids?
- whether to relocate to the other side of the world?

And there are a million others.

And, of course, no matter which direction you head in, some days your decisions will flow, and other days they'll feel too heavy and clunky to even think about it. But always remember these two things:

1. A decision can always be changed with another decision.

2. Not making a decision is *still* a decision.

## It was Fran who taught me that I could always make another decision

I'm blessed to have been sent many 'angels' in my lifetime.

I've had mentors. Teachers. Friends. People who've shown up in my life just when I needed their wisdom, guidance and love the most.

Fran – the woman you met in the Preface of this book – was one of them.

Fran came into my life when I separated from my husband back in 2005. She was smart, funny, kind, caring, quirky and generous. She was also full of wisdom that only an 'old soul' could know.

**While I was married, I didn't really think about my future.**

I just knew there'd be one. I knew it would be filled with family, friends, events, moments, holidays... the kind of stuff that families just did. The kind of stuff I'd assumed that *our* family would do too.

One day, I was talking with Fran about my decision to separate. I wasn't regretting it, but the enormity of what it meant was weighing heavily on me.

Suddenly I couldn't see anything in my future. It was all just white fog: completely empty. Woah! I realised that to fill up that future, *I'd* need to make some decisions.

And I'd need to make them by myself.

**"But what if I make the wrong decisions?" I asked Fran.**

"One door closes and another one opens... but it's hell in the hallway!" she replied from across the table. "So don't stay stuck in the hallway!"

I just looked at her and burst into tears... and I mean the hyperventilating kind!

In that moment, I was totally stuck in the hallway.

**"Jen, there ARE no wrong decisions," Fran told me.**

"There are just decisions. And every decision can be changed with another decision."

Of course, this didn't magically fix things. But it *did* give me a new perspective.

And suddenly, the weight of making decisions at this very new stage of my life didn't seem quite as heavy.

## Try just focusing on your next right move

**In the same speech I mentioned above, Oprah went on to say that a great question to ask yourself is, *"What is my next right move?"***

Martin Luther King, Jr. said something similar in his famous quote, *"Take the first step in faith. You don't have to see the whole staircase, just take the first step."*

Now, you may be wondering, "But how do I know what the right move is?"

Here's the thing about that question. Your next 'right move' is whichever decision *you* make. Because every decision you make moves you forwards in life. Through one door at a time.

There's just one decision I highly advise against: making no decision and staying stuck in the 'hell in the hallway'.

**I get it. It's so tempting to avoid taking responsibility for deciding.**

After all, if you don't make a decision, someone else will. And then, if you don't like the consequences, you get to blame them for it. (But, as I mentioned above, by doing this, you'll just be stuck with consequences you don't like.)

So, instead, you waver on the precipice of deciding.

You wait and see how it goes, while telling yourself that you don't know what to do.

You have endless conversations with endless people and get endless suggestions, but you never actually DECIDE which one to go with.

**That's what Fran meant by 'hell in the hallway'.**

So why do we stay stuck there?

You'll probably notice you get stuck on particular types of decisions. Often it's the big-ticket items like your career, relationships, business, family or friendships.

Of course, you won't tell yourself you're 'stuck'.

Instead, you'll insist that you're just waiting to see what happens. But really, that just translates into waiting for someone else to make a decision to miraculously get you 'unstuck'.

In other words, instead of creating your own life, you're allowing other people or situations to create it for you. Because that way, if it doesn't work out, you don't have to be responsible: you can just blame them.

So are you *really* OK with giving over control of the decisions in your life? Or do you actually want to be the creator of your life?

The only way to avoid the hell in the hallway is to decide for yourself! Because only you know the answer to any decision that needs to be made.

## The Practice – Getting out of the hell in the hallway

If making a decision still troubles you, the coin toss test is one of the most foolproof tests I've come across.

We've all done coin tosses before, right? You just grab a coin and allocate one side to one decision and the other side to the other decision.

But this coin toss comes with a twist.

**First, go ahead and allocate an outcome to both sides of the coin.**

Next – and this part is important – promise yourself that *no matter what*, the result determines your decision.

**Then toss the coin.**

But as you do, close your eyes.

While the coin is spinning in the air, your gut or heart will whisper which side you really want it to land on.

**And right there is your answer.**

Even if that's not how it lands, deep down you already know the answer to the decision you want to make. It may not be the answer you think you want. It may also not be an answer you're ready for.

But it *will* be your answer.

So don't stay stuck. Don't make a decision to not make a decision, because that IS a decision.

# Lesson 34

## HAPPINESS IS AN INSIDE JOB

 AKA It's nobody else's job
to make you happy

### Don't worry, be happy... now!

**Are you happy now, or are you waiting to be happy?**

What I mean is, do you think something has to occur *before* you can feel happy?

Does something need to show up in your life?

Do you have to be somewhere or achieve something?

**What if happiness didn't lie outside of you?**

What if it was completely in your control in this moment right now?

### Don't fall into the 'unhappiness void'

So what makes you happy?

Where do you find that feeling?

**First, realise that *your* happiness doesn't depend on anyone else's actions.**

Don't get me wrong, it's awesome when someone does something for – or with – you. Their actions can fill up your heart and put a smile on your face.

And who doesn't love sharing special moments with people they care about? Things like going to see live music or movies, lazy Sunday breakfasts or coffee catch-ups, trail running, going on adventures, watching sunsets and sunrises...

(OK, that's my list of things that make me happy. I'm sure you have your own list too.)

**But when you assume these are your *only* routes to happiness, an 'unhappiness void' can creep in.**

Over time, this void can grow and deepen as the people who are 'supposed to' make you happy don't (see Lesson 31 for more on the words 'supposed to'). Or perhaps your situation changes into one that no longer 'makes you happy'.

Or, even worse, when you look around, you realise that *nothing* in your life makes you happy anymore.

## Understanding this life lesson fundamentally changed my life

**A few years ago, I came upon this poem on the Internet.**

(I don't know who the author is – but whoever you are, thank you.)

*"Why Complicate Life?*

*Missing somebody?... Call*

*Wanna meet up?... Invite*

*Wanna be understood?... Explain*

*Have questions?... Ask*

*Don't like something?... Say it*

*Like something?... State it*

*Want something?... Ask for it*

*Love someone?... Tell it*

*We just have one life. Keep it simple."*

**One day, I was talking to a girlfriend who said she often sat alone at home on a Friday night.**

She'd feel sad, wondering why none of her friends ever invited her out for drinks, dinner or a movie.

Remembering the words in that quote, I asked her why, if she wanted to spend time with her friends, she didn't just do the inviting. Then I let her know I was probably at home alone on many of those Friday nights too. However, I wasn't sad about being there, because I knew I could create something different if I chose to.

**She looked at me quizzically in genuine surprise.**

In her unhappiness void, she'd just assumed that everyone but her was happily out having fun. In that moment, however, she realised she could *also* create something different if she wanted to.

She realised she could continue to create her own unhappiness, or she could choose again and create happiness instead.

**Have you ever done that too?**

Have you wanted something in your life to happen, but waited for someone else to take responsibility for creating it?

## We're all responsible for our own happiness

**At the heart of this lesson is the idea that happiness *doesn't* exist in the future or past.**

Nor is it something external that lies outside of you.

It's not something you wait for or hope for.

And under no circumstances is it something anyone else is responsible for giving you.

**Instead, happiness is an inside job.**

It's available to you in every second of every minute of every day.

And it's 100% within YOUR area of control to create it.

So why are you waiting for happiness to arrive?

As Yogi Bhajan put it, "*If you are happy, happiness will come to you — because happiness wants to go where happiness is.*"

## The Practice – Create a 'Happiness Jar'

This activity is not only a whole lot of fun to do, it's a great way to create your own happiness.

Here's how you do it:

**The essentials:** an empty jar, a notepad and pen, and your imagination

**Method:** on a blank page, write down one thing you love to do that fills your heart and soul and makes you happy.

Fold up the piece of paper and place it in the empty jar.

Repeat this a further 51 times with a new thing that makes you happy each time.

**How to use your Happiness Jar:** every week, pull out one piece of paper. Create a plan to complete the activity written on it over the coming week.

You can do the activity alone or with a friend or two. But YOU are in control of setting it up and then actually doing it.

**Outcome:** A whole year of self-created, self-funded, self-approved, self-loving happiness. And you didn't have to wait for happiness to come to you to experience it!

# Lesson 35

## LOOK FOR THE GIFTS

 AKA There's always something to unwrap

## When your rose-coloured glasses fall off

**Sometimes, life doesn't go the way you want it to.**

I'm sure I don't have to spell out for you that everything isn't always sunshine, lollipops, rainbows and unicorns.

Life DOES (occasionally) give us lemons.

Bad things DO (occasionally) happen to good people.

Your life WILL (occasionally) suck!

And no, you didn't DO anything to deserve these piles of crap.

Let me be clear: I don't personally believe the 'bad things come in threes' superstition, but I'm completely aware that shit sometimes happens.

# You might not be able to see the gifts immediately

So is there really a gift in that pile of crap?

The answer is, "Always!"

However, seeing that gift is a practice that, in almost all instances, operates in two parts.

**The first part is believing that life isn't happening to you. It's happening *for* you.**

Believing this means choosing to look for the gifts in every situation. It also means trusting that there are no mistakes: only opportunities to learn and grow.

If you can be open to this concept, you'll also accept that you can never NOT be on your path or being your purpose.

**The second part is realising that you'll often only see the gift after a period of reflection.**

You've probably heard the expression 'Everything happens for a reason', and you might even subscribe to it. But when you're smack bang in the middle of a crisis or questioning yourself or what's happening around you, it's often impossible to believe it.

I'm no stranger to experiencing those moments myself. And when I do, I remind myself that although I may not understand the gift right now, the time will come later – if I look for it – when I will.

# I discovered the gifts of losing my 'training wheels' in Sydney

**After leaving Tasmania for Sydney in 1989, I quickly found my feet.**

A couple I knew from Tasmania were already living there, and my plan was to rent their spare room. I'd been working at a credit union in Tasmania, and they'd arranged a job interview for me with a sister union in Sydney.

I had my interview and landed the job. My friends were a couple, and during the first few weeks, I met some of their friends while I settled into my new job.

Things were going along swimmingly. This was what I'd known in my heart was out there: new experiences, new people and an exciting new environment. Just as Dorothy found in *The Wizard of Oz*, I wasn't in Kansas anymore!

**Those first few weeks were exhilarating.**

My friends made slipping into Sydney life fun. I felt safe, happy and increasingly confident as I piggybacked onto their life. I couldn't imagine ever going back to Tasmania.

At least, I couldn't until my friends gave me the news that, due to their work, they were being transferred back to Tasmania.

No! This wasn't part of the plan!

**My first reaction was to pack up and move back to Tasmania too.**

My first few weeks in Sydney had been like riding a kid's bike with training wheels. But suddenly, it felt as though an adult had decided, "You've got this now!" and taken my training wheels away.

The thought of crashing and getting my first dose of gravelled-up knees and elbows was suddenly very real.

**As I mentioned previously, it's hard to find the 'gift' *during* moments of crisis.**

I certainly couldn't see any kind of gift in that moment.

In fact, if I'm being honest, for a twenty-something Tasmanian farm girl who'd left everything behind to move to Australia's biggest city, being all alone in it just *sucked*. I could hear all my friends and family saying, "We told you so. We knew you'd come back!"

But when I later chose to unpack the crisis, I found the gift.

**You see, I decided to stay in Sydney, even though being alone sucked.**

And over the next few years, not only did I find my way but I also surrounded myself with amazing friends. My career path also took me into the world of international hotels and travel.

I landed a job in an international sales office that was led by a female director, working with a team of extraordinary people who are friends to this day. And from them, I learnt incredible business skills and knowledge.

**I worked hard, gaining opportunities to travel the world.**

I got to showcase the company's five-star hotels all around the world to high-profile corporates and their executive assistants, as well as the travel agents who recommended their travel plans. The first ever international flight I took was in First Class, as were the next dozen or so. I remember one day looking down at Kerry Packer's Amex card details and realising just how far this young Tasmanian farm girl had come.

And all because something 'shitty' had happened.

So now, whenever I'm faced with a crisis of any kind these days, I look for the gift. Because I know there's *always* one to be found.

## Victim to life or victor of life?

**Look for the gift – it can be the difference between being in a crisis or being on the fringe of opportunity.**

It can be the difference between staying stuck in that crisis or trusting that you'll get something life-changing from it. And even if you can't see the gift right then, you know it's there and that, in time, you'll understand it.

That's the difference between living as a victim to life or victor of life.

The option to look is always available to you.

But it's up to you to trust that the gift you'll find is meant just for you.

# The Practice – Unpacking the gifts

Again, it's worth repeating that this practice – at least initially – is a tool of reflection.

As you practise, it may begin to help during moments of crisis. Often, however, it will be most useful afterwards.

Regardless of when you use it, simply follow these steps.

Step 1:   Remind yourself that there's a gift to unpack.

Step 2:   Notice your thoughts. Particularly, notice when you're asking yourself powerless questions like:

- "What's wrong with me?"

- "Why is this happening to me?"

- "What did I do to deserve this?"

Step 3:   Replace those thoughts with powerful questions like:

- "What is this here to teach me or show me that I can't yet see for myself?"

- "What can I learn from this?"

- "What would love do in this moment?"

Step 4:   Reflect on and journal about the answers to these questions.

# Lesson 36

## ASK FOR WHAT YOU WANT

 AKA If you don't ask, the answer will always be NO

### Do you find it difficult to ask for things?

Perhaps you find it hard to request something, so instead you say nothing.

Maybe asking for a pay rise freaks you out.

Or what about asking someone to look after your kids?

Do you feel like you're being a pain when you ask someone for something they haven't offered? Perhaps you even preface your request by saying, "Sorry to be a pain, but..."

If so, I totally get it!

This was me for most of my life.

## Are you telling *yourself* NO?

Are any of these situations familiar to you?

- **There are five of you at a restaurant and only four water glasses.** You say you're not thirsty because you don't want to hassle the waiter to ask for a fifth glass. The restaurant is full and they're clearly having a busy night. After all, you can just have a drink of water when you get home, right?

- **You need someone to pick your kids up from an event during school holidays, but you're working.** You don't like to ask your mum-in-law because she knows you need help in the holidays and she didn't offer to help out. After all, she would have automatically offered to pick them up if she could, right?

- **Your boss has asked you to work overtime again.** Although you know they value you, working unpaid overtime is becoming a habit. You say YES (even though it means missing Susie's soccer match) without asking to be paid for it. After all, your company never pays overtime anyway, right?

**Sure, sometimes when you ask for something, the answer will be NO.**

However, if you don't ask, you're telling *yourself* NO and cutting off any possibility of a different answer.

And that translates into believing that you're not worthy of a YES.

What this practice is about is understanding that asking for what you want is completely within your area of control. And if you *don't* take that control, the only life you affect in the long term is your own.

# I was devastated to discover I'd taught my kids not to ask for things

**When I was a little girl, manners were a really big deal.**

My grandfather always told us that manners cost us nothing but would take us places in life. And throughout my life, people have always complimented me on how polite I am.

Most of what I was taught about manners just made sense. Add to that my pop's sage advice plus the lifetime of acknowledgement I'd received myself, so teaching my kids what I'd learnt also just made sense.

**Now, for the most part, those manners were a good thing.**

Except for one, which I'd 'lovingly' passed on to my kids until I figured out its impact years later: *"When you visit family or friends, don't ask for anything. Always wait to be offered: asking is impolite."*

Having since cracked this one open, I now find it odd to even write about. It just seems ludicrous. But nevertheless, I schooled both of my children well in the practice of 'never asking for anything'.

**I'd like to tell you there was a defining moment when I first caught this in action.**

The truth is that a series of moments brought it fully into my awareness. And I didn't see it in my own world initially. Instead, I noticed it in my children's.

I first noticed it in my daughter. If we were in a cafe or restaurant, I noticed that she'd never place her order directly with the waiter. Instead, she'd look at me and tell me what she wanted.

I'd tell her to ask the waiter instead of me and she'd literally squirm in her seat. She couldn't even look directly at them as she spoke – she'd lower her head as she ordered.

It also showed up in my son. He regularly wanted to go out with his friends, and because I was a solo mum, we needed to get creative with transport. However, if I suggested he ask a mate for a lift, he'd often choose not to go, rather than asking.

**To be clear, asking ME for something they wanted came more naturally.**

But when they had to ask a friend, family member or (God forbid) a stranger, they really struggled.

Initially, it just annoyed the crap out of me. But as I'd taught myself (and as I've recommended throughout this book), I leaned into the annoyance rather than just dismissing it.

And what I noticed was confronting.

Not only was I asking my kids to ask for stuff (which I'd drilled them not to do) but I was also *asking them* to do the asking. I was actually passing my own 'asking' responsibilities off onto them.

And then I was getting annoyed when they wouldn't ask.

**So I shone the spotlight back on myself and asked, "Where did *I* avoid asking?"**

Obviously, I passed off the responsibility to ask wherever I could. Even to my own children.

But where else did 'not asking' show up for me?

I realised it showed up in my not choosing. If someone asked me what I wanted to do or where I wanted to go, my usual response was, "I don't mind. You choose."

Of course, that often resulted in me doing things and going places I really wouldn't have chosen for myself.

**What was I really afraid of? Being told NO?**

Maybe.

However, I suspect it was more likely that – just as I'd been taught and just as I'd taught my kids – I feared that someone would tell us we were being rude.

That meant they'd think poorly of us.

That, in turn, meant they wouldn't like us.

Over my life, as I've relentlessly unpacked these practices, it's always amazed me how hidden my habits, automatic responses and actions often are. And even more, it's amazed me how much these hidden habits have secretly impacted what's possible in my life – and, in this instance, in the lives of my kids.

**When I figured this out, the first thing I did was tell my kids I'd made a mistake.**

I explained to them what I'd unpacked and let them know I was wrong for teaching them not to ask for anything.

Then I told them how incredibly sorry I was, and that it was their birthright to ask – without expectation – for anything they wanted. It was also the respondent's right to answer with either a YES or a NO. Either way, it was OK to have asked.

**Now, of course this didn't instantly undo the years of conditioning for any of us.**

However, what it *did* do was create a new awareness around our old way of being. It opened up the possibility for each of us to choose differently and to see the meaning of the answer we received in a different light.

With practice, asking for what we wanted brought a complete shift. And my children each created a new, more powerful belief that they could hand on to their own kids.

## 20 seconds of insane courage

**By now, you may have realised how often you also stop yourself from asking for what you want.**

You may have noticed that you've let countless opportunities slip right on by, telling yourself that they 'didn't matter'. You may also realise that, like me, you've taught your kids to do the same thing.

If this has been your safe space to operate from, the idea of suddenly just asking for what you want may seem a little scary. You may feel tempted to still allow the 'little things' to slip by.

But what if, just for today, you gave yourself permission to ask for EVERYTHING you want?

In the film *We Bought a Zoo*, Matt Damon's character Benjamin Mee talks to his son about using '20 seconds of insane courage'.

What if *you* took a deep breath and summoned your own 20 seconds of insane courage to:

- ask for the water glass?
- ask for help from your mum-in-law?
- ask your boss to be paid for the overtime?

Because what's the worst that could happen? Is it just that they might say NO?

If you think this, remember the worst thing is actually that by not asking, you're telling *yourself* NO.

And the good news is that with just 20 seconds of insane courage, you may just get a YES instead.

## The Practice – Asking for what you want

This practice is designed to remind you that asking for what you want is always within your area of control.

Step 1: Begin to notice your internal dialogue around asking for what you want. In particular, look for any hesitation you have.

You may notice thoughts like:

- "It doesn't really matter."
- "I can manage this on my own."
- "It's not worth the worry."
- "I don't want to be a pain/nuisance."

Step 2: When you catch yourself having these thoughts, begin to count to 20 in your mind. As you do this, think about what you DO want, regardless of whether the person you'd need to ask replies with a YES or a NO.

Step 3: When you've finished counting, and without any expectation of a particular outcome, ask for what you want.

Step 4: Finally, regardless of the outcome, accept the answer you receive with gratitude both to yourself for asking and to the person who answered.

# Lesson 37

## NO IS A COMPLETE SENTENCE

 AKA How to say NO
when you mean NO

## This is the reverse side of asking for what you want

I purposefully wanted to follow the previous lesson with this one.

That's because the two of them kind of connect. In Lesson 36, I talked about the impact that not asking for anything had had on both me and my kids.

Ultimately, what triggered this was the fear that we'd be told NO. That, in turn, would mean that people were unhappy with us, think we were rude and wouldn't like us.

But if you thought being told NO was scary, you'll enjoy the irony that, at least for most of us, *saying* it is even scarier.

## It's natural to avoid things we're afraid of

**When we fear something, it's human instinct to not want to be around it.**

The best way to not be around something, of course, is to avoid putting yourself in a situation that brings you face to face with it.

For example, if you're scared of spiders or snakes, the last thing you want to do is to be anywhere near them! So of course, going into the bush, long grass or dark cobwebby spaces isn't high on your list of priorities.

**The fear of hearing NO is the same.**

If you're scared of hearing NO, you'll almost always fear *saying* it too. And probably for the same reason: you don't want the other person to be unhappy with you, think you're rude or not like you.

**Make sense?**

**Unfortunately, when you fear saying NO, one of two things occur:**

- You say YES when you actually mean NO.
- You make up a story (OK, a lie) to avoid having to say it: 'I can't' is so much easier to say than NO.

In either instance, however, you're not choosing. Instead, you're avoiding.

## It's not *their* fault you said YES

For me, discovering that it was OK to hear NO gave me the power to start saying it.

**Before I lived the practices in this book, however, that wasn't the case:**

- I didn't like saying NO to my friends – so I said YES to events I didn't want to attend.

- I didn't like saying NO at my work – so I said YES to giving away my time, attention and expertise for free if people asked me to.

- I especially didn't like saying NO to my kids – so I said YES when they wanted something I couldn't afford to buy them.

Because, in all of these instances, I feared that they'd no longer like/ love me if I did.

**Of course, avoiding all those NOs didn't do me any favours.**

I had almost no boundaries between my work and my personal life.

I'd get upset because, after giving away hours and hours of my time, I had no time left for me.

And after buying those things for my kids, I stressed about bills that I had to figure out how to pay.

The theme you're probably noticing here is that saying YES when I meant NO may have made the other person happy in the short term. In the long term, though, the person who was upset was me!

**But here's the kicker, which multiplied my upset...**

Often, if I'd said YES instead of NO, I'd change my mind or cancel at the last minute after making up some kind of excuse. That made me feel awful, and then I'd be even *more* upset.

So my life was filled with being upset – yet everything I was upset about was completely within my area of control. Not only that, but instead of being upset at myself, I'd get upset with the people I'd said YES to. How crazy was that?

The good news is that once I saw how this pattern was showing up, I could find a way to change it.

## Thank you, I love you, I appreciate the opportunity

**So how do you say NO when you mean NO?**

I'm not going to tell you it's easy in the beginning. Saying NO *will* feel clunky and those 'What will people think about me?' thoughts may creep up.

But I ask you – no, I implore you – to think about the giant pile of upset you'll be left to deal with if you don't. It will come from either giving up your time and resources, or from backing out of a YES you didn't want to say.

I also ask you to remember that it will be YOU who created all that upset.

**Now I want you to imagine the difference it will make in your life to actually say NO when you mean NO.**

For example, you could say:

- "Thank you for the invitation, and NO I can't make it. Please ask me again, though, as next time I may be able to."

- "This is an opportunity I really appreciate, and I'd love to help you. Can we book an appointment during business hours to talk about it?"

- "I love you and I'd love to get this for you. For now, it's not in our budget, but I'll see if I can budget it in soon instead."

Saying NO doesn't make you a bad person. It simply makes you someone who not only values those around her but herself as well.

## The Practice – Using the key phrases

As I mentioned in the previous section, I keep these three key phrases in my 'back pocket'.

Then I take them out and use them whenever I can feel myself being sucked into the vortex of saying YES. Here's how:

Step 1: First, know that if you initially say YES when you meant NO, it's never too late to change your mind.

Step 2: Next, try using the key phrases this way.

- When you're saying NO to someone you care about deeply, begin with, "I love you, and..."

- When you're saying NO at work, begin with, "Thanks for the opportunity, and..."

- When you're saying NO to a stranger, friend or acquaintance, begin with, "Thank you, and..."

Step 3: Note that using the word 'and' after your sentence starter instead of 'but' removes the element of not wanting to comply. Instead, it replaces that element with gratitude for the invitation/opportunity/request.

# Stage 4:
# Actualisation

"You've always had the
power, my dear, you just had
to learn it for yourself."

- Glinda the Good Witch
(The Wizard of Oz)

## Actualisation is the foundation that brings everything together

The word actualisation simply means 'bringing something into fruition'.

You could also define it as 'bringing something to life', 'bringing it out from the shadows and into the light', 'making it real' or simply 'creating it'. However you want to define it, it provides the platform that will help you to *keep* transforming your life.

All the lessons you've learnt so far are powerful practices that will help you to develop your experiential transformation superpowers. However, without support for those new superpowers, it's far too easy to slip back into a perspective where transformation remains stagnant in your mind as just an intellectual concept.

That support comes from the things you do every day: your day-to-day actions, habits and routines.

These things are what create your maintenance kit, which then ensures you keep *on* transforming – and helps you to continually develop and draw upon your other superpowers. That's why Actualisation is the fourth stage of experiential transformation.

In this section, we'll be looking at lessons and practices that will allow you to continue to make everything you've learnt 'real', while remaining centred, aligned and peaceful.

## Actualisation can't happen without the first three stages

**It's important to realise that Actualisation isn't a 'magic pill'.**

If you tend to skip to the end of books or look for shortcuts or quick fixes, you might have jumped to this section to find the 'gold'. If so, I want to tell you that it's here. However, you probably won't recognise it without first completing the practices in the previous three stages.

How do I know this? Because I spent over a decade myself searching for the answer without knowing the question.

In other words, unless you switch on your awareness spotlight, accept what 'is' and stand in your own area of control, diving into this stage won't help. Just like an answer without a meaningful question, the lessons in here will be unclear and make absolutely no sense.

## This is the final stage to living peacefully and powerfully

**It involves building a solid base to anchor your transformation superpowers.**

By embodying the practices in this stage, you'll create the final component in living a peaceful, powerful life. You'll understand how to drop your armour and defuse your dramas on an ongoing basis.

You'll know how to ensure that your internal navigation system is always in pristine condition. That means you'll be able to embrace the belief that your life is happening *for* you and not *to* you. You'll experience a centred stillness that radiates forth from you, which people around you will begin to notice. And powering this peaceful radiance will be the confidence that you can return to it in any moment of any day, regardless of what comes at you.

## This final stage completes your transformation superpowers

**But it's not the end of the transformation process.**

Transformation, as we've previously discussed, doesn't have an endpoint: rather, it's constant and ongoing. However, you *are* about to embark on the final practices that will build your foundations to ensure your transformation continues.

And by the end of this fourth and final stage, you'll have everything you need to keep your experiential transformation going. You'll never live the same way, love the same way, work the same way or parent the same way again.

Whilst life will continue to occur, the YOU who steps up and into that life will do so armour-less, drama-less, peacefully and powerfully.

# Lesson 38

## HONESTY IS NOT ALWAYS
## THE BEST POLICY

 AKA Will this add value to
the person or situation?

### Sometimes it's better NOT to tell the truth

If, like me, you were raised to always tell the truth, this practice
may seem odd.

Hang in there with me for a moment though. Let me explain what's at
the heart of this life lesson.

I want to shine a spotlight on the power and impact of truth-telling.
The hashtag #truth currently has almost 46 million hits on Instagram,
so it's fair to say the subject is an important one – at least on social
media, anyway.

However, while it's important to speak our truth, we all also have a
responsibility for the impact of the truth we speak.

# Are you being an igniter or a 'foof-er'?

**Think about the effect your words will have on someone's spirit.**

Many years ago, I was privileged to be in an audience of over 200 business women at an inspiring keynote address by Amanda Gore. Check her out on Google – and if you ever have an opportunity to hear her speak, I highly recommend taking it.

In short, Amanda is a communications and performance expert, the author of multiple bestselling books and an international speaker. However, she's perhaps most widely known as the foremost expert on the topic of joy.

**During her keynote, Amanda shared that we can think of other people's spirits as being like sparks or flames.**

Whenever possible, we want to ignite those flames and encourage them to burn brighter. By the same token, whenever possible, we also want to avoid stifling or smothering their light – in other words, 'foof-ing' it out.

That means the words we say to other people can either make us igniters or 'foof-ers'. My explanation of this is simply:

- If you're being an igniter, your words are encouraging someone's spirit.

- If, on the other hand, you're being a 'foof-er', your words are dousing someone's spirit.

# Judo Jen!

**As a personal trainer, I had countless opportunities to be an igniter.**

Often, my clients either hadn't exercised for a very long time or were returning from an injury. In either instance, their fitness was at a basic, foundational level.

In these cases, I'd always remind them that this was the best news ever. I'd tell them that building fitness slowly and focusing on the range of movement was paramount to minimising (further) injuries.

And then I'd let them know that this slow pace would support them in building sustainable fitness habits and routines.

**Now, did you see what I did there? I acted as an igniter!**

And whether you currently work out or not, I'm sure you felt supported by those words.

What was *never* beneficial to anyone was telling them that I was going to "smash them" in their first session or that they'd "be super sore tomorrow".

Now, of course, some soreness was likely, even with the most gentle start. However, I didn't 'foof' their spirit by pointing this out (and nor did I ever 'smash' a beginner).

**I changed my language from session to session and from client to client, depending on what I thought would be most encouraging.**

But I always started from the desire to lift each person up and remind them constantly of what they'd achieved thus far. I never talked about how far they still had to go.

If they'd done a combined walk and jog during their first kilometre, but now could jog the entire distance, I'd congratulate them and excitedly remind them of their achievement and progress.

If they'd never been able to complete a movement with a full range of motion (eg. a squat or push-up) but now could, I'd also focus on that achievement.

And the difference this made was phenomenal: some of these women even went on to complete full Iron Man triathlon events.

**As a complete contrast, a judo instructor I encountered was a real 'foof-er'.**

I met them in 1995, only a couple of years after quitting smoking. I was on a new-found fitness journey, and my friend and I decided we'd try a judo class. It looked like fun and the people we saw doing it were clearly very fit, however their advertising also clearly stated that beginners were welcome.

The instructor began the group session by getting us to run in a circle around the room to warm up. I don't know what happened, but somehow, I tripped over my own feet and fell flat on my back.

I thought it was very funny and so did my friend. Apparently, however, the instructor didn't. They called out to me to focus and pay attention. The other students just ran right past me too, staring straight ahead and not offering any kind of assistance to me as I lay flat on my back on the floor.

**Needless to say, I never went on to become a judo champion.**

In fact, I never went to another judo class ever again. Because, whether the instructor's intention was to encourage me or not, their words landed for me in a way that completely 'foof-ed' my spirit.

## It's not what we say, it's how we say it

**To be clear, this lesson is not about encouraging you to lie, or be condescending or dishonest.**

Yes, it's important to speak your truth honestly. Always. But you're also radically responsible (see Lesson 40) for the impact of the truth you speak. So the *way* you speak that truth is important too.

For example, "Does my bum look big in this?" is a well-known question that doesn't generally bode well for either the person who asks it OR the person who was asked.

So for this lesson, I want you to consider both positions.

If you *ask* a question like this and request 'complete honesty', you need to prepare yourself for what you get back. (You might also want to pray that the person you ask has read this book!)

**However, if you're *asked* for 'complete honesty', you have the opportunity to choose a response that can change the course of someone's life.**

If that seems dramatic, can I remind you that I never became a judo champion? And yes, maybe I never would have, even without my spirit having been 'foof-ed'. But we have no way of knowing whether I could have now, do we?

You ALWAYS have a choice. Always.

You can either ignite someone's spirit or 'foof' it.

Plus, by becoming an igniter in life, you can also create a profound ripple effect of love and peace on our planet.

## The Practice – Are you adding value?

This is a powerful practice for becoming an influential leader, an inspiring coach or a successful manager.

It can also help you to bring peace to your parenting and even ignite your own spirit.

Step 1:   Ask yourself, "How will what I'm about to say 'land' for that person? Will it add value to them?"

- If it will ignite them into positive action or move them positively towards a solution or outcome, choose to say it.

- If it will 'foof' their spirit, consider keeping it to yourself. Or, better yet, try to change the way you say it so that it WILL add value.

Step 2:   If you find yourself thinking, "I don't care how it affects them. I'm just going to say it anyway!" this might be because your ego is running the show.

If that's the case, ask yourself, "What would love do here?"

# Lesson 39

## WHO I AM IS ENOUGH

 AKA Why I knitted an oversized pair of slippers

## Our expectations of ourselves can be damaging

**As we talked about in Lesson 31, expectation is a dangerous thing.**

It's the number one factor in disappointment, heartbreak, self-defined failure, and feeling let down, unworthy or not good enough.

And though many people place expectations on others and their surroundings, your greatest (mis)placed expectations are often the ones you put on yourself.

This destructive habit leaves you fighting a never-ending battle to attain 'enoughness'. Not only that, but it also lures you into a false pit of worry that the world around you might discover how 'not enough' you are.

And the irony is that you're usually the *only* person who doesn't think you're enough.

## Do you ever think these thoughts?

Before we dive in, take a minute or two to consider the ways in which you might think that you're 'not enough'.

For example, do you ever think you're:

- not smart or successful enough?
- not pretty enough?
- not fit or 'in shape' enough?
- not 'mother of the year' or 'partner of the year' enough?
- not 'I've got my shit together' enough?

**Once you've identified the thoughts that are true for you, I want you to imagine that your best friend is beside you.**

Imagine yourself saying all of these things out loud to her, one by one. Begin each one with, "I am..." (eg. "I am not smart or successful enough.")

Now, what do you suppose your best friend will say in response? Will she reply, "Yep, those are all true! You are SO not enough!"?

Of course they won't (well, not if they're a real friend anyway). Instead, they'll probably look at you blankly and likely say something like, "Are you serious? That's crazy talk! You are TOTALLY enough!"

My point here is that *YOU* are the only person who thinks you're not enough in the first place!

# How knitting oversized slippers taught me I was enough

**2011 was an amazing year for me.**

My business was booming, and I had incredible clients who were achieving amazing things. I lived in my own home with my two beautiful kids, right near one of the most spectacular beaches in the world.

On top of that, I had wonderful friends and often went on exciting weekend adventures. I competed successfully at many sports events. I was in a relationship. And I was nominated for the Sunshine Coast Business Women's Network *Business Woman of the Year Awards* for the second year in a row.

Yet despite all this, I was the unhappiest I can remember being in my life.

To the outside world, it looked like I had it all. And the truth is that I did.

So why was I so unhappy?

**I just wanted to run away!**

Six months earlier, I'd met Jacqui, a modern-day hippie counsellor/ mentor/wise woman.

She lived completely off the grid in a hidden valley called The Grove, and her home seemed like the perfect place for me to run to. So within 48 hours of coming up with the idea, I had everything organised. I left the Sunshine Coast on a one-way ticket, not knowing when I'd be ready to return.

The day I left, I received the news that I was a finalist in the Business Women's Awards. However, I had absolutely no intention of going through with the award selection process and made a mental note to email them that I was withdrawing from consideration.

**When I arrived at The Grove, Jacqui was sitting around the fire with her partner and some of her family.**

It was like I'd just popped in from next door, instead of having travelled from hundreds of kilometres away. There was no TV – just conversation – and Jacqui was knitting slippers. She had a massive box of wool and needles beside her, and she invited me to knit a pair for myself.

Of course I looked at her like she was mad. "Slippers?" I sputtered. "I didn't come here to knit slippers! I came here because I thought you could help me!"

"Help you with what?" she asked.

"I don't know, just help me!" I replied, and she burst out laughing.

**"You're not broken," she said. "You don't need fixing!"**

I felt like such an idiot. I was completely exasperated, but I picked up the wool and needles. With a deep crease between my eyebrows, I began furiously knitting slippers.

Over the next few days, in between knitting those bloody slippers, I went for long walks and rode horses. I went to an art class and drew a very angry red kettle. I also cried many, many, many times. I had long, peaceful conversations with Jacqui – and short, fiery ones too.

What was wrong with me? I didn't know.

All I knew was that I didn't ever want to leave The Grove. The thought of going back to my life scared me.

**After a couple of weeks, Jacqui asked me what was so awful about my life.**

What was so bad that I never wanted to go back to it? What was I afraid of?

I told her I was scared that I wasn't strong enough, smart enough, capable enough or perfect enough to keep doing a good job in my life. I told her I was scared of letting everyone down – as a mother, as a partner, as a business owner and as a friend.

I told her that if I let any of them down, they'd realise I was a complete and total fake. And then they'd see all the areas in my life that I was barely holding it together most days.

"And yet you are here, Jen," Jacqui replied. "And you can be here because you're surrounded by people who love and support you exactly as you are.

Your children are enjoying time with their father, and your incredible team is running your business. Not *one* person in your life thinks you're not enough: it's only you who thinks that!"

**Then she said the words that changed my life: "Jen, you ARE enough!"**

I stared at her for a moment as her words sank in, then replied, "Yes I am. I AM enough. As a mother, partner, friend and business woman."

"NO!" she exclaimed. "Not as those things. You're missing the point, Jen. You're ENOUGH as YOU! You can never, ever be any more than that in this moment, the past moment or the moment to come. You're enough just as you are and just as you aren't."

**It took many minutes for that to wash over the 'stuck' part of me.**

And it took many *more* minutes for me to truly understand what she was saying. When I did, though, I realised that my thinking had completely created the dark place I was living in.

And I realised it wasn't just me, either. We're ALL enough. Just as we are and just as we aren't. With absolutely NO expectations to live up to. Right here and right now. In THIS moment.

WE'RE ENOUGH.

That night, I finished my slippers and booked my flight home.

When I tried them on, however, they were *miles* too big for me. Luckily, my son has size 13 feet, so he enjoyed them over the next few winters.

And seeing them on him always reminded me of the profound wisdom of this life lesson, which was knitted into those slippers: who I am is enough.

**A few weeks later, I stood on a stage, giving my acceptance speech to over 500 people.**

I'd been awarded the title of Sunshine Coast Business Women's Network Sportswoman of the Year.

In my speech, I acknowledged many, many people – especially Jacqui.

And I knew in my heart as I stood there, holding that amazing award in my hands, that with or without it, who I am would always be ENOUGH.

## You are enough just as you are AND just as you aren't

**In 2018, I created The Peaceful Warrior Woman Project on social media.**

It was essentially a 100-day photographic journey. It was a passion project that also allowed me to understand what was going on in the minds of women all around the world.

I asked them to send me their favourite photograph. Then I asked them to share with the world, in 25 words or less, what their inner peaceful warrior woman would tell their younger self.

Women of all ages and all cultures from all around the world began to send me their words and images. And I went on to share one per day for the next 100 days.

**The results were profound.**

Every time a new entry arrived in my inbox, I'd be brought to tears by the sender's heartfelt words of wisdom. And the most commonly shared words to each woman's younger self were, "You are enough."

Every time I read those words, it reminded me of my own discovery during the weeks I spent with Jacqui.

**There's no quick fix for the millions of women who've come to believe over time that they don't 'measure up'.**

But true transformation begins the second you become aware of the moments in which that idea shows up. Only then can you choose to replace it with the belief that you already are, indeed, enough.

## The Practice – Knowing that you're enough

When I came back from The Grove, I had the words 'Who I am is enough' tattooed on my left shoulder.

Now, I'm not in any way suggesting you do the same thing. I'm not even suggesting you knit yourself some 'Who I am is enough' slippers (although you can if you want to).

So if tattoos or knitting aren't your thing, try the practice below.

**Step 1:**   Write yourself a letter that begins with:

"Dear [insert your name]

This is your Divine Self, and I'm here to remind you of the burdensome expectations you've been carrying lately.

These are..."

Then write, write and write some more. Allow your Divine Self to speak to you and remind you of what the expectations you've placed upon yourself are.

You may only need one reminder or you may need several, but keep writing until you have nothing else to write.

When you've finished, complete the letter with:

"[your name], I'm now going to ask you to let go of the burden of these expectations.

I want you to write across each one, in big letters, 'WHO I AM IS ENOUGH'.

Because my dear, you ARE!

With love,

Your Divine Self"

**Step 2:** If it feels aligned to do so, burn the letter (safely in a fireproof dish in the open of course).

Or if you prefer, hang on to the letter for 30 days and each day, repeat out loud, "WHO I AM IS ENOUGH!"

# Lesson 40

## YOU ARE RADICALLY RESPONSIBLE FOR YOUR LIFE

 AKA Don't play the "blame game"

**Have you ever wanted something in your life to be different?**

**Perhaps you've wanted a situation you're experiencing to change?**

Or have you wanted a person to change the way THEY are?

Have you just known deep down that if just *one or two* things changed about that person or situation, you'd have the life you wanted?

What I've come to discover is that if you want your life to be different, the power to change it starts – and ends – with you.

# It can seem hard to take responsibility for creating what we want

**We don't always know what we want, but we somehow know what we *don't* want.**

This is as good a place as any to begin the process of taking radical responsibility, which means accepting *total* responsibility for everything you create (or don't create) in your life.

But so often we don't take responsibility for creating what we want, because we don't know what 'it' is. We are, however, very good at complaining that we don't have it.

For example, I complained that I didn't have the relationship I wanted.

I also complained that I didn't have the career I wanted.

And I sometimes complained that I didn't have the life I wanted.

But complaining about what I didn't want did NOT help me in any way to take radical responsibility for creating what I did want.

A problem I hear over and over is when people can't see how they can change something they're unhappy with. They believe that what they want depends on whatever's going on outside of them. So they keep saying things like:

- "It's not my fault my relationship is crappy. My partner won't commit to making it work."
- "It's not my fault that my business is flatlining. The economy is terrible right now."
- "It's not my fault my life sucks. It's because blah, blah, blah..."

For example, I have a friend who thinks she can't meet the right partner.

She often asks me, "Why do I always attract the narcissists?"

(Side note: I actually believe the word 'narcissist' is highly overused. I'm not suggesting that it's not a genuine psychological condition. However, nowadays, it's also used to describe someone who's just an arsehole. This can then sometimes precipitate avoiding responsibility for being in a crappy relationship.)

Meanwhile, another acquaintance tells me she has to continually step in to help her grown children.

"If I don't, they'll never be able to manage!" she says.

In all of these examples, whatever is negatively impacting our lives WILL NOT change just because we keep complaining (often continuously) about it.

**But you *can* change your life by taking 100% (radical) responsibility for it.**

Simply put, the life you want is waiting for you. You just have to give up playing the 'blame game' first.

## Two powerful words – 'not this'

**The two words 'not this' help to move you towards radical responsibility.**

I first heard these words during an interview with Elizabeth Gilbert that I listened to. In it, she was speaking about her bestselling novel *Eat, Pray, Love.*

What got my attention was the part in the book when she made the decision to leave her husband. To everyone on the outside –

including her husband – her marriage and life appeared normal, so leaving him made no sense. Yet she couldn't deny her soul screaming at her 'not this'.

**However, Elizabeth had no idea what the 'next thing' was.**

She had no idea what she'd do after leaving her husband. She had no plan. She didn't know what her life would look like.

She simply knew that she must take radical responsibility for whatever that would become.

**This happened in my life too.**

When I ended first my marriage and then a subsequent relationship, I too had no idea what my life would look like beyond them. But I also knew deep down 'not this'.

Nor, when I left my corporate job prior to writing this book, did I know what my life would look like beyond that.

But again, I somehow knew deep down 'not this'.

**A blameless 'not this' allows you to take radical responsibility for your life.**

It's tempting to attach a sense of blame to your 'not this'.

However, if you can move *away* from blaming what's going on outside of you, you'll start to recognise when your soul is undeniably telling you 'not this'.

Then, just as Elizabeth shared, you'll find an opportunity to take radical responsibility for moving powerfully forwards. That's true even if you're not yet sure where it will take you or what it will look like.

## Radical responsibility is about creating the life you want for yourself

Before we talk about what radical responsibility is, let's talk about what it *isn't*.

It's not about designing the life you want and then expecting someone else to do the work of building it for you. Nor is it about blaming the person who *tries* to build it for you that their creation doesn't look like your original design.

And it's certainly not about blaming them afterwards for fucking the whole thing up.

**Taking radical responsibility applies to every area of your life.**

In this lesson, I've used relationships as one example of taking radical responsibility. However, this practice applies to every single area of your life. For example:

- **If you have health issues,** is it really the fast food industry's fault? Or could you perhaps make some dietary changes (eg. eating fewer processed foods)?

- **If you're always scrimping and saving,** is it really the economy's fault? Or could you perhaps make some lifestyle changes (eg. setting up and following a realistic budget)?

- **If you're in a job you hate,** is it really too late for a career change? Or could you investigate different ways to do what you love (eg. doing some volunteer work to gain experience)?

- **If you haven't spoken to someone for an extended period of time,** are they the only one who can reach out? Or can you decide that reconciliation is more important than being right and initiate contact yourself (eg. sending a short message just to say hello)?

- **If your business isn't thriving,** is it really your customers' or employees' fault? Or could you take steps to reinvent the culture (eg. organising a regular team meeting or customer survey)?

- **If you're doubting yourself spiritually,** is it really because the world is a terrible place? Or could you look for a support group with like-minded people (eg. finding a local meet-up group)?

**It doesn't matter WHAT it is in your life you want that you don't have.**

Whether it's your body, your job, your finances, your partner or your success, you have two choices. You can continue to be miserable and unhappy OR you can stop blaming what's outside of your control and instead take radical responsibility for the choices you can make within it.

The point is that you and you alone have the power to change any aspect of your life.

But that will *only* happen if you're willing to take radical responsibility for it.

# The Practice – Moving away from blame

The first step in taking responsibility for what you want is to recognise what it is.

To do this:

Step 1:  Choose an area or situation you're currently unhappy with or that isn't working the way you'd like it to. You may find yourself saying 'not this'.

Step 2:  Ask yourself what you can identify specifically about this situation that you don't want but are tolerating. Be completely honest with yourself here.

Step 3:  Now ask yourself, "If I wasn't tolerating this, what would I choose instead?"

Step 4:  Once you can see what you actually want, write a list of five actions you could take to move you towards it.

NOTE: sometimes, taking radical responsibility may require compromise on the path forward.

However, there's a difference between creating an acceptable compromise and tolerating a situation. A compromise doesn't require you to betray your values and ideals, while tolerating a situation does.

# Lesson 41

## SPECTACULAR EFFORT BRINGS SPECTACULAR REWARD

 AKA Choose *your* best effort in every moment

## Have you ever committed to doing something outside your comfort zone?

**We've all been there.**

In a blind moment of inspiration, motivation, determination, indignation or just sheer impulsiveness, you said YES (out loud) to 'something'.

This 'something' can take many forms. It might be:

- something simple like agreeing to an early morning training session or meet up

- something longer-term, like not drinking alcohol or eating chocolate for a month

- something *much* bigger, like a 12-week challenge or a life-changing bucket list goal.

Sometimes it's something physical and sometimes it's not.

Regardless, you said, "Yes, bring it on!" And initially, you were excited.

You shared your 'big decision' with everyone you knew. Maybe you even made a public declaration on social media. Your energy and enthusiasm were riding high, and you felt on top of the world!

## Then the inspiration passes, and your motivation goes AWOL...

**After a few days, however, your inspiration starts to fade.**

Suddenly, all your pumped-up motivation decides to take long service leave. Suddenly, the reality of getting up at 5am, not sipping champagne at your sister's wedding or not getting a chocolate rabbit this Easter sinks in.

Maybe 12 weeks now seems forever – and really, was that 'life-changing' thing ever *actually* on your bucket list?!

**So then you start making exceptions to the rule.**

You think to yourself, "OK, I'll just change the 5am to 5pm," or, "I'll just give myself a free pass for my sister's wedding (oh, and for Easter too.)"

You decide you'll just coast through the 12 weeks and tell yourself you did your best. And you downgrade that life-changing bucket list statement to something that would 'be great if it happened, but no biggie really'.

**Now, this isn't an integrity lecture (although I *am* a fan of integrity).**

And it's not about passing judgement on yourself either.

Instead, it's about YOU deciding how much effort you'll bring (or not) to each moment in your life.

Because whilst life is out of your control, your *effort* isn't.

# I learnt this lesson from a body sculpting competition

I've spoken before about my crazy decision to train for and compete in a body sculpting competition in 2009.

To help me succeed, I hired a coach. (Side note: if you really want to achieve something huge, hire a coach/mentor who's actually achieved it.)

There were two events one week apart in May 2009 and, like the unconscious overachiever I was back then, I thought, "What the heck, I'll do both!"

My coach created a training plan and I began the work. First, there were three months of pre-comp preparation, followed by a little break over Christmas. Then came five months of solid competition preparation, combining disciplined nutrition with 10–15 hours of weekly training and posing practice.

I never planned to do this sport on an ongoing basis.

I knew, however, that I wasn't going to invest my precious resources and eight months of my life into just arsing about.

So when it came to effort, I'd absolutely give it a red-hot crack!

I wanted to be 100% sure that when I stepped on that stage on 17 May 2009 I could ask myself one question and answer it honestly.

That question was, "Have I brought *my* best effort to every moment in this process?"

If I could answer YES, it didn't matter whether I finished in first place or twenty-first place. I'd still be a winner. If I answered NO, I knew my result would reflect that too.

And I'd *still* walk away knowing that my result equalled the effort I'd brought to each moment of the process.

Now, during my eight months of training, I was often (and I mean OFTEN) plagued with thoughts like, "Will it reeeeeeally matter if I...

- do 15 reps instead of 20, or only do 30 minutes on the cross trainer instead of 45?"

- don't weigh my food precisely or have an occasional glass of wine?"

- buy healthy takeaway food occasionally instead of carrying my pre-prepared meals around with me EVERY DAY?"

- sleep in and skip training just this once?"

- refuse to hand-glue hundreds of crystals on my costume or skip my daily posing practice?"

- blow off the fake tan, hair, makeup and stripper shoes?" (I far preferred hundreds of squats to all that stuff!)

**Because who'd know if I didn't do these things, right? And who'd care?**

The answer was 'Nobody'. Not even my coach would lose sleep over it.

I'm the only one who'd ever know.

So only I could decide if any of those things would really matter. Then, based on that decision, only I could choose how much effort I'd bring to each of them.

Knowing this helped me to change my attitude from one of 'Ughhhh, I *have* to do this thing!' to 'I *want* to do this thing'.

## Flipping 'I have to' to 'I want to'.

**Please understand that this life lesson isn't about winning or losing.**

It's not about body sculpting or competing either. And it's absolutely not about martyrdom. Rather, it's about understanding that, whatever you do or want for yourself in life, you have the power to create it through whatever effort you choose to bring to each moment.

**I mentioned above that this isn't about self-flagellation or martyrdom.**

Sometimes your 'best effort' in one moment might be supporting yourself to allow the best version of you to show up in a future moment.

For example, if you have an injury, your 'best effort' will be to rest and avoid exacerbating it. Or, if there's an important family event coming up, your 'best effort' may be to forgo your training that day and reschedule it to later in the week. Or maybe your 'best effort' is to just stop and breathe for five minutes.

**So what do you do if you're not sure what your 'best' effort is?**

A power question to ask yourself is, "What's the one thing I can do right now that will move me towards what matters most?"

This is about helping yourself to seal up the 'Will what I choose reeeeeeally matter?' escape hatch. It's about becoming aware of what's important in *this* moment. Only then can you ensure that your choice moves you intentionally in the direction of your 'something', which we talked about back in the first section.

**Curious about how all my body sculpting efforts paid off?**

Well, as it happened, I stepped out on stage wearing fake tan, stripper shoes and the least amount of fabric I've ever worn in public... and I won. But, because I understood this lesson, I knew I'd had absolutely NO control over where I placed in the competition.

I also knew it didn't matter.

Don't get me wrong: winning is great – and it's possibly the ultimate 'spectacular reward'. But it's not the *only* spectacular reward.

If you've truly brought your spectacular effort to any goal, THAT's your spectacular reward in itself – regardless of the outcome.

## The Practice – Becoming more intentional

**The question I asked myself above is great for self-awareness.**

It's served me – and the clients I've coached – very well, and I hope it will help you too.

So when you find yourself asking, "Will what I choose really matter?" turn the question around and ask,

**"What's the one thing I can do right now that will move me towards what matters most?"**

Think about what you're aiming for. Now look at the choices before you in *this* moment. Then choose the one that will best move you towards your 'something'.

# Lesson 42

## THE FLOW OF KNOWING, DOING AND BEING

 AKA How to live an aligned, creative, purpose-fuelled life

### Have you ever felt like you're working your butt off and getting nowhere?

**Maybe you sometimes feel like *all* you do is work.**

You might even be feeling completely burnt out and not see much progress for your efforts, even though you're exhausted at the end of each day.

Or perhaps you're in a frenzy of learning, so you can qualify for whatever it is you really want to do?

Or maybe you're going around in circles in your head, thinking about launching something huge, but waiting for a sign that the timing is right?

In each of these instances, despite feeling busy and overwhelmed, you probably feel like you're not achieving anything. Somehow, your momentum in life seems to have stalled.

**If so, you may be out of flow.**

And it may be because you're inadvertently caught in one element of what I call the 'Knowing, Doing and Being' paradigm. As a result, you're not in 'flow' with your purpose (or your 'divine plan', 'path', 'journey' or whatever description resonates for you).

Regardless of what you call it, when you're stuck in one of these elements, life will seem harder than you know in your heart it ought to be. And chances are that you just can't seem to put your finger on why.

## How do you get into 'flow'?

**The concept of flow was popularised by Mihaly Csikszentmihalyi.**

Mihaly is a renowned psychologist, and the author of the bestseller *Flow: The Psychology of Optimal Experience*.

His research on this topic suggests that what makes you genuinely enjoy something is being in a state of consciousness called 'flow'. This occurs when both the challenge of your task/goal and your skillset pertaining to the challenge are at optimal levels.

He believes that if you're in this state, your experience will be one of deep enjoyment, creativity and total involvement with life.

His book made total sense to me. However, after reading it, I became aware of three key elements that were also integral when it came to me being in 'flow'. I refer to these elements as 'knowing', 'doing' and 'being'.

And, more importantly, I realised that when I *wasn't* in 'flow', it wasn't just about the level of the challenge or my skillset. It was usually because I was also stuck in one of those three elements.

**Here's how each of them can show up in your life.**

*Are you a know-it-all?*

Know-it-alls know, well, *everything*. And if they don't know something, they'll research the crap out of it until they can hold a 'facts and figures' conversation with anyone. If you're a Google queen, this is probably you.

Know-it-alls generally find it difficult to take action because they're never quite ready. They never have enough knowledge to act – so they continue reading, researching, attending seminars and making truckloads of notes.

Sound familiar?

*Perhaps you're more of a control freak?*

Control freaks like things to be done a certain way (their way). They often 'do it themselves because it's just quicker'. They like to plan things down to the final detail, and they freak out if something derails their plan.

And even if they're overloaded, they still take on more.

If that sounds like you, maybe you're a do-er. Don't be fooled: a do-er's control freak tendencies can show up in different ways. For example, perhaps you're not a 'nitty gritty details person', but a 'just hand it to me, I get shit done' person instead.

Both of these tendencies are thinly veiled disguises for a control freak – and common attributes of a classic do-er. If you're a do-er, you need to be in control with your sleeves rolled up, head down and bum up – constantly doing.

*Or maybe you're 'waiting for a sign'.*

If you're happily coasting along with life, waiting for something outside of yourself to change, you're probably a 'be-er'. If this is you, you're not learning anything new, making decisions or taking action.

Maybe you're *planning* to do something, but you're waiting for the right circumstances, for the right moment or for Monday. Or maybe you're just happy to 'see how things go'.

Sometimes you might wait for messages. You might meditate on the answer, or check the oracle cards and crystals, read your stars, check your numerology or reset your chakras.

**To be clear, there's nothing *wrong* with any of these elements.**

In fact, when you're in 'flow', they'll all be present and you'll be harnessing the positive attributes of each one. That means you'll be seeking information, applying it to your actions and then remaining open to all outcomes and opportunities.

However, if you stay stuck in any one of the elements for long periods of time, its negative attributes begin to dominate, inhibiting your 'flow'.

You see, what I've discovered is that to connect to our 'flow' state, we need to 'know', 'do' and 'be' *simultaneously*.

## Can you guess what my default is?

**If you've read the book up to this point, my default will come as no surprise.**

Yes, I'm a do-er.

I'm not super detailed – I'm more of a big picture person. But I regularly deal with life's challenges by 'doing'. Whenever I feel unsure, lost or confused, my coping mechanism is to just get busier.

I've already spoken about becoming aware of my 'overachiever within'. And whilst she sometimes serves me well, I'm now acutely aware of when she's operating without my consent. This is also when I notice I become stuck in the 'doing'.

If I'm busy, I make myself busier. If I'm snowed under with commitments, I take on a couple more. If I want to avoid dealing with something, I'll look for a big, fat, juicy goal I can sink my teeth into – regardless of whether the goal serves any purpose or not.

However, that's not the only element I've been stuck in.

**Remember how my 2017 was filled with big, fat, juicy goals?**

I literally *couldn't* have made myself any busier. But what I now know is that all that busy-ness was because I was avoiding writing this book. Why? Because I wasn't confident that I could or even if it was what I was supposed to do.

Funnily enough, since I made the decision to write it – after I'd applied some knowing (research), doing (writing) and being (trusting in myself) – the book has flowed. So has everything around me to make it possible.

However, just after I decided to write it, I found myself stuck in 'being' for a short time. I kept looking for a sign that I was 'meant' to do it.

**And at another time, I got completely caught up in 'knowing'.**

Just after I first qualified as a personal trainer, my experience and confidence were both limited. So I set about reading, googling and attending every workshop I could find, so I could learn to be a better trainer.

Now whilst learning is of course necessary to become more proficient, it was counterproductive if I used it to avoid actively recruiting clients. (Yes, even though I had more knowledge in my head than many newly qualified trainers.)

**Nowadays, I know the first step in dealing with being stuck is recognising it.**

Once I've done this, I'll look at where I'm spending the majority of my time – and I'll often discover that I'm caught in one of these three elements.

As soon as I become aware of this, I can bring balance to all three. And then, just like magic, my life gets back in flow.

## Which is YOUR default: knowing, doing or being?

The easiest way to identify your default is to look for how each element impacts you – both positively and negatively. Each one has benefits that will help you move forwards in life – but each also has negative attributes that will block you.

### Knowing

The positive attributes of 'knowing' are learning, expansion, growth, education, knowledge and wisdom.

The negative attributes of 'knowing' are procrastination, becoming a know-it-all, staying stuck in the search for the 'right' knowledge, and fearing not knowing enough or the unknown.

If you're stuck in the negative of knowing, you're on a quest to seek out information and answers, but you're not prepared to act on any of it.

## Doing

The positive attributes of 'doing' are production, achievement, action, task completion and the physical act of progression.

The negative attributes of 'doing' can involve becoming unfocused, misdirected or misguided. They can also involve becoming closed to new, more efficient actions (because you want to do it the way you've always done it). And, of course, we've already talked about burnout, spinning your wheels and doing *anything* rather than nothing.

If you're stuck in the negative of doing, you describe your days as 'super busy' and complain of exhaustion, needing a holiday and that 'your plate is overflowing'.

## Being

The positive attributes of 'being' are about being open to all perspectives. They allow you to set intentions without attachments and mean you can happily take quiet time out for stillness, meditation, self-love and self-awareness.

The negative attributes of 'being' include sticking your head in the sand, looking for signs, scrolling social media, being easily distracted and jumping from one idea to the other.

If you're stuck in the negative of 'being', you're most likely daydreaming, staring into space and imagining how you want your life to look. What you're not doing, however, is taking any action towards having it look that way.

## Why do we get stuck?

When you activate all three 'knowing', 'doing' and 'being' elements simultaneously, you can create purposeful, effortless flow. So why is it so easy to get stuck in their negative attributes?

Mihaly Csikszentmihalyi would say it's because either the challenge level of your task or your own skill level isn't optimal (or both). And whilst I do subscribe to his theory, I don't think it's the whole story.

I think we sometimes unconsciously set ourselves up with skill or challenge levels that aren't optimal because we're just not ready to expand.

But mostly, I believe we get stuck in our default element because it comes naturally to us. At least that's how I noticed it in my own life – and when I did, I knew I could restore flow instantly.

## The Practice – Getting unstuck and into flow

**So how do you recognise when you're stuck in the negative attributes of your default element?**

And, once you've recognised it, how do you move back into the simultaneous positive flow of all three?

Try this practice:

Step 1: Look at an area of your life where you feel stuck, unhappy, unsure, uncertain, lost or confused. Write down what this is.

Step 2: Ask yourself which element of knowing, doing and being is receiving the majority of your focus and attention at this time.

Step 3: Identify three things you can do in the other two areas to create some forward momentum with them.

**Step 4:** With this new awareness, create a seven-day plan. Start with a double A4 page and title it with the area you want to work on. Divide the pages into seven columns, one for each day. Next, divide each column into three rows, and name those rows 'Knowing', 'Doing' and 'Being'.

Then, in the relevant square for each element, list three things per day to focus on and pay attention to.

The purpose of this practice is to become consciously aware of balancing all three elements simultaneously and thus return to your flow state.

# Lesson 43

## WHAT YOU FOCUS ON GROWS

 AKA What you think about you bring about

## Have either of these situations happened to you?

**Have you ever bought a car? Or has someone close to you bought one?**

Before the purchase, you never saw that make, model or – in particular – colour anywhere. Never. Now suddenly, you're seeing *that exact car* everywhere!

Did all those cars just 'magically' appear? Or were they always there but you'd never noticed them?

**Something else you may notice is a phenomenon that psychologists call 'the cocktail party effect'.**

This happens when you're in a noisy room filled with hundreds of people – for example, at a big cocktail party. However, you might also be in the middle of a busy shopping centre or at an airport.

Wherever you are, despite all the background noise, voices and maybe music, if your name is spoken – even from across the room –

you hear it loud and clear. It's like your brain somehow filters out all the external noise and focuses on that one sound.

Wait, what? How does that even happen?

Well, in the world of self-development, it's considered to be your reticular activating system (RAS) at work.

## Your mind is *always* looking for evidence of what you think

**Scientifically speaking, your RAS is a physical network of neurons located in your brainstem.**

It's sometimes referred to as 'your brain's attention centre', and it's responsible for keeping you alert and awake during the day. However, it also processes outside stimuli and may act as a filter for the billions of bits of information that come at you daily.

Think of your RAS as a little microprocessor that filters out anything you're NOT thinking about and allows in the stuff you ARE focusing on.

So, of course, it doesn't matter whether you're thinking about something real or made up. What matters is that you end up bringing it about simply by thinking about it.

**Another way you might have heard this described is as a 'self-fulfilling prophecy'.**

It doesn't just show up when you buy a car and hear your name in a noisy place either. For example:

- If you think you're 'bad with directions', do you notice that you get lost far more often than your friends?

- If you think you're 'lucky', do you notice that it's always *your* raffle ticket that's pulled out of the hat (unlike your 'unlucky' sister)?

- If you think you're 'clumsy', do you notice that you have far more accidents than the rest of your family?

- If you think people always 'let you down', do you notice that the people in your life disappoint you more often than they disappoint your optimistic friend?

**You might think that you're simply observing an overwhelming mountain of evidence that just proves what you think.**

My experience, however, is that it works the other way around. What you think begins with an isolated piece or two of evidence.

You think about that evidence.

You imagine it happening again.

You feel the way you'd feel if it were happening in reality

And you do this *over and over again.*

That's how whatever you think or believe to be true becomes your self-talk.

**All that self-talk is then like programming code in a computer microprocessor.**

It tells your mind (via your RAS) to look for evidence that proves what you think and then discard everything else.

So, over time, you end up with an overflowing file of evidence to support whatever you believe, regardless of whether it's real or imagined.

In short, what you focus on grows.

## Is that stick moving?!

I first came upon the concept of 'bringing about what you think about' in 2007.

I was studying for my life coaching certificate, which opened my mind to some of the great philosophers and self-development gurus from earlier decades. And through my studies, I came upon the teachings of Maxwell Maltz.

Maxwell was famous for his 1960 book *Psycho-Cybernetics*, which has since sold over 30 million copies. He didn't specifically use the term RAS, but he referred to the same concept as both a 'servo-mechanism' and a 'creative mechanism'.

As I understand it, Maxwell says that activating this servo-mechanism in our brains will actually help us to create whatever we're thinking about.

**But in order for this to happen, three things are necessary:**

- Our thoughts need to have some emotion attached to them.
- We need to imagine the thought vividly.
- We need to repeat the thought over and over.

**I saw this happen clearly when I used to go trail running.**

One of my favourite pastimes is trail running. Where I live, we're spoilt for choice when it comes to bushland and hilly trails.

Of course, in Australia as a whole, we're also spoilt for choice when it comes to venomous creatures. And one type of venomous creature that loves bushland trails as much as I do is snakes.

**One of my running buddies is absolutely petrified of snakes.**

Truth be told, more than one friend of mine is scared of them. However, you could say that this particular friend is *paranoid* about them.

She talks constantly about how much they terrify her, how afraid she is of coming upon one on the trails and how she worries that every stick is a snake. And she shares this over and over again with anyone she runs with.

**I, on the other hand, don't fear snakes at all.**

Perhaps it's because I grew up on a dairy farm and saw plenty of them. Of course, my dad taught me to be careful if I saw one – to give it a wide berth and tell an adult – but otherwise, to leave it alone.

And perhaps because I saw my dad never feared them, the self-talk I created meant I didn't either.

So my friend's self-talk programmed her mind to see snakes, while my mind didn't.

Now, for years, my friend and I have run – both together and separately – on many of the same trails. Can you guess who's come face to face with a multitude of snakes over those years and who almost never sees them?

**Of course, it's my friend who sees them.**

And I believe she does so because:

- She has a very emotional response to the thought of them.

- She imagines seeing them vividly.

- She does this over and over again.

And her RAS delivers in spades.

Your RAS doesn't decipher whether what you're thinking about is true or false, fact or fiction. It simply searches for the evidence from your outer world to support your thoughts and then discards everything else.

## With great power comes great responsibility

It's important to state here that this is NOT about 'thinking positively'.

If my friend just tried to think positively about snakes, she'd still notice them on the trails. She'd just try to force herself to believe that she was happy about it (probably without much luck, given how deeply entrenched her fear is).

Instead, it's about using Maxwell's 'emotion, vivid imagery and repetition' to powerfully program our thoughts to create what we DO want. In my friend's case, this might be vividly imagining the peace and tranquillity of the natural bushland. It might also include imagining how happy and energised she feels at the end of each run.

Alternatively, let's say you're annoyed that your partner never helps out around the house.

If you just try to think positively about them not helping out, the best-case scenario is that you'll just be 'happy' about doing everything yourself. (Again, though, it's more likely you'll try to convince yourself you're happy, but end up even more annoyed because you focus on the 'not helping' even more.)

Instead, I recommend thinking about how happy you are when they actually DO something to help out. Really feel into the emotion of appreciation for their help.

*Then* imagine ways in which their help might show up. Imagine that they make the bed, unstack the dishwasher, mow the lawns or whatever it is. Imagine the joy and gratitude you feel. Then imagine that scene – and your response – over and over again.

**The final step ALWAYS needs to be taking action.**

For my friend, this might involve actually going out for a trail run, and – if she didn't see a snake – journaling about all the good things she experienced. In the housework example, you might leave a loving note or two that asks for your partner's help with particular tasks.

And you'll probably also need to retrain your current thinking. If my friend's self-talk tells her RAS that she'll keep seeing snakes, she probably will. If you've programmed yours with the self-talk that your lazy partner never helps out, that's all you'll see – even if they do occasionally give you a hand.

If you program your RAS and self-talk with what you want to see using repetition, vivid imagery and some emotion, however, what you focus on WILL grow.

**Try this exercise to experience how it works:**

- Close your eyes and think of a single colour. For example, yours might be red.

- For the next 30 seconds or so, keep thinking of nothing but this colour. Think of all the things that you know are (or could be) red and how much you love the colour too.

- Now, open your eyes and look around you. Do you notice that your attention goes immediately to red objects?

This happens because you've temporarily programmed your RAS to notice red things. If you kept repeating this exercise consistently, you might find yourself noticing and being drawn to far more red things in stores compared to things of other colours. So, over time, you might end up buying more red things and, slowly but surely, your home would indeed become more and more red.

That's how your RAS can help you create the things that you desire – but first, you need to tell it clearly what exactly that is.

## The Practice – Focusing on what you want to grow

Now that you've experienced the process above, let's start to bring a clear focus to whatever you want to grow in your life.

Follow these steps:

Step 1: Write down your goal, intention or thing you desire more of in your life.

Step 2: Now tap into the emotion behind what you want to create. Focus intently on that feeling and draw it into your body. Truly breathe in the emotional energy.

It might help to close your eyes and visualise yourself actually *having created* what you want. Feel the emotions, notice who's with you and their emotions, see all the colours and hear all the sounds.

Make it as real in your mind as you can. When you're finished, open your eyes and journal what you experienced.

Step 3: Draw or find a picture of what you want. If you're creatively minded, perhaps create a vision board that reflects your visualisation.

**Step 4:** For the next 21 days, repeat your goal/intention/ desire out loud as you look at the image and feel the emotions behind why you want it.

Do this as often as you can throughout the day.

**Step 5:** Keep a journal record of all the evidence that begins to show up. This becomes your confirmation that 'what you focus on grows'.

# Lesson 44

## OPPORTUNITY KNOCKS REPEATEDLY

 AKA But you have to be home to answer the door

### Have you heard of 'FOMO'?

**FOMO is a 21st century acronym that stands for 'Fear of Missing Out'.**

Social media has not only been the catalyst for creating this acronym but it's also been a breeding ground for the concept itself to rise to fame.

Here's one way the Urban Dictionary defines FOMO:

*"FOMO | fōmō | noun: a state of mental or emotional strain caused by the fear of missing out.*

- *A form of social anxiety – a compulsive concern that one might miss an opportunity or satisfying event, often aroused by posts seen on social media websites.*

*ORIGIN: acronym from FEAR OF MISSING OUT"*

# FOMO may be distracting you from YOUR opportunities

**I'm going to go out on a limb here and suggest that if you're on social media regularly, you'll have experienced FOMO.**

It may have just been at a specific point, and it may have only been briefly. But I bet you've experienced it.

I know *I* certainly have.

So I feel like I know a little something about the opportunities that succumbing to the pressure of FOMO can lead you to miss out on. It's a pressure that the bullet point in the Urban Dictionary definition above totally nails.

**Social media has become a part of almost all of our lives.**

And, sometimes, the 'Fear of Missing Out' it creates can translate into a 'Fear of Missing Opportunities' – particularly opportunities that other people have chosen for themselves.

This, in turn, can lead you to question your own choices and decisions. Are you doing the 'right thing' in business? What about as a parent? In your personal life? At school? The list just goes on...

So you begin to second-guess yourself and ask:

- What if I miss out?

- Will I be left out?

- Will I be left behind?

Does this sound familiar? If so, I get it. I really do.

But here's what I learnt a few years ago: while FOMO is distracting you, you're actually missing the real gold. The REAL opportunities.

**Because opportunities come along EVERY second of every day.**

However, they can slip right on by if you're looking the other way and aren't aware of them. If you're busy worrying about what everyone *else* is doing and whether or not you should be doing the same, you won't see those real opportunities.

You'll be too busy focusing on whether you're missing out on something you weren't even considering until you saw someone else doing it!

**It's easy to assume that the grass is always greener on the other side.**

I want to warn you to beware of FOMO astroturf (you know – the fake grass they sometimes use in playgrounds). It might seem to be a brighter green... but it's *nothing* like the real thing.

Instead, consider that perhaps the real grass is greener wherever you're standing right now. And consider further that it'll be even greener if you water it!

Napoleon Hill said, "*Your big opportunity may be right where you are now.*" – possibly because FOMO was less of a thing in his day.

## I used to go to the opening of an envelope

**The area in which FOMO affected me most was business.**

It still *would* if I hadn't had so much practice at recognising its intoxicating pull.

You see, when I first started my fitness business, I was an eager business woman who was passionate about sharing my brand. It was fresh and unique, and it made fitness fun for all women.

I found myself seeking out networking events in my area to meet new people, engage with other businesses and grow my own profile. I'd scour the internet for groups, scroll social media and *literally* attend anything that I came upon.

**I wasn't in any way being strategic – I just attended event after event.**

Before long, I began to get this sense that I 'had' to attend them.

Even when I was tired from a long day or would need to miss out on dinner with my kids I'd think, "But what if I miss meeting my ideal client or business opportunity?"

FOMO was setting in.

Around this time, I was chatting to a business mentor.

We discussed my typical business week and where I spent my time. To say they were surprised by all my networking events was an understatement.

**And they pointed out that going to everything to avoid missing potential opportunities meant I was actually missing out on some REAL ones.**

For example, my business was for women – so it made sense to streamline my networking to focus on women's groups only. Perhaps, for balance, I could maintain *one* other business group – but the rest should relate to my ideal clients.

Instead, spreading myself so thin because of FOMO was impacting the quality of my networking. It was actually *diluting* my opportunities to connect to the right people for my business.

Interestingly, the business women's group I connected with as a result of that conversation became a ten-year relationship. I even went on to become a member of the committee and received a 'Business Woman of the Year' award.

And I'd probably have missed all of these opportunities if FOMO had continued to drive my networking decisions.

## Stay in your own lane

**Consider for a moment where FOMO might be pulling you away from your own course.**

What opportunities might be there around you already? How might they enhance your life?

I've noticed that FOMO has the most power over me when I'm unsure about what I want or am striving for in my life. If this is true for you, it's because you think that having or doing the same as everyone else will magically bring you what you want.

All it really does though is pull you out of your own lane and into theirs.

**Now, I'm not suggesting closing your eyes completely to what's going on around you.**

I *am*, however, saying that putting on blinkers occasionally may help you stay focused on what will support you, your intentions and your life.

So to hell with FOMO! Stay in your own lane, and be ready for the golden opportunities you'll find there when you start to look.

## The Practice – How to get back in your own lane

Here are some steps to help you get back on course when you're under the influence of FOMO:

Step 1: Choose an area of your life that you'd like to focus on, eg. your business, finance, relationship, family.

Step 2: Ask yourself what the ultimate outcome you're striving for in this area is.

Step 3: Make a list of any distractions that may be pulling you away from this outcome.

Step 4: Next, make a list of three things you could do that would bring your focus *back* to that outcome.

Step 5: Now actually DO those things.

Once you've reset your focus onto what you want and have taken action towards it, notice the opportunities that now 'magically' appear.

# Lesson 45

## DO ONE THING

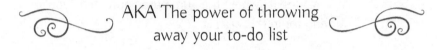 AKA The power of throwing
away your to-do list

### Are you a list-maker?

**What's the first thing you do when you have a lot on?**

Do you get your trusty pen and paper out, and start writing a list of everything you want to achieve?

Maybe you write out all the things you want to achieve for the day. Maybe your list is for the month. Maybe it's even for the whole *year*!

Regardless, if you're a list-maker, I understand. I used to do exactly the same thing – and I know it's not just me.

In fact, truth be told, I still tend to do this.

But my lists serve a very different purpose these days.

# What Maslow's Hierarchy of Needs has to do with your to-do list

**In 1943, psychologist Abraham Maslow published his *Theory of Human Motivation* paper.**

This paper has since formed a fundamental part of our knowledge and understanding of human psychology. Many people now know it as 'Maslow's Hierarchy of Needs'.

Maslow breaks our needs as humans into three main groups:

- basic needs
- psychological needs
- self-fulfilment needs.

He then breaks basic needs down into physiological needs and safety needs, and psychological needs into belongingness, love and esteem needs.

If that all sounds a bit complicated, you can see it laid out visually in the diagram below.

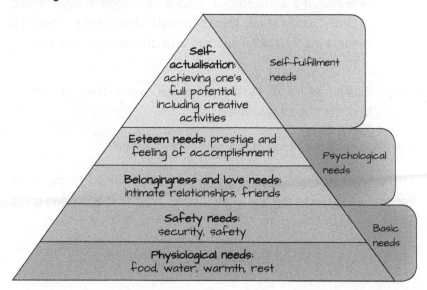

**Maslow's original theory stated that we're always motivated to fulfil our basic needs first.**

This motivation is something 'primal' – a 'must' rather than choice. We start at the bottom of the hierarchy and move upward from there. As we fulfil each level, we move on to the next.

For example, think of the reality TV show *Survivor*:

- When competitors first arrive in the middle of nowhere, they work well together to build their shelter, find water and food, and create a fire. This means they're taking care of the bottom level of physiological needs.

- Next, they ensure they have some level of safety. At this point, all their basic needs are met.

- Once they've met those needs, they're inherently motivated to create friendships and alliances.

- Next, the producers throw in challenges that give the competitors a sense of purpose and accomplishment. At this point, they're also meeting all of their psychological needs.

- However, if a competitor LOSES a challenge, they're forced to drop back a level. This then motivates them to shore up friendships and alliances to 'save themselves' from being voted off.

- Finally, self-actualisation happens when they go on to become the sole survivor.

**But what if we get stuck at the self-esteem stage?**

At the heart of this lesson is our unconscious human tendency to become addicted to the 'self-gratification buzz' that achieving gives us.

In Maslow's terms, this is the stage before self-actualisation – the one that relates to our self-esteem. THIS is the stage where most people are (perhaps unconsciously) happy to remain.

You might even think of it as your 'comfort zone'.

So why do we so often get caught here?

Because we all love to feel good about ourselves – and, of course, by definition, that's how we feel inside our comfort zones!

**What does this have to do with creating to-do lists?**

And how do they hold you back from attaining your full potential of the 'self-actualisation' Maslow speaks of?

That sense of achievement is so alluring because when you experience it after completing something, your brain releases a cocktail of 'feel-good chemicals'. And as with anything that feels good, you have a very human tendency to want more of that feeling.

As a result, your self-esteem and the short-term gratification from your achievement hold you hostage. And that's where your to-do list comes in, because the good feeling only grows stronger every time you tick something off it.

## It took '2017: the year of the overachiever' to help me throw away my to-do list

**This is why I no longer have a perpetual to-do list.**

Yes, that sense of achievement is intoxicating: it feels good – and, well, I'm achieving stuff, right?

But that addiction to the feel-good chemical flood I get from ticking off things that I know I can achieve also keeps me from achieving my full potential (self-actualisation). Because why would I be motivated to stretch to *that* place when I'm already feeling pretty fulfilled where I am, thank you very much!

**By the way, setting goals is just creating another type of to-do list.**

Originally, I couldn't see that, however. It took the mighty '2017: the year of the overachiever' list before I recognised what I was doing.

And I didn't just set myself a to-do list of massive goals to tick off that year either. Inside *each* of my big-ticket goals, I created smaller to-do lists that I could also tick off.

It was a nonstop sense of achievement with the associated feel-good chemical rush in my brain.

**But somehow, I never got to the thing that truly mattered to me.**

The one thing I cast aside that year (and the previous year as well!) was writing this book. It was the *one* thing that I knew would stretch me, take me out of my comfort zone and bring me face to face with my full potential.

Of course, I'd never focused all my attention on just 'one thing' before.

Ever.

So, not surprisingly, the idea of writing this book scared me. If I stretched myself to use ALL my attention and resources on this 'one thing', I'd have to let go of my to-do list addiction.

I knew deep down that writing the book would not only step me up and towards my potential but that it would serve the world as well. My self-esteem, however, got nervous.

So I did everything BUT write it.

Now I'm not suggesting that everyone needs to write a book.

Instead, I'm recommending that you take a look at the chaos and busy-ness that a never-ending to-do list may be creating in your life.

Ask yourself whether the items on it are things that really matter to you. Are the activities you're filling your days with moving you towards anything you truly want?

Or have you just become addicted to the 'tick'?

## How to create a different kind of list

**Please note: I'm not telling you to give up to-do lists entirely.**

Granted, that might be necessary for some people. Maybe it could be useful for you if, after reading this, you can already feel the tugging of your true potential. If this describes you then:

- You might feel like you're here to do something big with your life and are just never doing it.

- You might have a sense of 'something missing' or 'feeling lost'.

- Perhaps you're constantly questioning what your purpose is.

- Or maybe, like me in 2017, you keep setting massive goals (each with a million to-dos), but shortly after you tick them off, you feel empty and unfulfilled.

**Others, however, are *sure* they can't function without a to-do list.**

If you're sitting there, scratching your head, thinking your life would fall apart without yours, I get it. Remember: I used to be that way too.

The good news is that there IS indeed a place for making lists. You just have to create them a little differently.

And you need to think hard about what you put on them.

**I want you to consider making two kinds of lists in the future.**

- **A 'daily reminder' list:** this list will be just for things you need to *remember* to do and you can put as many things as you like on it.

- **A 'self-actualisation' list:** this one will be something else and will only ever have ONE thing on it at a time. That one thing will be whichever action will move you forwards the most towards whatever matters most to you.

I got this idea from the bestseller *The ONE Thing: The Surprisingly Simple Truth Behind Extraordinary Results* by Gary Keller and Jay Papasan.

It's a book I highly recommend you read – but even just this one practice will have you on your way to reaching your full potential.

## The Practice – Pick ONE thing

**So how do you know what 'one thing' to do?**

These steps will help you figure this out.

**Step 1:** To begin, write down everything you want to achieve. It's OK if there are 10 things, 20 things or even more. Just keep writing until you're completely done.

**Step 2:** Now ask yourself, "What one thing on this list will move me forwards the most towards what matters most to me?"

**Step 3:** Take that one thing and put it on your 'self-actualisation' list.

Your only focus now is to do that one thing.

**Step 4:** Once you've done it, return to your list, cross the thing off, and repeat the process from Step 1.

# Lesson 46

## PAY IT FORWARD, NOT JUST BACK

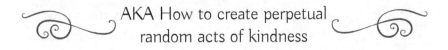 AKA How to create perpetual random acts of kindness

### Remember the movie *Pay It Forward*?

**Back in 2000, the movie *Pay It Forward* was released.**

The film is set in the Las Vegas of the time and chronicles 11-year-old Trevor McKinney's launch of the goodwill movement known as 'Pay it Forward'.

Although the movie was only moderately successful at the box office, the concept of 'paying it forward' has since developed a strong following on social media. Many non-profits, charity groups, foundations and community groups also use it as a core practice now.

Essentially this concept means that if you benefit from a random act of kindness yourself, you then 'pay it forward' by doing a random act of kindness for someone else.

**Many of us have been taught to repay good deeds.**

For example, if someone does something good for you, it seems natural to do something good for them in return. The problem with this is that if that's ALL you do, it stifles any ripple effect. It brings the good deed to a stop.

Paying it forward, on the other hand, keeps the favour moving – well – forward.

## Paying it forward makes a HUGE difference in the world

**It could do the same in your life.**

When I first saw the film in 2000, I was 34, married and a mother of two small kids.

To say it impacted me would be an understatement. Yes, I cried at the end – but the feeling it left me with lasted for weeks and weeks. I wasn't happy, exactly. Nor was I sad. I was just definitely moved in some kind of massive way.

I couldn't stop thinking about the 'pay it forward' concept and the power it could have in the world.

Keep in mind that this was long before social media, so I wasn't aware of the power this movement would garner over the years. I had no idea that it would become a concept that the world would come to know and embrace.

Perhaps you've been on the receiving end of a random of act of kindness?

Maybe someone did something for you that just blew you away and you already practise paying it forward in your life. If so, here's a giant high-five!

If not, though, I want to share with you the peaceful power that this practice can create. You can use it whenever you receive a kind gesture (and even when you don't).

## Here's how paying it forward changed ME

Back in the year 2000, I couldn't stop thinking about how to implement paying it forward in my life.

Eventually, I realised that all I needed to do was simply make the decision to do just that. And I realised that, rather than wait for someone to do something for me that I could then 'pay forward', I could actually start the process with me. Every single day.

So I began with always paying two tolls at the toll gates.

I'd pay for my car and the car behind me. I never looked to see who was behind: it was never about them and their gratitude. Instead, it was about me and my newly adopted principles.

In fact, sometimes there *wasn't* a car behind me at all and the toll dude would calmly point this out (thinking, perhaps, that I'd lost the plot). And I'd always reply, "I know. But there will be soon."

**The toll booths were eventually phased out, but the practice of paying it forward remained in my life.**

I didn't do this because of what it potentially gave to others. Instead, I did for what it gave to *me*.

Every time I 'paid it forward', I felt a massive sense of peace and power all in one incredible internal feeling.

- Peace, because it reminded me how the smallest of gestures could create a 'pause point' in someone's day so they could also feel peaceful.

- Power, because of the enormous ripple effect that my one small gesture could have on the world.

I'd sometimes imagine that the person who benefited from my gesture might be about to do or say something that would potentially negatively impact another person. But maybe – just maybe – the 'pause point' I created for them would shift their mindset. Maybe it would change what they did next.

And then *they* might pay it forward to someone else. And so on and so on.

My tiny pebble might create a giant ripple.

## I believe paying it forward is *bigger* than gratitude

**As I said above, this isn't about earning someone's gratitude.**

I'm not paying it forward in the hope that something good will happen to me in return. Nor am I looking for acknowledgement of any kind.

I'm doing this because it fills my imagination with possibilities – possibilities of what might happen next differently in that person's life. For example:

- I imagine how it might change a conversation they're about to have.

- I imagine how it might change a course of action they're about to take.

- I imagine how it might change a decision they're about to make.
- And then I imagine what that change might lead to... and so on... and so on.

So for me, paying it forward isn't just about paying people's tolls. It's about creating whole new possibilities in the world.

**There are so many ways you can pay it forward:**

- When you fill up your coffee reward card, leave the 'free coffee' on a random car's windscreen. Or ask the coffee shop that offers the card to pass it to the next person once you leave.
- If you win money on a scratchie, cash it out into $1 scratchies and place them on random car windscreens. You could even just buy ten $1 scratchies and do the same thing.
- Another simple idea is to handwrite a bunch of notes that say, "I hope you have an amazing day! ☺" and leave these in random places.

Plus, whenever actual random acts of kindness happen to you, consider how you can pay them forward. Perhaps if you were let off a traffic fine or parking ticket, you might pay for the fuel of the person behind you next time you fill your car up.

**It doesn't have to cost you money either. You could also:**

- mow your neighbour's lawn
- wash your friend's car
- volunteer for a couple of hours at a local non-profit.

And if you receive a random act of kindness, then do any of these things (or something of your own) and let people know that you're paying it forward. Perhaps tell them the story that prompted you to do this and the random act of kindness you received. Planting the notion of this practice in anyone's mind also creates a ripple effect.

**Now don't get me wrong: I'm a huge fan of gratitude, and we can all practise that every day too.**

But for me, paying it forward is about something bigger. It's about:

- a ripple effect
- a tipping point for change
- a shift in the status quo
- a different way of thinking
- a different way of being.

## The Practice – Pay something forward

**This lesson's practice is SUPER simple.**

Step 1:  Choose one of the examples mentioned above (or come up with your own).

Step 2:  Give it a go.

Step 3:  Notice how you feel and anything else that changes in your life afterwards. Journal about what you felt and experienced from this.

And, of course, 'rinse and repeat' this practice as often as possible.

# Lesson 47

## GIVING AND RECEIVING IS
## A BEAUTIFUL DANCE

 AKA Don't be afraid
of asking for help

### Do you hate to ask for help?

**Back in Lesson 34, we talked about asking for what you want.**

But there's a type of asking that most of us find especially hard: asking for help.

Although the two lessons are closely linked, asking for help often requires us to be vulnerable. This is something that women in particular are very, very good at protecting themselves from at all costs.

Many of us would rather go without or just shoulder our way through and do something ourselves rather than reach out and become vulnerable by seeking help.

In her bestselling book *Daring Greatly*, Brené Brown defines vulnerability as 'uncertainty, risk and emotional exposure'.

For most of us, this also sums up how it feels to ask for help.

## Let's face it – asking for help can be hard

**Perhaps it just feels easier to say, "I can do it myself!" for the little things.**

You know, things like:

- preparing the family dinner after the end of a long day
- cleaning the house on a Saturday when you'd rather be at the beach
- doing the grocery shopping.

**And although you *can* manage, wouldn't it be great to be able to ask for help with the bigger things?**

Imagine asking for help with:

- dropping the kids off to school or picking them up
- minding them for a couple of hours so you can go out and see a movie
- minding them for an entire *weekend*, so you and your partner can have some much needed 'alone time'.

**Of course, help isn't limited to your family home either.**

What about in business, especially if you experience the isolation of working from home? What if you could ask for help with:

- a brainstorming session with a mentor or colleague about an idea you have to grow your business?

- understanding the latest social media trends and business tools?

- creating a referral network in your area that would help both you and other businesses?

I get it. I really do.

**I used to try to just 'do it all myself' too.**

I did my best to figure it out on my own.

But by not asking for help, you're disabling your ability to receive. You're keeping your heart closed to love.

You're also limiting your own potential and that of those around you.

## I love thinking of giving and receiving as a dance

**It was around 2009 that I first heard someone refer to giving and receiving as a 'beautiful dance'.**

I was at a full moon meditation, sitting on a yoga mat in a circle with around 40 other people.

In the middle of the hall's darkened room sat an intricate display of crystals, flowers and candles that was truly mesmerising. We were all offered freshly brewed chai tea that tasted like Christmas in a cup (which then started my love affair with chai tea).

**This was my first guided group meditation, and I was completely awestruck by the energy, the people and the atmosphere.**

The facilitator was like some sort of red-haired mystical being. Her aura and energy just poured from her into the room, and I thought she must be some kind of 'Earth Angel'.

I felt as though her words were captivating and calming all in one. I don't remember everything she said that night (although I'll never forget the feelings I experienced). What I *do* remember is this one phrase she spoke: *"Practise giving and receiving. It's a beautiful dance."*

**She talked about how most of us are really good givers.**

We're not, however, so good at receiving. At the time, I was deep into my solo parenting gig, and what she was said totally resonated with me. For me, asking for help meant I couldn't manage by myself. It was a sign of weakness that meant being completely vulnerable.

But what she said next made the biggest impact on me. It's why I can now both ask for and receive help.

**She asked us all to imagine a friend asking *us* for the help we needed.**

How would we react to that friend? Would we say, "Yes," and help willingly, or would we answer, "No," and flat out refuse?

I thought about this for a moment, pondering the last few times I'd needed help. And I knew without hesitation that if anyone had asked for my help in the same situation, I'd have absolutely said, "YES!"

It's hard to put into words, but I *immediately* felt a large weight lift from my body. I knew from that day on that I could ask for any help I needed and then receive it.

It didn't mean I couldn't manage by myself, nor did it mean I was weak.

## Asking for and receiving help creates connection

**When two people dance effortlessly, it's often because they're exchanging equal amounts of energy.**

Giving and receiving help is exactly the same. It's a light, effortless and equal exchange of energy.

And when you move about your day, just doing what you do best and being authentically you, you never know just who you might be touching, moving and inspiring.

That night in the hall, I was touched, moved and inspired by an authentic and beautiful person. In that moment, she effortlessly gave, and I (along with 40 other people) effortlessly received.

**Imagine being able to experience that kind of effortlessness between you and another person.**

This may require you to take small steps at first – especially if, like I was, you're attached to 'doing all it yourself'.

Perhaps you might begin by sharing this practice with a good friend. Let them know that you'd love to be able to give and receive effortlessly, and invite them to join in with you. You could then both spend the next week practising asking each other for help. You might even agree on a set number of 'asks' each.

What you'll begin to experience is the beautiful energy that exists in both asking for and receiving help. You'll realise that this flow of help invites connection, communication and a strong sense of community between the two of you.

So this simple practice that you've been scared to do actually contributes to something so much bigger than either of you.

## The Practice – Asking for help

**If you find it difficult to ask for help, try this.**

**Step 1:** First, imagine someone asking you for the same help that you're about to ask for.

**Step 2:** If you know that you'd say, "Yes!" without hesitation, allow the other person to offer that gift for you.

**Step 3:** If you'd hesitate and perhaps answer, "No," consider how you might reframe the request. Could you perhaps offer an exchange that brings a lighter energy to the request? For example, could you say something like, "I'd be happy to do x for you if you can help me with y"?

Asking for help is an opportunity to bring the beautiful balance of giving and receiving together not only in *your* life but in the lives of those around you as well.

# Lesson 48

## DON'T CHASE BUTTERFLIES

 AKA There's nowhere to get to: you're already there

### Happiness is like a butterfly...

**There's a famous quote about happiness:**

*"Happiness is like a butterfly: the more you chase it, the more it will elude you, but if you turn your attention to other things, it will come and sit softly on your shoulder."*

Depending on what you google, there's evidence that two literary greats – either Henry David Thoreau or Nathaniel Hawthorne – penned this quote. There's also a suggestion that neither of them did.

In any case, it sums up our quest for happiness perfectly: there are literally *thousands* of books written about happiness and our pursuit of it.

# It's easy to assume you'll be happy 'when'

**We've talked about happiness a few times in this book.**

Back in Lesson 7, you learnt to hone your awareness of happiness. We also talked about the danger of assuming that you can only be happy when something outside of you changes.

Then, in Lesson 34, we talked about happiness being an inside job – something that's totally within your area of control.

**Now, in this lesson, I want to talk about happiness from the perspective of actualising it within your life.**

Just as the concept of 'being right' packed a powerful punch across three lessons, 'happiness' is also a biggie that requires more than one lesson. And just like the butterfly in the quote, it's something we seem to insist on chasing, rather than allowing it to land upon us.

Have you ever found yourself thinking:

- "I just need to finish this one thing, and then I'll be happy"?
- "Once I get to the end of [insert issue], I'll be happy"?
- "If only this didn't happen, I'd be happy"?
- "If only this *would* happen, I'd be happy"?

**I'm not here to rewrite the book on happiness.**

However, the practice in this lesson is about reminding ourselves that happiness is available to us right now. Right here. In this moment.

*If* we choose it to be.

Eckhart Tolle's bestsellers *The Power of Now* and *A New Earth* helped me fully understand what it means to be present in the current moment.

I realised that whenever I get attached to feelings of the past or need to feel something in the future, I completely miss what's right here in this moment.

Now I'm sure this concept isn't rocket science to you.

**But how do we actually focus on the present moment?**

The key to understanding this is to forget about happiness for just a moment. Instead, let's bring the real protagonist of this story – suffering – out from behind the curtains and shine our spotlight on to it:

- When you're worried about, or stuck or caught up in what's happened in the past, you're suffering.
- And when you're worried about, or stuck or caught up in what will happen in the future, you're *also* suffering.

However, both of those places – past and present – are actually impossible for you to exist in. The only place you can truly be (where suffering can't exist, but happiness can) is the present.

And, just as a physiological side note, when you're suffering, your nervous system releases the fight-or-flight hormone cortisol. This compound can actually be toxic in large or repeated doses – so doesn't it make sense to reduce your suffering as much as humanly possible?

## I learnt to connect with the present moment through meditation

**Back in Lesson 42, I talked about getting stuck in 'doing'.**

I learnt the practice that enhanced the way I meditated from Alexi Panos and Preston Smiles during a seminar they gave.

(Incidentally, these guys are the bomb dot com, so go find them on social media or google them. You can thank me later!)

It was during the Q&A at that seminar when I *finally* recognised that my comfort zone was 'doing'. Whenever I was 'doing', I was sleeves up, head down, shouldering my way through life. It was my avoidance mechanism to keep me in my zone of comfort.

And, as we previously discussed, when one element dominates, your flow state disappears.

**Alexi and Preston suggested that I do something they called a 'soul sabbatical'.**

The rules were that I had to take myself into nature with no phone, no pen or paper, and no food or water, and just 'sit' for one hour without sleeping. They recommended that I do this once a week for three months.

To some people, this might sound like bliss, but it actually freaked me out. And it took what I'd been doing as 'meditation' up to that point to a whole new level.

All I could think of was everything I could be 'doing' in that one hour. However, with the awareness I'd now been practising for many years, I realised that the very fact I felt triggered was a reason to lean into it. Only then could I learn from it.

**So, that first week, off I went into nature and just sat, staring into space.**

It was AWFUL. I hated every second of it.

My thoughts flitted between the past and the future; for not one moment was I present.

I recognised, however, that my anxiety had nothing to do with the moment I was in. Instead, it was attached to something I couldn't change or something that hadn't even happened.

**As the weeks rolled by, I began watching myself and my thoughts.**

When I noticed them heading into the past or future, I gently brought my focus to the present.

Blip!

And there it was. That tiny blip was the present moment.

Now, I know that you probably know *intellectually* what it means to be present. So did I. But for the first time in my life, in that moment, I'd experientially accessed it.

The present was no longer an intellectual concept for me. Instead, it was something I'd physically, mentally and emotionally experienced.

So I could now access it at any moment I chose to become aware of it.

## Learning to meditate is simpler than you think

**First, consider where your thoughts are in this moment.**

Are they in the past or in the future?

If so, consider that without even realising it, you may be flooding your body with cortisol. Also consider that you may be completely missing out on the peace and happiness that exists in this moment.

Because – as we said above – in this moment, there *is* no suffering.

In *this* moment, all needs are met.

One of the most powerful, beneficial, do-anywhere practices to release suffering and reconnect with the present moment is meditation.

If you've never meditated before, or if you've tried and just didn't 'get it', I want you to notice that *that* is a thought about the past. (See how much your thoughts are running rampant?)

Of course, just 'being' is something that many of us – especially mums – struggle to do. We're all natural worriers. But I want you to begin to notice that if you're worrying about anything, you're suffering – either about something in the past or the future.

The second you even *notice* this, right there is your 'blip'.

The trick is to practise allowing the 'blip' to become a 'bleep'.

And then a 'bleeep'.

Then a 'bleeeeeeep'.

Then a 'bleeeeeeeeeeeeeeeeeep'.

And so on.

## The Practice – Noticing your thoughts

You don't need to take a soul sabbatical to meditate (although I highly recommend it).

Instead, the practice here is to simply notice your thoughts. You can call it meditation if you want to, or you can just call it 'noticing' or 'being still with your thoughts'.

Regardless, you can have your eyes open or closed and either sit up or lie down. Then, once you're comfortable:

**Step 1:** Take a deep breath and notice what you're thinking.

**Step 2:** As you take your next breath, notice whether your thoughts have changed and what you're now thinking about. Are you in the past or the future?

**Step 3:** Wherever your thoughts are, bring them back to this moment. Don't judge them. Simply accept them as you move your attention back to now.

**Step 4:** Keep focusing on noticing your thoughts and repeat the above steps.

**Step 5:** Just start with a few minutes and then gradually build up from there.

Oh, and by the way, if you do this practice, you actually *will* be meditating.

# Lesson 49

## MOVE OFTEN,
## PLAY OFTEN,
## HAVE FUN!

AKA How to reconnect and
come back to "YOU"

### It's about what you gain, not what you give up

**It's probably no surprise that I'm a big fan of movement.**

My background in the fitness industry happened because regular
activity positively impacted my life in a big way – and because it
enabled me to positively impact others.

However, I've also come to understand that exercise is immensely
valuable for our human potential, creativity and mindset. It's about
*so much more* than calorie burning, deprivation and working out so
you can eat that piece of cake.

Instead, it's about the life-changing benefits of movement, play and
having fun.

This lesson is an invitation to pause the power hold that maximising metabolism and minimising food has on most of us.

Rather, I invite you to start thinking of wellness as something you can gain in your life, rather than something you have to sacrifice to attain.

When you do this, you'll begin to actualise the all-encompassing benefits of movement for your mind and body. You'll be able to turn on the feel-good chemical tap in your brain at will and drink in all of the many benefits it brings.

Imagine being able to love who you are, how you look and how you feel now – and that it didn't require sweating, starving, shredding or sacrificing.

## Change your shape, change your state

The phrase "*Change your shape, change your state*" is well known in yoga.

It refers to the way that moving your body from one position to another (changing your shape) also changes your mood, mindset and emotional state.

Now, I'm not suggesting that you need to be or become an athletic goddess. That's a common misconception about movement that I really don't want to perpetuate.

Instead, I'm saying that any kind of movement is beneficial – with the best kind being the kind you enjoy most. And I do mean *any* kind of movement. You can shift from one position to another, from one room or place to another, or from indoors to outdoors. And, of course, there's also the movement from any kind of physical activity.

I'm also saying that the practice of movement – in *whatever* form it takes for you – is as good for your mind as it is for your body.

**Where does play come into this?**

Far from being a frivolous use of time, play connects us to our creativity and helps us to become present.

Kids do this effortlessly in their early years. However, once they grow up, the adult world they enter is often far more logical, linear and outcome-based.

This is a major loss, because research confirms that play can stimulate imagination and creativity in adults. It can also enhance problem-solving skills and improve both relationships and connection to others.

**So when did you last play, just for the sake of playing?**

You might be thinking, "But Jen, I don't have time to play!" If so, you're not alone. For many of us, play stops sometime between childhood and adulthood.

George Bernard Shaw was attributed with the quote: *"We don't stop playing because we grow old. We grow old because we stop playing."*

To bring some play back into your life, ask yourself what you loved to do when you were a kid. What games do you remember loving to play? Were there:

- inside games?
- outside games?
- physical games?
- imagination games?
- board games?

**Then, finally, there's fun.**

Ask yourself when it was that you became so *serious*. When did you forget how much you loved life? When was the last time you really had some fun? And when did you last smile, giggle or laugh until you cried?

When you're having fun, you're automatically present. And, as we talked about in Lesson 48, the present is where happiness exists.

**These three elements – movement, play and fun – are integral to accessing the authentic 'YOU' within you.**

They help to break through the outer 'you' who's armoured herself up so she can grimly shoulder her way through life. The 'you' who's been taught that movement is a necessary evil, play is a waste of time and fun is just for kids.

And when you can access the true 'you' – the 'you' who's present, aligned and following the essence of who she is – that 'you' is the most peaceful and powerful 'you' there is.

She responds to life, rather than reacting to it.

And she's present to the life she was always destined to live, even if she's wandered off course.

## Movement, play and fun changed my life

**I wasn't always this fired up about movement.**

You might assume that it's easy for me to do this stuff because I've made my living in the fitness industry, so it's already part of my life. I'd almost agree with you... except for the fact that there was a time in my life when I had cigarettes and coffee for breakfast – in that order.

You see, my husband and I were both smokers when we were first married. To be honest, I really loved smoking back then. However, one day, my hubby decided that he was going to quit and that I should too.

I told him that I *liked* smoking, so I wouldn't be quitting any time soon.

Knowing me as well as he did, he replied, "Well, it's actually really hard to quit. You probably wouldn't be able to anyway."

Of course, with my personality, that was like a red flag to a bull. So following his comment, I stubbed out my cigarette and have been a non-smoker ever since.

**Now, one of my dearest friends back then was extremely health-conscious.**

She was delighted that I'd quit and encouraged me to go running with her one afternoon. I thought, "Why not?" Since I was no longer smoking, improving my health and fitness made sense.

I think we'd run about 200 metres before I thought my lungs would explode and my legs would drop off! I was gasping for breath, bent over as I looked up at my friend skipping along and bursting with happiness. She seemed to be having the time of her life.

Panting heavily, I wheezed, "Are you kidding me? Why are you so happy? This is shit!"

**And we both burst out laughing.**

We alternated walking and jogging the rest of the way and, by the end of it, I actually felt amazing! Now, of course, at this point, I was *not* a runner. However, the combination of walking and jogging had delivered a cocktail of feel-good chemicals to my body.

On top of that, the playfulness and laughter of simply hanging out with my friend and having fun lifted me up to a place I'd forgotten about.

The world just looked different.

I looked different. I felt different. And powerful, uplifting ideas I'd never thought of before started popping in my mind like popcorn.

All because I'd moved my body to the best of my ability and made it playful and fun.

**My friend and I began to meet up regularly.**

Eventually, I added some team sports, club squash and some gym classes too. And although all of this could be classed as 'exercise', it was the social, playful, fun elements that were so addictive.

It was never about punishing myself to 'lose weight' or 'get healthy'. Rather it was about doing something that added so much value to my mental clarity, mood, posture, body and social connections.

Whenever I start straying from this profound formula of movement, play and fun (like I did in Lesson 8 for my body sculpting competition), my inspiration and motivation both wane. When that happens, I notice I get irritable and moody, lack energy and my spark for life dulls.

So no matter what activity I choose to do these days, whether it counts as 'exercise' or not, it needs to tick three boxes:

- It has to include some kind of movement.

- It needs to have an element of play.

- And it absolutely MUST put a smile on my face and be FUN.

## Movement doesn't have to be your worst nightmare

**Movement, play and fun all come fairly easily to me these days.**

They can do the same for you too, no matter what stage of life you're at and what your fitness or physical capacity is. (Yes, even if you've been injured.)

- It might mean going to the gym, running or lifting weights for you – or it might not. (Maybe it's just a gentle walk or going to a cafe you've never been to before.)
- It might involve thinking, strategic game-based play – or it might not. (Card games, board games, memory games – they're all valid.)
- It might involve being social – or it might not. ('You time' on your own is important too.)
- It might be actively participating in something – or it might not. (You can be a spectator or volunteer to help with admin as well.)

**Movement, play and fun can be whatever you want them to be.**

They just require you to start with the premise of 'what *can* you do?' rather than allowing you to get stuck in 'what you can't do'.

They're whatever you want them to be, as long as they don't create any kind of conflict within you. In other words, they shouldn't make you feel bad, hurt you or embarrass you in any way. They don't have to be competitive either, and they're *never* a punishment to yourself or your body.

**So what could they look like for you?**

Here are just a few things that movement, play and fun could be for you:

- dancing

- games with your kids
- walking or biking
- yoga, meditation or tai chi
- gardening
- ten pin bowling
- fishing
- sit-down games and puzzles (including computer games!)

As I said above, they can be absolutely anything!

Give one or all of these options a go, or create your own. Just remember that if you're NOT having fun, you can always change your mind and try something else. (See Lesson 33 about changing a decision with another decision!)

## Try experiencing the joy of play right now

**Here's a quick way to get yourself in the mood for movement, play and fun.**

First, close your eyes. Now, imagine yourself skipping along a path, beach, trail or wherever you enjoy being.

OK, are you back? Great.

Did you notice that you were smiling while you skipped? Either in your imagination or possibly in reality too?

Unless you consciously decide not to, it's almost impossible not to smile in some way while you're skipping.

It matters not whether you can actually skip or not, this simple visualisation will be enough to remind your heart of the joy of movement, play and fun.

## The Practice – Finding the kind of movement that lights you up

This practice helps to remind you of the types of movement, play and fun that most light you up.

Perhaps it's something you used to do and have stopped for whatever reason. Perhaps it's something you've always wanted to do, but put off.

Step 1:   Make a list of the games or activities you played as a child that you can connect to a memory of having fun. Circle the one that makes you smile the most when you think about it.

Step 2:   Make a list of anything you've always wanted to do, where the prospect of trying it gives you a sense of joy and excitement. This could involve *anything* from games to activities to joining a club or community volunteering.

Step 3:   Now, with both lists, note down as many ways as you can think of to connect to a sense of movement, play and fun – either actively (ie. participating) or non-actively (ie. volunteering).

Step 4:   Over the next two weeks, schedule in one or two of them.

Step 5:   Journal about how you felt after completing the activity. In particular, write about any new thoughts or ideas that may have come to you.

# Conclusion

I am you,
You are me,
We are 'She'.

## Congratulations! You're ready to 'take your notebook home'!

**It's been quite a journey since you first picked up this book...**

And if you've truly absorbed the lessons and practices on its pages, then just as I was ready to take my notebook home, so now are you.

If you've tried out a few practices, you may have already begun to see the changes occurring in your life, at work, with your kids or in your relationships. You may be feeling a foundation of peace that now exists within you. You may also find it difficult to see your life, or the people in it, the same way anymore.

Perhaps those around you may tell you they've noticed a change in you too.

**This is the positive impact of your peaceful power.**

I do need to remind you, however, that passively reading, analysing, pondering or intellectualising any of the lessons won't create transformation in your life.

You need to bring them out of the pages of this book and *into your life*.

Yes, it may well feel clunky at first. It did for me too. And yes, you'll absolutely need to practise, practise and practise some more. That's what I still do every day.

But YOU are all you need to harness your peaceful power.

## Wielding power from drama and disturbance only creates more drama and disturbance

Just like anything of great power, your *peaceful power* comes with great responsibility too.

These lessons and practices are only effective when you apply them internally – within yourself. Wielding them externally like a weapon on those you love or on situations you encounter will only bring more drama.

It will also leave you frustrated and wondering why this shit isn't working!

In contrast, when you responsibly, internally and consciously embody these practices with the utmost love for yourself, your power comes from a foundation of peace. This means there's nothing else possible *other* than a peaceful life.

**You get a life where you can defuse your own damn drama!**

Here's an example of what you can expect when you begin to apply the miraculous wisdom and practices in these pages and bring them into your daily life.

It happened to me whilst I was creating this book, and it shows you how I still (almost every other day) consciously and internally transform my own dramas. And in doing so, I reconnect to my peaceful power.

**The drama started sometime around Lesson 28.**

I don't recall exactly where, but I do remember that it was during the very first round of editing.

My written-from-the-heart manuscript was well and truly in the process of transforming from a newborn into an adult, and my learning curve was more vertical than curvy.

So let's just say that the drama of a childish tantrum was about to unfold.

Up until that point, I'd been ploughing along with my editor and loving the process. But suddenly, two or three teeny-tiny (constructive) editing comments plummeted me into a downwards trajectory that you're probably familiar with.

**For the purpose of this story, let's call it 'I-suck-ville'.**

There I was, spiralling out of control, into the world of being a human with very human responses. And the fuel for the journey was nothing but a few constructive comments.

I could feel it happening and could notice my thoughts... but I couldn't prevent the process. The thing is that I knew I didn't need to. I knew I could allow myself to consciously feel all the feelings that were creating my thoughts and reactions to the feedback.

**I felt distracted, anxious and worried about my ability to write this book.**

Of course, my thoughts found *lots* of evidence for my fears. So – as you do – the next thing I did was jump ahead and read the editor's notes about the forthcoming lessons. And what do you know, I found more (made-up) evidence about my (in)ability to write this book.

I was spiralling downward into the overwhelming drama I'd created.

So I paced the house.

I walked the dog.

I scrolled social media.

I moved restlessly from room to room.

And still, the thoughts and feelings were there.

**So I decided I needed to email my editor to share my concerns.**

I began by thanking her for her incredible work, then I let her know I was feeling overwhelmed and bullet pointed my specific worries. For example, I told her:

- "I don't think I'm a good writer."
- "I don't have the credibility to write this book."
- "I don't think anyone will read it."

And finally, at the root of my fears...

- "I suck."

And then I signed off with a final sentence: "By the way, my ego and fear are writing this email, and I am here too."

**How powerful is it to be *that* conscious of what I was experiencing in the moment?!**

## I literally had an out-of-body experience

I was conscious and aware, watching myself from the moment I felt the drama begin through to the feeling of disturbance and rising anxiety. I was with the 'me' who walked the dog and patiently accompanied the 'me' who moved agitatedly from room to room.

**You see, that's the power of the practices you've just discovered in this book.**

They do more than simply give you instant access to defusing your own dramas. They also allow you to lovingly support yourself whilst you create a truce with your ego and fear, and actually *listen* to what they have to say.

So I stood beside the 'me' who sat at my laptop and placed my hand lovingly on 'my' shoulder. I gave my 'upset self' permission to hit the button that would send my ranting email to my editor.

I knew that doing so would allow me to move *through* my feelings rather than trying to manhandle my ego and fear into submission. I didn't need to make myself wrong for my feelings. I didn't need to feel silly for sending the email, because I knew that my 'upset' had nothing to do with my editor.

In fact, I suspect that before she'd even read it, much less replied to it, I'd already moved through my upset feelings. I'd learnt what I needed to, acknowledged my ego and fear and given them their moment, and reopened my heart and reconnected with my peaceful power.

**And I used the four stages of experiential transformation to achieve this:**

- **Awareness** allowed me to have my out-of-body experience, notice the drama and be aware of myself within it.

- **Acceptance** gave me access to the self-love I needed to support myself through my human experience and let go of any judgements.

- **Area of control** helped me to own and internalise my way through my 'tantrum'. I controlled my controllables, which in this instance meant sending the email without making myself (or my editor) wrong for it.

- **Actualisation** is why, after reflection, I can verbalise the experience to both myself and you with a clear perspective. And it's also why I can consciously reopen my heart to myself and my life.

## So what now?

**How do you ensure that you don't slip back into the powerlessness of intellectual wisdom?**

How do you truly bring forth the life-changing power of these lessons and practices?

If you've completed the practices at the end of each lesson (or even just some of them), your transformation will have already begun.

You'll already be experiencing your life and the people in it differently. Try as you might, you just won't be able to go back to the 'you' that ever saw them any other way. Nothing and no one will seem the same to you. Because *you* won't be the same.

It will be as if some kind of miracle had occurred.

You'll also start noticing your own patterns, responses and ways of being. Then, with this new awareness, you'll start making conscious choices that bring loving, peaceful outcomes.

And chances are that you'll notice a whole load of 'stuff' that just doesn't seem to upset you as much (or even at all) anymore.

**So if you haven't yet completed any practices, that's your first step.**

I strongly suggest you go back to the first stage of experiential transformation, Awareness, and begin there.

Remember: seeking transformation intellectually will render this book as much use to you as a torch without batteries. If you try to use it, you'll be forever in the dark, fumbling around clumsily, bumping into sharp objects, and getting angry and upset. You'll be cursing the dark because you can't see – much less put your hands on – the life you want.

Experiential transformation involves applying the wisdom in these lessons by doing the practices. It allows you to put the batteries into your torch, so you can 'see' exactly what you do and don't want.

## There it is: the secret that the pages of this book hold

If you're prepared to take action, experiential transformation will occur in *every* area of your life.

Of course, if you'd like more help, you can always go to my website www.jenniferforster.com to find further resources.

You can also stay connected to me on Instagram and Facebook (find the links on my website), where I'll keep sharing my own personal experiences and pieces of wisdom. You'll also find the support of other like-minded, peacefully powerful women there.

I am SO ridiculously excited for you, beautiful woman.

I know that you're holding in your hands *everything* you need to drop your armour, harness your peaceful power and defuse any drama.

And what's waiting for you is the life YOU want – the life that YOU will have created.

Imagine a world filled with women who know that their most potent power comes from being armour-less, drama-less and peaceful. With this book, you have the tools to become the embodiment of a peacefully powerful woman who may also be a mother, partner, sister, business woman, thought leader, influencer and changemaker – or all of them.

**And how do I know this?**

I know it because:

I am you,

You are me,

We are 'She'.

She is your light and she is your shadow

She is your voice and she is your wisdom

She is your peace and she is your power

And... SHE knows the way...

 x

# Acknowledgements

**Bringing this book to life has been one of my grandest adventures.**

In doing so, I've come to realise that my life overflows with incredible people! Seriously, there are just so many of you. If humans were treasure (and let's face it, they really are!) then my life is truly an Aladdin's cave.

I could fill an entire book writing about each of you (note to self for my next project), but to keep my editor happy, I've done my best to be somewhat restrained. However, it must be said that every single human I've met has played a part in my evolution and, ultimately, the creation of this book. So I acknowledge and send love and gratitude to you all.

In particular, however:

**To Alexander and Isobel:** my babies, my children, my greatest teachers, my loves. Thank you for always and in all ways believing in me and supporting everything I do. Thank you for being my loudest cheerleaders, for loving me, for choosing me and for always calling me forward into my gifts. I love you more than cookies.

**To my incredible family:** there are so many intricate, beautiful layers to the tapestry that weaves us all together.

- My mum and dad (Pam and Athol, both passed): long before I would ever truly understand the meaning, you taught me that no matter the question, love is the answer. It's that same love, not blood, that bonds me to my brother Chris and my sisters Sal and Moozle. I could not love you more.

- My modern, crazy, functional, dysfunctional, divine and grounded family – Tony (the father of my children) and Tania (their stepmum): what a team we make. Our kids are so blessed!

- Alice, my kindred free spirit and fellow adventurer: for reminding me always to nurture my heart and soul with the things that light me up.

- My extended family – nans, pops, grandmas, grandpas, aunts, uncles, nieces, nephews and cousins: you're the solid foundation from which I've grown.

I love you all with all my heart.

**To my amazing friends:** there are so many of you from all around the world. You're my technicolour dreamcoat of cool people who span cultures, countries, communities and creeds. Each of you has, either knowingly or often unknowingly, been the love-fused catalyst that has helped me to unwrap the gifts in my life (even when they didn't look like gifts!)

You've helped me to expand and grow, lovingly and gently held my hands during the challenges, and patiently waited with me whilst parts of me fell away. You've celebrated my joys and supported me through my tears. You've been right beside me during some magnificent, fun-filled adventures and trusted me when I've said, "Come on, it'll be fun!"

In particular, thank you to every Goal Power girl, the entire 'Fatties' family, my Parkrun family, the Sunshine Coast Business Women's Network, the Magic Sisters, the Enchanted Sisters, The Garmigos, and my besties Annette, Melinda, Vickie, Jodi, Melanie and Mikey. I thank you and love you!

**To my mentors, guides and teachers:** some of you I've met, but so many of you I haven't. Yet I've listened to each of you, learnt from you, and drawn upon your wisdom and inspiration to continue moving forwards towards my purpose and towards birthing this book into the world.

Thank you most notably to Elizabeth (Liz) Gilbert, Michael A Singer, Oprah Winfrey, Kyle Cease, Gabby Bernstein, Brené Brown, Rebecca Campbell, Jacqui Segal, Alexi Panos and Preston Smiles, Linda Pesavento, Carren Smith, Kim Morrison and Craig Harper. You have all shared words of wisdom that have been pivotal to my growth and expansion, for which I will be eternally grateful.

**To my wonderful friend, Alex Fullerton:** publisher, editor and woman at the helm of the ship that is Author Support Services.

**To Alex's team of wordly wizards – in particular, Tanja Gardner:** you're all masters of your craft and I'll be forever grateful for your patience, support, humour and friendship.

**To Alex's design team of creative superstars – in particular to Sylvie Blair:** I knew instantly that the universe had sent you to me. Thank you for infusing my book with her very own life and personality.

**To Paula Brennan:** The artistic genius behind the cover shot and images throughout. You are just magnificent – thank you for capturing the true essence of ME! I adore you and your masterful creativity, your ability to see beyond the lens, and the ease, grace and joy you put into all that you do. www.paulabrennan.com.au

**To the fur kids who kept me company:** Ego, Sassy, Hugo, Pixie, Nikki Nuu, Jimmy, Arlie, Pebbles, Angel, Pippa, Lucy, Fergus, Chloe, Ajax, Spyrro, Francis, Effie, Toby, Charlie, Alfie, Lily, Hugo, Flora, Riddles, Astro, Gracie, Miah, Chicco, Boy, and one non-furry friend, JRoo – your input was priceless!

**Finally, to Fran:** none of us can ever know the paths that lie ahead of us. But I'll always be forever grateful that our paths intersected. I love you, beautiful woman.

# About Jennifer

Jennifer Forster's life is a kaleidoscope of experiences and qualifications, spurred by her love of adventure. From a humble childhood on a Tasmanian dairy farm, she commenced her business career in Sydney with an international deluxe hotel chain and went on to create a boutique chocolate shop, found an award-winning fitness business and later a magazine publication on the Sunshine Coast. Her love of adventure also took her abroad to pioneer a health and wellness program for women in a vocational college in Saudi Arabia.

In late 2016, she took up the role of Executive Manager of an innovative new business back on her beloved Sunshine Coast. Entrusted to establish and develop this company with her entrepreneurial skills, she grew it from a business plan to a profitable enterprise within six months.

Jennifer could never deny her love of adventure and her life has included travelling around Australia and many other countries, trekking to Everest Base Camp, being an Australian representative in body sculpting and a trail ultramarathon competitor.

With a Masters in Business Administration, Jennifer is an entrepreneur, a qualified fitness professional, life coach, solo mum, mentor, speaker and, now, published author. Prior to writing her first book, Jennifer has been featured in regional and national publications as well as being a guest contributor in two international best-selling books.

But according to Jennifer, these are just the facts. Here's what you really need to know to understand the true essence of the woman she is:

- Jennifer talks a lot and her voice is LOUD
- Jennifer is ambivert

- She loves dark chocolate and red wine

- She has identified an overachiever who lives inside of her, whom she has fondly named Odette. These days, Odette serves Jen, not the other way around

- Jennifer believes connection is critical to wellbeing and abhors cruelty or bullying

- Her heart expands when she's in nature and contracts when she ignores its whispers

- Her family is her life force and her friends are her oxygen

- She adores all creatures great and small and dreams of owning a rescue farm one day

- She no longer subscribes to societal business norms and has traded business plans and marketing strategies for heart plans and soul shares

- She focuses on what's right as opposed to what's wrong, as a practice to open her heart and expand her soul.

Behind her drive, determination, gypsy spirit and constantly curious nature is a woman who covets, above all else, her inner peace.

# Peaceful Women Rising Together

"There is no power for change
greater than a community
discovering what it cares about."

– Margaret J. Wheatley

I care about *you*, beautiful woman, and there is a multitude of ways that we can stay connected and continue to rise, peacefully and powerfully, together.

My focus and intention are to connect women globally to the power of their inner peace, which is why I am committed to creating content that is relevant, that resonates, impacts and inspires. This means my programs and workshops are constantly being updated, reinvented and revised so we all continue to expand and grow.

Take a look below, and peruse the various sites and pages where you'll find everything from Facebook groups to online programs, free resources and live events. Or you can simply join the conversation on my social pages. I love connecting in real time with our community. I know your heart will guide you to what resonates for you.

I am so grateful to you for being committed to your own expansion and, ultimately, a world filled with peaceful women rising together.

*Jen* x

Website: www.jenniferforster.com
Email: hello@jenniferforster.com
Facebook: www.facebook.com/JenniferMForster/
Instagram: @jenniferforster_

Printed in July 2019
by Rotomail Italia S.p.A., Vignate (MI) - Italy